T0190358

Mastering 3D Printing

A Guide to Modeling, Printing, and Prototyping

Second Edition

Joan Horvath
Rich Cameron

Apress®

Mastering 3D Printing: A Guide to Modeling, Printing, and Prototyping

Joan Horvath
Nonscriptum LLC, Pasadena, CA, USA

Rich Cameron
Nonscriptum LLC, Pasadena, CA, USA

ISBN-13 (pbk): 978-1-4842-5841-5
https://doi.org/10.1007/978-1-4842-5842-2

ISBN-13 (electronic): 978-1-4842-5842-2

Managing Director, Apress Media LLC: Welmoed Spahr
Acquisitions Editor: Natalie Pao
Development Editor: James Markham
Coordinating Editor: Jessica Vakili

Distributed to the book trade worldwide by Springer Science+Business Media New York, 233 Spring Street, 6th Floor, New York, NY 10013. Phone 1-800-SPRINGER, fax (201) 348-4505, e-mail orders-ny@springer-sbm.com, or visit www.springeronline.com. Apress Media, LLC is a California LLC and the sole member (owner) is Springer Science + Business Media Finance Inc (SSBM Finance Inc). SSBM Finance Inc is a **Delaware** corporation.

For information on translations, please e-mail rights@apress.com, or visit http://www.apress.com/rights-permissions.

Apress titles may be purchased in bulk for academic, corporate, or promotional use. eBook versions and licenses are also available for most titles. For more information, reference our Print and eBook Bulk Sales web page at http://www.apress.com/bulk-sales.

Any source code or other supplementary material referenced by the author in this book is available to readers on GitHub via the book's product page, located at www.apress.com/978-1-4842-5841-5. For more detailed information, please visit http://www.apress.com/source-code.

Printed on acid-free paper

For everyone who contributed to the RepRap project to start this revolution.

Table of Contents

TABLE OF CONTENTS

About the Authors

Joan Horvath and **Rich Cameron** are the cofounders of Nonscriptum LLC, based in Pasadena, California. Since 2015, Nonscriptum has consulted for educational and scientific users in the areas of 3D printing and maker technologies. Joan and Rich find ways to use maker tech to teach science and math in a hands-on way, and want to make scientific research cheaper and more accessible to the public. This book is their eighth collaboration for Apress. They have also authored additive manufacturing online courses for LinkedIn Learning (formerly Lynda.com). Links for all of these are on their website, `www.nonscriptum.com`.

In addition to her work with Rich, Joan also has taught at the university level in a variety of institutions, both in Southern California and online. Before she and Rich started Nonscriptum, she held a variety of entrepreneurial positions, including VP of business development at a Kickstarter-funded 3D printer company. Joan started her career with 16 years at the NASA/Caltech Jet Propulsion Laboratory, where she worked in programs including the technology transfer office, the Magellan spacecraft to Venus, and the TOPEX/Poseidon oceanography spacecraft. She holds an undergraduate degree from MIT in aeronautics and astronautics and a master's degree in engineering from UCLA.

ABOUT THE AUTHORS

Rich Cameron (known online as "Whosawhatsis") is an experienced open source developer who has been a key member of the RepRap 3D printer development community for many years. His designs include the original spring/lever extruder mechanism used on many 3D printers, the RepRap Wallace, and the Deezmaker Bukito portable 3D printer. By building and modifying several of the early open source 3D printers to wrestle unprecedented performance out of them, he has become an expert at maximizing the print quality of filament-based printers. When he is not busy making every aspect of his own 3D printers better, from slicing software to firmware and hardware, he likes to share that knowledge and experience online so that he can help make everyone else's printers better too.

Acknowledgments

The consumer 3D printing ecosystem would not exist in its current form without the open source 3D printing hardware and software community. We appreciate how much we learn by looking at projects made by everyone at maker events large and small.

The Apress production team was there for us to solve problems as they arose and let us have great creative freedom otherwise. We dealt most directly with Natalie Pao, Jessica Vakili, and Welmoed Spahr, but we also appreciate the many we did not see. This book includes some materials from our other Apress 3D printing titles, notably the 2014 *Mastering 3D Printing* and the 2018 *Mastering 3D Printing in the Classroom, Library, and Lab*.

Much has changed from the first edition, but Diego Porqueras of Deezmaker, Metalnat Hayes, and Peter Dippell's invaluable inputs back then still echo in this edition. We also particularly thank Michelle Lowman, the editor of the first edition, for taking a chance on us back in 2014 when this was so new.

We talked to many 3D printing professionals and maker-educators as we worked on this book, and we are grateful for the advice, images, and in some cases permission to use screenshots or photographs of their work, credited in more detail in the text. We want particularly to call out Steve Wygant of SeeMeCNC; Shelley Sun of MAKEiT, Inc.; Mara Hitner and Dave Gaylord at MatterHackers; Cody Casale of Casale Design LLC; Will and Jewelyn Co of CoKreeate; Nicole York of 3D Systems; Gabe Bentz of Slant 3D; David Shorey of Shorey Designs; Marius Kintel and the other OpenSCAD developers; and Ultimaker for allowing use of Ultimaker Cura screenshots. We are also grateful to the teams at Formlabs, SprintRay, The Virtual Foundry, and Procusini for discussions and images and to Desktop Metal and Markforged for insights for the metals chapter.

ACKNOWLEDGMENTS

Educators (and their students) who particularly inspired us were Simon Huss, Regina Rubio, Tri Nguyen, and others at the Windward School; Will Kalman of Granada Hills Charter High School; Nicole Endacott and Alexis Hopper of Pasadena's Institute for Educational Advancement and our students there; and maker-educators, Lucie deLaBruere and Rodney Batschelet. We were encouraged to create 3D printable educational models for visually impaired students by discussions with people in the community of teachers of the visually impaired, notably Mike Cheverie, Lore Schindler, and Yue-Ting Siu.

We also appreciate the resources at various libraries, notably the Los Angeles County Library South Whittier branch, the Pasadena Public Library, the Santa Monica Public Library, and the encouragement of Vivienne Byrd at the Los Angeles Central Library.

Finally, we want to thank our families for putting up with us in the thick of a long book project, and all their encouragement during the process. We could not have done it without any of you! Any errors are, of course, ours alone.

Introduction

We have been astonished at how much the 3D printing industry has changed since the first edition of this book, which was published in 2014. Amazingly little has remained constant since then, except perhaps for a sense of wonder about what might be possible. That sense now is informed by more sober realities about the challenges that remain, as well as more realistic ideas about good applications.

In this book, we want to give you a path to get started with 3D printing, as well as enough insight to go a considerable distance down the road to using it to create useful things. 3D printing still is not all that straightforward, and we have tried to create a balance between telling you enough so you can get started without drowning in too much detail and not telling you enough. We have minimized the use of step-by-step screenshots, for example, since those get out of date quickly. Instead, we have given a few examples and tried to tell you what we were doing and why, so that you can do the same thing in whatever system you are using.

3D printing now is largely a materials game. Whether you want to print in metal or plastic, and the mechanical characteristics of the final part, will drive the choice of printer type (filament, resin, or powder) and thus price point. Printer hardware design innovation continues. However, we expect to see faster evolution of materials that will allow seamless creation of a prototype and first production run with a 3D printer, then moving on to injection molding for high-volume parts. Dentistry has emerged as a key early adopter, along with general product prototyping and creation of tooling and fixtures.

We expect this book to be used by a wide spectrum of readers, from K-12 teachers to plant managers. As such we have included a variety of examples to give you ideas on what is possible. Since we have heard that some people used the first edition as an ad hoc textbook, in this edition we include questions at the end of each chapter. If you are using this to learn on your own, you may find reflecting on the questions useful to focus your understanding as you go.

New in this edition is a discussion of printers that use liquid resin, which was far less ubiquitous in the consumer market in 2014 than it is now. By their nature and heritage, the many brands vary more among manufacturers than filament printers do, and we have accordingly tried to keep things generic but with enough information to get you started. We also dip into what is possible with powder-based printers, particularly those used to create metal parts.

The book is divided into three parts. Part 1 covers 3D printing hardware and software, starting with the basics of understanding when using a 3D printer is a good idea (Chapter 1), what technologies are generally available (Chapter 2), and the overall workflow and software environment for actually using a printer (Chapter 3). Chapter 4 discusses how to select a printer based on what types of parts you will want to print. Chapter 5 gets into how creating a print works, and what to do to resolve common problems. Chapter 6 winds up the section with a discussion about how to post-process a print so that it is suitable for its ultimate use.

Part 2 is focused on designing models to be 3D printed. Like all manufacturing techniques, it is possible to design a part that is easy or hard to fabricate with a 3D printer. Chapter 7 reviews common computer-aided design (CAD) software and the strengths and weaknesses of various types. Chapter 8 gives you some design rules for creating a part. Chapter 9 describes part geometries that require special handling.

Finally, Part 3 describes applications, starting with manufacturing plastic parts (Chapter 10) and moving from there into the many options for printing in metal (Chapter 11), some of which are surprisingly affordable. We wrap it up with chapters on visualization and prototyping (Chapter 12) including innovative uses in surgery planning, a discussion of 3D printing in the classroom (Chapter 13), and wind up with a survey of applications in their early stages now (Chapter 14) like specialty food printing and bioprinting.

We hope you find the book useful and a jumping-off point to getting started or to going to the next level. At the end of Chapter 1, we have noted other resources we have created. We hope you will invent the next amazing application for future editions of the book.

PART I

3D Printer Hardware and Software

In this section, we describe the available 3D printer technologies and their advantages and disadvantages and the basics of what you need to know to operate one. In Chapter 1 we cover the situations when one would want to use a 3D printer. Chapter 2 discusses materials available for 3D printing and how your material choice may drive your printer hardware selection. Chapter 2 moves on to cover the *slicing* software that takes a design and makes it printable.

In Chapter 4, we move on to helping you make a purchasing decision for your printer, and in Chapter 5 we walk you through how to actually operate it and troubleshoot common problems. We wind up Part I with Chapter 6's review of techniques to use on a finished print for cosmetic or functional reasons. You will then be ready to think about how to design something to print (Part II) and 3D printing applications (Part III).

CHAPTER 1

Why Use a 3D Printer?

3D printing has been around since the 1980s. It has exploded in popularity since key patents began to run out in the 2000s, and by the mid-2010s low-cost 3D printers were everywhere. In the ensuing excitement, there was a lot of hype and a sense that soon everyone would have a 3D printer at home and would manufacture some large part of their consumer goods.

Reality has turned out to be both more and less interesting than that. Learning to use a 3D printer requires two distinct sets of skills. First, a user has to be comfortable with computer-aided design (CAD) tools or have access to models created by someone else. 3D printers require that you have a 3D computer model of your object in an appropriate format. A photo or other 2D image is not enough, since you need to have data that is stored as a full 3D model of the object (although scanners that take many pictures from different angles can use software to create a 3D model from them).

Then, to actually print it, some understanding of the physical properties of the real materials and the structure of your part in the real world is needed too, so that it will not fall apart during printing. People often come in from one side of that divide or the other and are surprised by how much they need to learn to be successful. Software is starting to bridge some of that gap as the market expands.

© Joan Horvath, Rich Cameron 2020
J. Horvath and R. Cameron, *Mastering 3D Printing*,
https://doi.org/10.1007/978-1-4842-5842-2_1

The home market makes sense for people who are comfortable with computer-aided design and like to make things in general, and thus who have a less-steep learning curve to climb. However, professional manufacturing has started to embrace 3D printing in earnest. Needing skills in both design and fabrication is nothing new for a factory, and 3D printable versions of common materials are becoming available.

This means that factories can do one-off prototypes and small batches of product and then seamlessly jump to very high-volume traditional techniques only if there is proven demand. Lower-cost ways of 3D printing metal are becoming available too. Printing molds and fixtures can likewise replace other methods that are far more costly and time-consuming.

Additive Manufacturing

3D printers create objects one layer at a time. The way they do that—by extruding melted plastic, by sintering materials, by hardening resin with UV light—can vary. But the basic premise is the same: a layer of material appears, controlled by a digital design stored in a computer, then another, and so on until the object appears, seemingly by magic. The key distinction from most other means of manufacturing is that 3D printing is *additive*—material is not cut away, but is added to a piece as it is built (Figure 1-1). Consumer-level 3D printers are very simple robots. We often say that they are, more or less, computerized hot glue guns (using a somewhat different plastic, though).

3D printing is a form of *additive manufacturing*. Additive manufacturing starts with nothing and builds up parts by laying up material on some sort of build platform. A lot of conventional manufacturing is *subtractive,* meaning that you start with a block of material (like metal or wood) and start cutting away material until you have the part that you want plus a pile of sawdust or metal shavings.

Figure 1-1. *A 3D print in progress*

History of Robotic 3D Printing

Charles W. (Chuck) Hull is generally credited with developing the first working robotic 3D printer in 1984, which was commercialized by 3D Systems in 1989. These machines were systems that used a laser to harden liquid resin, and many machines still use this technology. Other early work was taking place at the Massachusetts Institute of Technology (MIT) and University of Texas.

A flurry of patents followed in the early 1990s for various powder-based systems. These systems use inkjets to deposit a binder very precisely on the surface of a bed of powder to create layers on a downward-moving platform. These inkjet 3D printing patents became the basis for Z Corp, now part of 3D Systems. Alternatively, a laser can be used to fuse powdered plastic or metal together, called *selective laser sintering (SLS)*.

Meanwhile, S. Scott Crump and Lisa Crump patented fused deposition modeling (FDM) in 1989 and cofounded printer manufacturer Stratasys, Ltd. This technology (more generically called FFF, for fused filament fabrication) feeds a plastic filament into a heated extruder and then precisely lays down the material. When key patents expired in 2005, this technology became the basis of the RepRap movement described in the next section. This book mostly focuses on this type of printer, but we have some forays into resin stereolithography (SLA) printers and the various descendants of SLS as well.

The RepRap Project

When some of the key patents expired on the FFF printing method, it occurred to Adrian Bowyer, a senior lecturer in mechanical engineering at the University of Bath in the United Kingdom, that it might be possible to build a filament-extruding 3D printer that could create the parts for more 3D printers (except for readily available electronic and hardware-store components).

Furthermore, Bowyer decided he would put the designs for the parts for his 3D printer out on the Internet available to anyone with encouragement to others to improve them, with the requirement that anyone who wanted to distribute an improved version had to do so under the same license terms (an *open source* license). He called this concept the *RepRap* project, and obtained some initial funding from the UK's Engineering and Physical Sciences Research Council.

Bowyer's team called their first printer *Darwin*, released in March 2007, and the next *Mendel*, released in 2009 (for more details, see http://en.wikipedia.org/wiki/RepRap_Project). The printers were named after famous evolutionary biologists, because they wanted people to replicate the printers and evolve them as they did so. Files to make the plastic parts were posted online, freely available with alterations and improvements encouraged. Necessary metal parts were ideally available at a hardware store or able to be made in a garage. More exotic metal parts like gears to grip filament and nozzles to push it through became available for online purchase pretty early on from entrepreneurial printer builders with access to machine tools to make them. Stepper motors and some of the electronic components needed to drive them were already available online, but became much cheaper and easier to find as the 3D printer market increased the demand for them.

The early printers were difficult to put together and to get to print well. In the Czech Republic in 2010, Josef Prusa released a design now called the *Prusa Mendel*. It simplified the original Mendel design, and after that, there was an acceleration in printer designs as people tried out the open source designs, modified them, and posted their own. Prusa Research (`www.prusa3d.com`) is now one of the larger consumer 3D printer companies, still based in the Czech Republic.

After a while, there was a transition from just making files for printer parts downloadable to making whole printer kits available for purchase. One of the better-known kits was the *MakerBot Cupcake CNC*, which started shipping in April 2009, and which was superseded by the *MakerBot Thing-O-Matic* in 2010. These were mostly made of laser-cut wooden parts with some 3D printed parts (plus of course motors and electronics). Eventually, MakerBot became one of the earlier commercial consumer printer companies, and was purchased by Stratasys in 2013.

Crowdfunding and Makers

What really caused a blossoming of different designs, though, was the availability of funding for hardware projects through *crowdfunding*—websites that allow entrepreneurs to put out early-stage products and take contributions from the public to fund development and early production. Since the key patents had run out, entrepreneurs typically did not have any type of proprietary technology, which made traditional startup funding difficult to obtain.

By 2009, 3D printer development largely split into two camps: those supplying large, industrial printers (typically with some proprietary technology) and a big informal network of people working on open source RepRap or similar filament-based consumer printers.

On April 28, 2009, the *Kickstarter* crowdfunding platform was launched (`www.kickstarter.com`). Kickstarter is one of many *crowdfunding* platforms which allows an entrepreneur to post a project and ask people to support the endeavor. Various crowdfunding platforms have different rules about the type of project that is acceptable, and open source 3D printers are a very good fit for crowdfunding because most crowdfunding sites require a clearly defined project. Developing a 3D printer is a project with a natural endpoint, and often people offer a printer as the reward the person gets for supporting the development.

Since an open source printer, by definition, is not patented, it can be difficult to raise money in conventional investment forums. However, it is a good philosophical match for crowdfunding, extending the we-will-all-build-it-together open source ethos to also raise the money for launching a new 3D printer design.

In 2012, the *Form 1* stereolithography printer raised nearly three million dollars on Kickstarter. Many other 3D printers have raised in the six figures on Kickstarter and other platforms.

Figure 1-2 shows two RepRap heritage printers. Rich designed the 2011 RepRap *Wallace (a proof of concept machine, never sold commercially)* and was a key team member in the design of the 2013 Deezmaker *Bukito, which was launched on Kickstarter.*

At the same time that open source hardware was becoming common, open source or free software also began to stabilize and be useful to a nonexpert consumer. Software to design models and to prepare them for printing made great strides around this time. Today, some printers come with proprietary software, but printers that support generic protocols can use free or open source software end to end to create models and print them.

Figure 1-2 shows how rapidly open source printer design matured in a little over two years. Since then, many 3D printer companies have been started, and many have gone out of business or been acquired. Much of the actual manufacturing of printers and materials has moved to China and other lower-cost markets, and only a handful of companies that were around at the beginning of the consumer boom still exist.

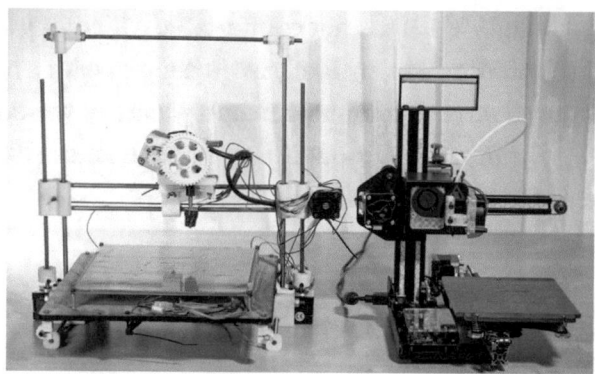

Figure 1-2. *The RepRap Wallace (L) and Deezmaker Bukito (R)*

Note   One good outcome of this heritage is that many 3D printers run on the same software base as each other. This means that if you are used to one printer you will be able to learn others fairly easily, and there are some software packages that work for many of them. In this book we will focus on Ultimaker Cura, which works with many different printers, but you should be able to translate if you use one of the other packages. We have much more about this in Chapter 3.

Kit or Fully Assembled?

Up until about 2013 or so, most consumer 3D printers required at least some assembly. It was worth mentioning in marketing materials if the assembly did not require soldering, since kits in those days often consisted of bags of wires, screws, and small parts. Currently, kits usually require minimal assembly, typically involving tightening a few screws and plugging a few electrical connectors, all of which are clearly labeled and keyed to prevent you from doing it wrong. The cost can be a lot lower, since often printers have a few pieces that will fit well in a small package when disassembled, leading to lower shipping costs.

Obviously, though, if you are not comfortable with doing some assembly and calibration, you are likely to be happier with a fully assembled printer. Even this minimal assembly teaches you something about how the machine works, though, so you will be more likely to know how to fix something that goes wrong.

When to Use a 3D Printer

3D printing is a very versatile technology, but there are times when other technologies are preferable. For example, laser cutters and small computer-numerically controlled (CNC) machines may be more appropriate tools in some circumstances. Of course, sometimes you can just use a piece of cardboard and an X-Acto knife to make something too.

Leaving that last one aside, we can do a comparison of the three common forms of *digital manufacturing*, machines that make something based on a computer file containing machine commands that result in a physical part. Laser cutters work from a 2D file (a .dxf or .svg format, typically) and 3D printers and CNC machines from 3D files in one of several formats (a common one for both being G-code) and manufacturer-dependent levels of interoperability among brands. All three have come down in price, although 3D printers probably have made the biggest strides there. The "maker movement," a renewed interest in making physical things, has created a market for these machines, which then bubbled up into professional applications.

For the details on the 3D printer options, see Chapter 2 for different types of printer and Chapter 3 for software and workflow issues. Chapter 4 discusses criteria to use when buying one based on what you want to do. In a nutshell, one of the challenges with low-cost 3D printers (as well as most of the higher-cost ones) is that prints take a long time. A twelve-hour or even multiday print is not uncommon, which might mean you want a gang of printers if you are going to depend on them for production. Second, either you can buy an expensive machine with expensive proprietary raw materials, or you can learn how to use more generic systems with some trial and error. The material cost difference can easily be a factor of 10 or 20, so this is a tricky thing to trade off. In an industrial environment where people's time is very expensive, the trade-offs may be different from those in a resource-limited school.

Caution   Be wary of marketing metaphors between resolution of 3D printers and that of printers on paper, since "dots per inch" does not make a lot of sense when you are laying down hot plastic (see the discussion of 3D printer resolution in Chapter 4). Similarly, "all in one" machines that incorporate a 3D printer, scanner, CNC machine, and even laser cutter via interchangeable heads are a much more challenging proposition than "all in one" 2D paper copier/scanner/printers. Since the tools have such different requirements to run optimally, we advise diligence before buying such a machine. If your budget is limited, buy just one tool now (we would vote for a 3D printer) and consider branching out in the future.

Laser Cutting vs. 3D Printing

Laser cutters use a laser to burn through material. The bigger the laser, the more challenging the material they can cut through. The keyword here is "burn." Since laser cutters basically are vaporizing a thin line of raw material, one has to exercise a lot of care that something unfortunate is not cut. For example, common plastics with some chlorine content (like PVC) will emit chlorine gas when cut with a laser cutter. At best, this destroys the machine; at worst, it injures the operator.

Therefore, a laser cutter, particularly outside a manufacturing environment, needs very strict protocols to make sure that only things that can be cut safely are ever placed in the machine. A fire extinguisher (along with training on how to use it) is critical too, since sometimes a cut line will catch fire in the machine. Fires are caused by failing to cool the surrounding material while depriving it of the fuel/oxygen mixture required to sustain a fire. For example, this can happen if the laser cutter's air nozzle gets blocked. For that reason, laser cutters need to always have someone watching so that any fire does not get out of hand. Laser cutters need to either be vented to the outside or used with a specialized air filter.

Having said all that, laser cutters are a lot faster than other digital fabrication for anything that is essentially a thick 2D slab. So, if you have 2D pieces that can be slotted together, or something is a flat cutout (like a stencil), then laser cutters are great. Most consumer-level ones can cut paper, acrylic and fabric, perhaps leather, and maybe etch metal, depending on the power of the laser. If you need to make 30 of something in a morning and the geometry and materials fit, a laser cutter might be the way to go, if you can create secure processes for operating it.

Some lower-cost machines are available with significantly less powerful lasers. These are often called laser engravers, but are sometimes (somewhat deceptively) marketed as laser cutters. These machines use smaller and cheaper diode lasers, closer to an overpowered version of what you would find in a Blu-ray disc player than in a real manufacturing tool. These devices are powerful enough to etch the surfaces of a range of materials and even cut some very thin materials like paper. Still there are risks from trying to use these machines on the wrong materials. Eye safety is also a big concern, since these machines often lack the metal enclosures and safety lockouts of more powerful machines.

A safer option is to use machines like those sold by companies like Cricut and Silhouette. These machines are commonly called *vinyl cutters* and use CNC instructions to move around a small blade that they use to cut thin sheets of material. Some, like the Cricut Maker, have tools available that are even capable of cutting thin wood or leather. While producing mechanically useful parts with them is unlikely, they provide a safer and friendlier experience for craft applications.

Laser cutters are usually between 10 and 20 times the cost of an equivalent-quality 3D printer, but then, they usually have the ability to cut a relatively large part. One trade-off is whether to buy a bunch of 3D printers or one laser cutter? Because of their versatility, we would likely vote for the 3D printer, but your circumstances and what you want to fabricate might warrant a different decision.

CNC Machine vs. 3D Printing

Small CNC machines have, like 3D printers, started to drop in price (and size). Ones that can handle cutting small pieces of wood are available now in desktop-scale sizes. These may have some limited ability to cut soft metals like aluminum, though they need to do so slowly and carefully. Ones designed to cut other metals are still pretty beefy though and are beyond most hobbyists' expertise level. Obviously if you want to make things out of a material that a 3D printer cannot make but a small CNC can cut, that can be a discriminator.

CNC machines are subtractive and start with a block of raw material. They make a lot of dust in the process, and how well they provide for containing and removing that dust can vary greatly. Their speed to make one of something is more comparable to a 3D printer than a laser cutter. Like 3D printers, cost rises rapidly with size and range of materials the machine can work with.

CNC machines have been around for a long time, and they for the most part run on a low-level language called G-code. (Most 3D printers run on G-code as well.) However, unlike lower-cost 3D printers which grew up around an open standard, CNC machines tend to all have proprietary "dialects" of G-code that they use, and so there is less commonality in how they work than there is for 3D printing. In either case, G-code should be considered specific to a certain model of machine, and is unlikely to work entirely as expected on another.

Unlike 3D printers, which usually use common slicing software to produce instructions in one of a few common G-code dialects (or "flavors"), the G-code for CNC machines is generated by CAM (computer-aided machining) software that is usually integrated into the CAD software used to design parts. Some CNC operations are simple enough, or the instructions sophisticated enough, that it is not uncommon for skilled CNC operators to write these instructions manually. This is not feasible for 3D printing and generally not recommended for hobbyist CNC operation.

One popular hobbyist application for CNC machines is making DIY circuit boards. By carefully milling away areas of the surface of copper-clad PCB material, producing custom electronics is fairly fast and cheap. Higher-quality circuit boards have become fairly easy to obtain using online services offered by professional circuit board manufacturers, but these are often expensive, slow to arrive, or both.

Caution   It is usually a bad idea to put a CNC machine, wood carving machinery, or anything that makes lots of fine dust in the same room as a 3D printer, especially if one or both machines are unenclosed. The dust will get picked up on the filament and clog the nozzle.

Table 1-1 summarizes key parameters for 3D printers, laser cutters, and CNC machines. Fundamentally 3D printers and CNC machines are complementary. Both work in 3D but some part geometries are more suited for one than another. Laser cutters are faster, but can really only produce parts that are "2.5D" (think something that can be cut out with a cookie cutter). As we will see, different 3D printer technologies vary widely in their cost and the demands they make on facilities, but the broad outlines in Table 1-1 will give you a starting point for comparison.

Table 1-1. *Digital Manufacturing Comparison*

	3D Printers	**Laser Cutters**	**CNC**
File type	3D (.stl, .obj), G-code instructions produced by a slicer	2D (.dxf, .svg)	2D or 3D, G-code instructions produced by CAM
Speed	Slow	Fast	Slow
Machine cost	Low (filament), moderate-high (metal, proprietary materials)	Moderate	Moderate to high
Materials	Plastics, some higher-end machines print metal or composites	Wood, acrylic, paper, cardboard, some plastics, etch metal	Wood, PCB material, soft metals, most other solid materials
Ideal part	Complex 3D	Complex 2D	Simple 2D/3D
Facility needs	Some	Moderate	Moderate

Complexity

One of the favorite mantras of 3D printing is that complexity is free. That is true, to a point. If a part is designed to be 3D printed (as we will discuss in Chapter 7, in particular), then it often does not matter that a shape is complicated. This does matter, a lot, for subtractive technologies since it is sometimes physically impossible to carve certain types of pieces. Subtractive technologies are good if the shape of the final part is not very different from your block, or rod, or sheet of raw material so that not a lot will need to be cut away.

For a 3D printer, the main thing that determines how much time a print will take is how much plastic it contains, including any support material that needs to be printed. There are some exceptions to this, but by and large a simple and complex shape with similar amounts of plastic will take close to the same time to build with a 3D printer. Because a typical 3D print is mostly hollow, the surface area of a model is usually a better predictor of the print time than the volume. The part in Figure 1-3 is a good example of a complex part that takes a while to print, but has no real challenges. It would be very difficult if not impossible to machine.

Figure 1-3. *A complex 3D printed part*

Size of a print, however, matters a lot. As printers get bigger, their cost rises very quickly. Typical sub-$2000 3D printers can build things from a few inches to a foot or so in each dimension. Getting much bigger than that may involve either glue or other assembly techniques to make a large piece out of smaller ones.

Beyond This Book

In this book, we will attempt to give you a good survey of the state of the art in 3D printing. We also try to give you a solid start in using filament-based printing and, to a lesser degree, resin printing. There is a great deal of free material out there too. Some of it is accurate, and of course some of it is not. Without a guide, it is challenging to figure out where to get started and how to pick a path through all that material. Here we have attempted to give you a path to get started and to be able to evaluate those other resources better.

In this book, we have tried to find a balance between the industrial user and the educator/hobbyist one. We have written several other books for Apress that might be of interest to the educational user, including the 2018 *Mastering 3D Printing in the Classroom, Library, and Lab*, and two books of 3D printable science projects, *3D Printed Science Projects* (2016) and *3D Printed Science Projects Volume 2* (2017).

If you are more interested in applying 3D printing to manufacturing, you can look up our courses on LinkedIn Learning (formerly `Lynda.com`). Here we have given references for more study where a specific one was reasonably freely available.

Summary and Questions for Review

This chapter gave a brief summary of 3D printing and other digital manufacturing techniques and their relative strengths and weaknesses. More specifically, we discussed the trade-offs among fabrication with a 3D printer, a laser cutter, or a CNC machine. We also gave a brief history of 3D printing and the emergence of lower-cost 3D printers in the 2010s. Finally, we wound up with some suggestions for further study.

Answer the following questions based on your review of the material in the chapter:

1. Name one type of part that could best be fabricated with (a) a 3D printer, (b) a laser cutter, and (c) a CNC machine.

2. Does a complex shape take more time than a simple one to print on a 3D printer? Why or why not?

3. Why can it be challenging to create a large print on a 3D printer?

CHAPTER 2

3D Printers and Printable Materials

In the last ten years or so, 3D printers have gone from being large pieces of industrial equipment to hobbyist novelties, to classroom staples. This chapter reviews the range of technologies that all fall into the broad category of 3D printing. There are many different 3D printers, but fundamentally they all create an object by building up one layer at a time on some sort of platform. As we discuss in Chapter 1, the basic idea of 3D printing (or additive manufacturing, if you prefer) is that you create objects by building them up one layer at a time.

The commonest type of 3D printer works with spools of plastic (called *filament*), which it melts and lays down to create objects. Others use lasers or projectors to harden light-sensitive resin. Still others either sinter powder or lay down binders to form objects from powder. The sheer number of technologies can be overwhelming. There is a lot of experimentation going on in the field at the moment, and hundreds of companies are developing new printers on what seems like a daily basis. The materials available have proliferated too.

In this chapter, we survey the field and give you a basic idea of what each of the technologies is and what it can do. We explain some basic vocabulary so that you can understand what we will be talking about later in the book. Later chapters focus more on the how-to aspects: the

© Joan Horvath, Rich Cameron 2020
J. Horvath and R. Cameron, *Mastering 3D Printing*,
https://doi.org/10.1007/978-1-4842-5842-2_2

software of 3D printing (Chapters 3 and 7), things to consider when buying a printer (Chapter 4), and how to fit a printer into your space and daily routines (Chapter 5).

Note   The 3D printing world uses metric measurements, and you will need to get comfortable with them if you are not already. The commonest measures you will encounter are millimeters (mm) and degrees Celsius. If you are used to Imperial units, 25.4 mm is an inch. To convert temperature in degrees Celsius to Fahrenheit, multiply the temperature in Celsius by 9/5, and then add 32 degrees. So, an extruder temperature of 210 C is the same as 410 F.

Filament Printers

By far the commonest consumer-level 3D printing technology is *fused filament deposition manufacturing*, sometimes called FDM (which technically applies to just one manufacturer) or more generically FFF for *fused filament fabrication*. In this book, we just refer to these printers as *filament 3D printers*. These printers pull plastic filament off a spool, melt it, and lay down the melted plastic in a fine line, typically around 0.2 mm high and a few times as wide.

Figure 2-1 shows a typical filament printer, which would have a spool of filament next to it if it were running. We have also labeled the common convention for naming the axes of a printer. The x axis here is left to right, the y axis is toward and away from you, and the z axis is vertical.

There are several different architectures of filament printers, which we can divide into *Cartesian* and *non-Cartesian*. Cartesian printers (like the one in Figure 2-1) have one motor or pair of motors for each drive axis. Non-Cartesians have no particular relationship between any one motor and axis.

Figure 2-1. *A typical consumer 3D printer*

The commonest non-Cartesian architecture is the *delta* printer, or *deltabot*. These owe some of their heritage to "pick and place" robots used in factories to pick up things and place them precisely somewhere else. The head that lays down filament is at the end of three independently moving arms. A typical delta is shown in Figure 2-2. Deltas are commonest for applications needing big build areas. Figure 2-3 is a photo of the giant demonstration deltabot, the Part Daddy, made by the same manufacturer as the consumer printer in Figure 2-2.

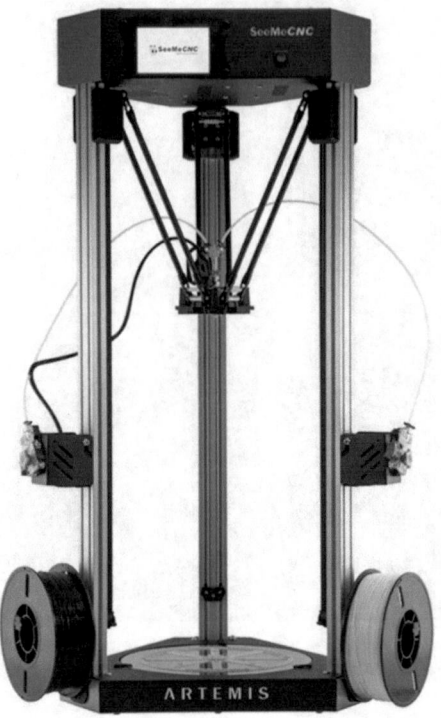

Figure 2-2. *The Artemis deltabot (courtesy of SeeMeCNC)*

Note   There are philosophical debates about whether Cartesians or deltas are "better" for any purpose, somewhat along the lines of debates about the virtues of Windows vs. Mac personal computers. In the end, the quality of manufacture and the features you need should drive your choice.

Figure 2-3. *The Part Daddy demonstrator*

Parts of a Filament Printer

A filament printer is pretty simple—a common analogy is to call it a computerized hot glue gun. However, there are several critical parts that affect reliability, print quality, and what kinds of materials you can use.

Stepper Motors

Consumer 3D printers usually have four or more *stepper motors*, commonly called *steppers*. As the name implies, these are precise motors that move their shafts in predefined angular steps. The availability of very reliable, precise, yet cheap steppers like those in Figure 2-4 has been an enabler for many consumer goods.

Typically, one motor drives each axis (sometimes two, on the vertical, or z, axis) by being coupled through pulleys to a belt or cable, or to a drive screw for an axis (often used for the z axis). Another motor drives the extruder gear. The steps per millimeter of your gears (how much an axis, or the filament, moves as the motor turns) is one of the things limiting how accurate a 3D printer can be, although it is not usually the principal limitation. Motors for 3D printers typically have 200 steps per revolution.

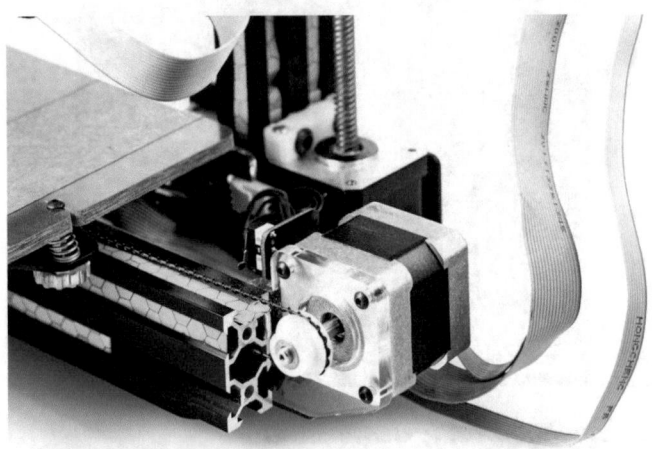

Figure 2-4. *A stepper motor*

Control

3D printers are controlled by microcontrollers. Many of these use a processor that is an adaptation or descendant of the Arduino open source microcontroller standard. Surprisingly, many printers run on very little computing horsepower. As of 2019, many consumer printers still use *open-loop control*, meaning that they do not have sensors checking that the printer is running as planned, except for sensors monitoring temperatures of the print bed and extruder. Deltas take more processing power than Cartesians, generally speaking, and you may want a more powerful controller on a delta to keep up.

Most printers do not need to be tethered to a computer. If they are, it is to feed the commands to create a model, not to directly control the motors and temperatures.

A printer runs some sort of firmware on its controller to do that low-level control. *Firmware* is just software that is used to control a machine. Many printers that are descendants of the RepRap project described in Chapter 1 run a variation of the open source Marlin firmware. Older MakerBots and their distant cousins and clones tend to run a version of the Sailfish firmware.

3D PRINTER CONTROLLERS

The most common type of 3D printer controller is based on the ATmega2560, an 8-bit microcontroller that runs at 16 Mhz. The first 3D printer controller to use this processor was the RAMPS board (short for RepRap Arduino Mega Pololu Shield). This was a shield, or daughterboard, designed to be used with the Arduino Mega development board that was designed to carry several small stepper driver boards in a form factor originally designed by electronics manufacturer Pololu. Most modern versions have the ATmega2560 chip onboard rather than using a separate circuit board, but many are still designed to use replaceable stepper drivers in the Pololu form factor. More advanced stepper drivers are now available in pin-compatible formats that allow you to upgrade your printer or replace a damaged driver.

There are several different projects developing open source firmware to run on these 8-bit microcontrollers. The most common of these is the Marlin firmware. Some newer controllers use 32-bit ARM microcontrollers running at 48–120 Mhz. Most of these are divided between those designed to run the Duet firmware and those designed for Smoothieware, and not compatible with one another. Marlin 2.0 (in development as of this writing) adds support for 32-bit controllers, including many of the existing boards designed for other platforms.

Build Platform

Prints are created on a flat platform, interchangeably referred to as the print *bed* or print *platform*. Most are equipped with a heater, which allows you to use more materials, as we discuss in detail in Chapter 4. Depending on the printer design, the print bed may move in one or two directions, or not at all.

Extruder

The *extruder* is the part of the printer that melts and moves the filament. It is made up of several parts. We have already mentioned the extruder drive gear and its motor, which push the filament into the hot end. The hot end in turn is comprised of a heater, a nozzle, and a sensor (called a *thermistor*) to sense how hot the nozzle is.

The nozzles are very precise. They typically measure 0.35–0.50 mm in diameter and can be made entirely of metal, or they may be lined with a material called polytetrafluoroethylene (PTFE) to minimize jamming. All-metal hot ends are required for printing many materials.

The hot end includes a heating element and a sensor to regulate temperature, a thermal transition zone (often with a heatsink and fan on the cold end), and a nozzle that is usually made of brass. Recently, hardened-steel and ruby-tipped nozzles have appeared—some filaments are very abrasive, and these are more resistant to abrasion. Figure 2-5 is a close-up of a nozzle. It is the triangular object under the "O" in "HOT."

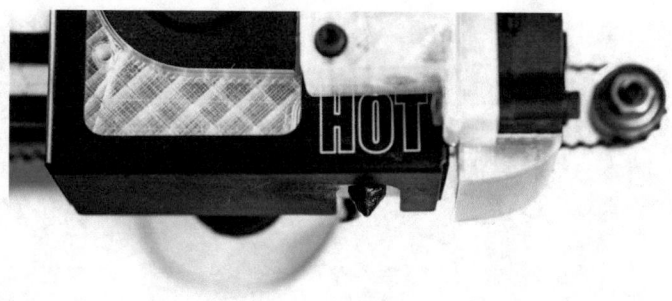

Figure 2-5. *A nozzle*

How Printing Works

First, filament has to be pulled from the spool into the printer, usually with a gear driven by a stepper motor. There are a variety of geometries for this. Sometimes a gear is right next to where the plastic will be melted (the hot end), and sometimes it is separated by a flexible tube, called a *Bowden tube*.

Extruders with a gear pulling in filament without an intermediary tube are called *direct-drive* extruders. Confusingly, the same term is used to distinguish extruders with the drive gear mounted directly to the motor from ones that have a gear reduction. In either case, the gear gripping the filament is called the extruder *drive gear*. Figure 2-6 shows the drive gear on a Bowden-style printer.

Figure 2-6. *Extruder gear on a printer with a Bowden tube*

Some manufacturers like direct-drive extruders; many have moved now to some form of Bowden extruder. The main advantage of having the gear right at the extruder is simplicity, though it also means that the motor is being carried around with the hot end. This can in turn mean slower printing and other issues.

A print starts with a 3D CAD, which is turned into a series of commands for the stepper motor and the temperature controls. This process is discussed in detail in Chapters 3 and 7. Once those commands are loaded onto the printer, via cable, SD card, or wireless connection, the printer will first heat up the nozzle and the platform (if it has a heater). Once everything is up to temperature and the printer performs whatever self-checks it is capable of, printing begins.

The first layer of the print has to stick well to the platform. There are various techniques for ensuring this. Some involve software settings (Chapter 3), and others are related to using the correct platform surface for the material you are printing (Chapter 4). Assuming that the print sticks, as a layer builds up, there are areas that do and do not have plastic within one layer. This means that the nozzle will be extruding during some parts of the layer, and not during others.

During the time that the printer is not laying down plastic, the extruder gear will first pull the filament back a bit to relieve pressure in the nozzle. This is called *retraction*, and getting it right is something of a black art that involves a process of trial and error for particular combinations of printer hardware and filament material. Poor retraction settings can make a print stringy or blobby, like the one in Figure 2-7.

Figure 2-7. *A print with poor retraction settings*

If the print fails to stick, most printers do not know that and will happily continue to print. This will result in a big pile of plastic (Figure 2-8). It is something of a rite of passage to leave a printer for a while and come back to a big hairball. Take a picture, sigh, and take comfort that you are now an official member of the 3D printing tribe.

Figure 2-8. *A failed print*

Suppose that you were printing something that had a part sticking out, like someone reaching out an arm. As you built up your print layer by layer, you would eventually reach the first layer of the bottom of the arm. But as you laid out plastic to form the first layer, it would just fall down since there was nothing to support it. To address problems like that, we use support material. *Support* is extra material that is added to the model to allow it to print a layer at a time. Figure 2-9 shows a print with support. The process of creating support is discussed in Chapter 3.

Printers can handle *overhangs* of about 45 degrees—the subsequent layers overlap a bit and allow you to print these moderate slopes. Printers can also *bridge* over open areas. If you are printing a hollow cube, for instance, the top will be over open space, but supported on all four sides. Many of the support and bridging decisions that need to be made are somewhat automated these days, but in Chapter 3 we talk about the human intervention that is still required.

Figure 2-9. *A print with support*

Assuming that everything went well, you will have a print that builds up from the platform layer by layer. The layers will be more visible in some filaments than others. Layer height is something that most printers allow you to set; common heights run from about 0.1 to 0.3 mm. Figure 2-10 is a close-up of the output from the Part Daddy giant printer in Figure 2-3, which is a little easier to see than some. (This printer uses plastic pellets rather than filament, which is why the colors are variable.)

Figure 2-10. *A close-up of layers*

Filament Choices

There are many choices for 3D printer filament. Your printer, however, will likely only be able to handle a subset of them, and will either use 3 mm or 1.75 mm diameter filament. The quality of your 3D printing filament will make the difference between endless frustration and a good experience, so let us go over what "filament quality" means first.

Consumer 3D printers, as we have just seen, are really not all that sophisticated. They have, in a way, outsourced their complexity to their filament. Consistency and quality is better now than it was a few years ago, but can still be uneven.

If you are 3D printing, you need a pair of digital calipers to check your filament's diameter. A "3 mm" filament will typically be about 2.85 mm. A 1.75 mm filament will usually be about that. If you have a printer that uses cartridges, you will need to assume that the extra money you pay for your filament is taking care of this step for you. Be sure to adjust the filament diameter setting in your software (Chapter 3) to the actual value of your filament diameter. Typically, we just leave the value at 1.75 or 2.85 without adjustment most of the time these days. Figure 2-11 shows checking filament diameter with a pair of calipers.

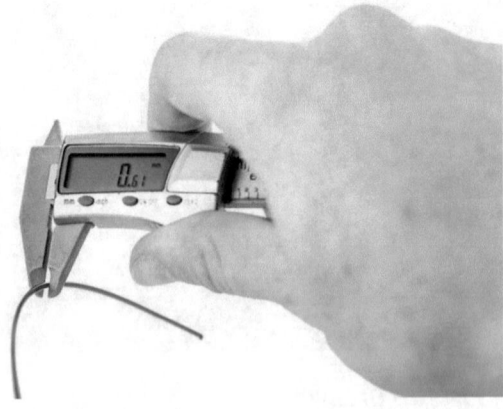

Figure 2-11. *Checking filament diameter with a pair of calipers*

Tip   If your printer stops extruding mid-print, your first suspect should be a bulge in the filament, which will jam the extruder. The extruder gear will also usually chew into the filament and therefore have a lot of ground filament in it. Brush the ground filament out gently and measure the filament. If it is significantly wider than you expected, break off a few meters and measure again.

The other filament problem that can cause this symptom is filament impurity or poor color mixing. Again, try breaking off some and printing again. If your printer has a restart function, it probably will not work in this case, because you do not know how long the filament has been grinding. You will probably have to restart from the beginning.

There are a lot of different filaments available. We discuss some of the commonest ones, and what 3D printer hardware and software you need to use them.

Tip   Filaments come labeled with a range of appropriate temperatures for the extruder and the platform. Often the temperature range is really large, so it is not that helpful. There may be a label on the spool or on the website where you ordered it. If in doubt, start in the middle of the range. See the discussions of settings in Chapter 3 to see whether you should move up or down if you do not like the results.

Filaments need to be kept in a cool, dry place. Do not open a spool of filament out of its shrink wrap until you are ready to use it, because keeping it sealed will keep moisture out of it. After a while, you will have a bunch of partial spools on the go. We keep ours in airtight plastic boxes—a

5-gallon paint bucket with a good lid works well; Joan is partial to 22-liter stacking plastic boxes with good seals. Resist the urge to use your spools as a colorful wall display, since that is asking for both dust and moisture contamination of your filament.

Nylon is particularly sensitive to humid conditions. If nylon gets damp, the water will pop and sizzle out as it heats up, leaving pits and gaps in the print. If you live someplace with routinely high humidity, you may want to explore reviews of the various filament-drying systems out there, or DIY equivalents.

Dust is an issue, too. Keep the filament clean; in Chapter 5 we have some suggestions on how to do that. Do not try to do 3D printing and other fabrication that creates dust (ceramics, woodworking, machining) in close proximity.

Caution   Many low-cost printers have no temperature limiters in their software or hardware and will be perfectly happy trying to heat the nozzle to the point where it will burn, or the heated bed to beyond its design temperature. Check your manufacturer's limitations before trying a filament that your printer was not designed to use.

PLA

By far the commonest filament material is PLA, polylactic acid. It is a biodegradable, corn-based (sometimes sugarcane-based) plastic. It melts at a relatively low temperature and will stick to a variety of platform surfaces. PLA usually requires an extruder temperature of around 210 degrees C.

One of the reasons it is so popular is that PLA does not require a heated platform. Low-cost printers usually suggest that you put blue painter's tape (1.88-inch wide 3M ScotchBlue 2090 works well) and use that as your surface. If you *do* have a heated platform, follow your manufacturer's suggestions for what to put on the bed. Often it will be plain glass, or you might smear on some glue stick first. The adhesive found on painter's tape is not suitable for use on platforms heated much beyond room temperature.

The downside of PLA is that, well, it melts at a low temperature. A PLA print on a hot car dashboard will warp and creep. (*Creeping* is a tendency to flow slowly under pressure—for example, a PLA print might develop a dent if something is pressing against it in a warm room.) If that is not an issue, PLA is a very good material for quick prototypes, student projects, and the like.

There are specialty *filled PLA* mixes that contain stone, wood, metal, or glow-in-the-dark fine particles. Objects made with this can look surprisingly like they are made of the respective substance, with a bit of polishing. However, these mixes are hard on nozzles and tend to abrade them; hardened or ruby nozzles can get around this problem. There are also formulations of PLA that have a nice sheen without any post-processing. Experiment a little (many filament sellers have sample packs) to see what you might like to work with.

Silk PLA is PLA mixed with lignin fibers. The fibers expand a bit when printed and make the layer lines nearly invisible, which gives a sheen to the material that can look like burnished metal. Figure 2-12 shows a piece printed in silk PLA.

Figure 2-12. *Vase printed in silk PLA*

Figure 2-13 shows the bad side of PLA: a garden sign that sat out in the California sun for about two years gradually sagged under its own weight.

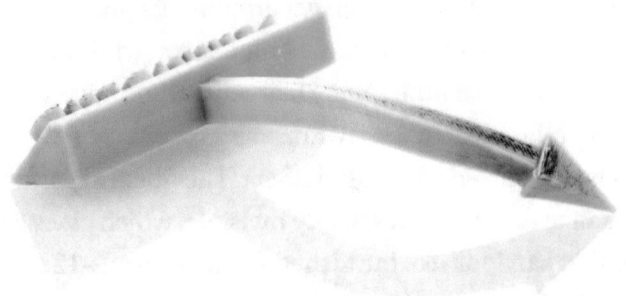

Figure 2-13. *PLA sign after time in the California sun*

PET

PET (polyethylene terephthalate) is a very common plastic in the non-3D printing world, used for water bottles and many other things. PETG is a type of PET that is often used in 3D printing; some varieties are translucent. You can in principle print PETG on blue tape, although people use heated beds if they have one. It needs an extruder temperature higher than PLA—around 230–260 C. PET filaments are typically a little more expensive than PLA, sometimes as much as twice the price. But they can look really good, particularly if you want something transparent, and they are not as vulnerable to warm temperatures as PLA is.

ABS

Acrylonitrile butadiene styrene (ABS) is the plastic used for LEGO bricks, among many other things. It is durable and far less vulnerable to warping in warm temperatures. The flip side of that is that it requires a high nozzle temperature—from about 220–260 C. A heated bed is also an absolute requirement for ABS, at 90–110 C. People often use PET or Kapton tape on a heated bed for ABS. As ABS cools, it wants to shrink and will pull up from the bed, as you can see in the print that was stopped after a few layers shown in Figure 2-14. Some trial and error is required to get it to stick and lay flat.

Figure 2-14. *An ABS part that pulled up from the heated bed*

Caution   Although we recommend ventilation with any 3D printer, ABS fumes in particular are an issue. However, blowing a fan directly on the print will tend to make it fail. Arrange your ventilation if possible to be pulling air off the print rather than blowing on it.

ABS can be smoothed and post-processed in a variety of ways. We talk about some of those in Chapter 6, where we focus on what happens after the print comes off the printer.

Nylon

Nylon is a strong printing material, which also requires a high temperature of around 240–270 C. Be sure your nozzle is all-metal before trying to print with nylon, because nozzles lined with plastic cannot handle that high a temperature.

The biggest challenge with nylon, other than the high extruder temperature, is that it does not want to stick to anything. The best platform material we have found for nylon is a cold platform made of Garolite LE, a type of composite. Failing that, we have heard that glue stick on a platform heated to about 75 degrees C will work. As noted earlier, nylon also needs to be kept very dry, or pitting can result. Nylon can be dyed after printing with dyes appropriate for it.

Challenging Filaments

Some materials are difficult to print well. Filaments that are very strong tend to require correspondingly higher temperatures and often want to peel up from the print bed. Some printers can handle materials like polycarbonate, which typically requires higher nozzle and bed temperatures than consumer machines can achieve safely.

There are also filaments that are flexible which can create parts that also can flex. However, they tend to jam in the extruder, particularly for printers using 1.75 mm filament and Bowden tubes.

Dissolvable Support

Some printers have more than one extruder. One reason for buying such a machine is to allow the use of support material that can be dissolved away, either with water or other chemicals.

The commonest water-soluble support, PVA (used ambiguously for the closely related water-soluble polymers polyvinyl alcohol and polyvinyl acetate), is basically Elmer's glue. As you might imagine, it has a tendency to clog nozzles, and it has to be extruded fairly cold. Check your local rules about disposal—you should not put water full of dissolved glue into your plumbing. PVA has to be kept extremely dry, for obvious reasons. It also tends not to stick well to the other materials you are using to make your print.

Other materials like HIPS (high-impact polystyrene) dissolve in *limonene* (a solvent made from oranges), but this leaves you with a rather smelly mess to deal with.

In other words, this is not a particularly easy route to go. You will need to talk to your local waste-disposal person to see how best to handle your waste stream. In the end, you may decide to stick with support you can pull off with pliers. We talk more about support in Chapter 3's discussion of software settings.

Multimaterials vs. Multiple Extruders

The other reason you might buy a printer with multiple extruders is to print objects in more than one color at a time. With only one extruder, 3D printers print with just one color of filament for the entire print. In essence, you develop two interleaved computer models, one for each color, and the printer alternates extruders in each layer. Because the extruders would interfere if they tried to print at the same time, typically dual-extruder prints take longer than single-extruder ones do because one extruder prints, then wipes itself off (so it does not dribble on the layer once it is done), and so on, back and forth.

Alternatively, some machines now come with a device that can take filament from multiple spools and splice a mixed filament to mimic what multiple heads would have done, but with one nozzle. This is an interesting development to watch; there are some aftermarket devices available as add-ons to existing printers.

Aftermarket Upgrades

If you want to be able to print some materials that will not stick to your original print bed material, there are now a variety of aftermarket materials you can stick on to your platform. A commonly used one is BuildTak (www.buildtak.com), which can be glued on to your existing platform. The only issue is that some materials stick *too well* to BuildTak, and getting the prints off it is challenging. You will need to recalibrate your printer if you add a clip-on or stick-on platform on top of your original. See "Calibrating Your Printer" in Chapter 5.

Similarly, there are replacement third-party nozzles. Here, however, the replacement process is more sophisticated. If you are not a tinkerer who is comfortable with building a printer from a kit, you probably should not go that route.

Advanced Filament Printers

As the consumer and higher-end "prosumer" markets expand, some specialty printers have emerged. Some are very large, having a build volume of a cubic meter or more. Some have up to five extruders, or one of the multimaterial extruders we mentioned earlier.

Another niche is occupied by Markforged (`www.markforged.com`). This company has a printer that lays down nylon in parallel with another head that lays down one of several continuous fibers. Thus, they are 3D printing carbon fiber or other composite parts; Markforged has stated in webinars that its early adopters often use their printers to make tooling. Some Markforged printers use a filament with chopped carbon fiber filler, which increases the stiffness of the base nylon. This evolution of materials with custom printers is probably a niche that will grow as specialty applications emerge; novel materials are now driving a lot of the 3D printing universe as the printers become more commoditized.

Markforged is also one of several companies developing printers that are designed to print with filament (or, in some cases, rods) with a high percentage of metal filler. Metal-filled filament is available for many printers, but while most of these filaments can only give the appearance of metal, these machines are designed to create real metal parts by allowing you to put the printed parts into some combination of a chemical bath and furnace that will remove out the plastic matrix material and sinter the metal particles together. Chapter 11 has more detail about 3D printing with metal.

3D PRINTING PENS

3D printing "pens" (Figure 2-15) heat up 3D printing filament (usually 1.75 mm) and allow you to freehand draw with the melted plastic. They are useful for welding together broken prints, since you can use a thin line of the same material as you are using for your 3D print. In other words, they are more or less hot glue guns that use 3D printer filament.

The pens can also be used to do 3D freehand drawing. However, unless you have really steady hands, it is not as easy as it looks. Cover a piece of cardboard with the same blue painter's tape you would use on a cold 3D printer platform and use it as your work area.

Vendors sell short strips of PLA filament to use with these devices, but you can use 1.75 mm regular 3D printer filament, which is much cheaper. We usually cut a few meters or so off at a time to use because the regular spools can be annoying to use with a pen. You can use as many colors as you want in one design, since you will just load strips of filament one at a time to create an object. We usually save the last few meters of filament on a spool to use with pens.

Figure 2-15. *A 3D printing pen*

Some pens can use both PLA and ABS, with an ability to set temperatures appropriate for both, and most have a speed control to manage how much plastic you are using at a time. Using one of these pens can be a good exercise in building your intuition about what a 3D printer is doing, as you will most likely make a stringy mess the first time you use a pen.

Concerns about ventilating an area where you are melting plastic, ABS in particular, still apply with a pen. And of course the pen tip gets very hot, just like the extruder on a 3D printer. If you are using PLA, you will need to have some sort of airflow anyway to cool the material as it hardens out of the pen if you want to build in 3D.

There are stencils and such things too; search online for "3D art pen" for examples and videos. Eiffel Tower models are the aspirational thing to build, but you obviously should not start there. No computer modeling is required to use a 3D pen, but manual dexterity and a bit of artistic ability help. Pens with good temperature control and ability to use multiple materials cost about $50–$100.

Resin Printers: SLA, DLP, and LCD

The consumer resin printer market has been coming into its own recently with a great deal of experimentation. There are three types of resin printer on the market right now: stereolithography (SLA), Digital Light Processing (DLP), and a variation of DLP that uses a liquid-crystal mask (LCD) with an LED illumination source. Technically, all are SLA, but the terminology is used somewhat ambiguously. Laser SLA printers use optics to move around an ultraviolet laser spot to cure UV-curable resin within one layer at a time. This layer is peeled off the bottom of a tank (or dropped down into the tank, in the older but now less-common top-down orientation), and then the next layer is cured, and so on. Figure 2-16 shows a Formlabs Form 2, one of the higher-end consumer SLA machines.

DLP, on the other hand, uses a projector to cure a whole layer at a time; LCD printers are similar but use an LCD mask illuminated by LEDs to illuminate a layer at a time. Some low-cost resin printers use a modified cell phone screen in place of the projector. In Chapter 4's discussion of purchase decisions for these printers, we go into the pluses and minuses of these in more detail, and the operational issues.

Figure 2-16. *A Formlabs Form 2 SLA resin printer*

Printing Process

Resin 3D printers have an ability to create far finer detail than filament-based printers. A resin printer is limited by its laser spot size (SLA) or the pixel size (DLP and LCD). This means that resin prints can have very smooth surfaces relative to those created by a printer using filament.

Resin printers still need to create support, but the nature of the support is a little different. Typical printers are "bottom-up" and build a layer at a time, which is peeled off the bottom of a tray. To survive the peeling process with every layer, support is required. However, the object prints upside-down and support primarily withstands the forces associated with peeling off the bottom at the end of each layer. Figure 2-17 shows a print building upside-down on a Form 2. The greenish glow is the laser.

Printers that use a laser to cure resin use a series of coordinates that the laser spot moves through, philosophically similar to the commands that control a filament-based printer. They can generally move the laser spot much faster than a printer can move a heated nozzle, though. Although most have proprietary software, some of them have adapted software developed for filament printing.

Printers that use a projector need a series of 2D images, one for each layer. Some of these printers have an HDMI port as an input, and their software treats the printer as a second monitor on which it displays those images. A popular way to run these machines is to connect a Raspberry Pi running NanoDLP to avoid tying up a larger computer. This avoids potentially ruining a print or even damaging the printer if the computer tries to display something else on that "screen."

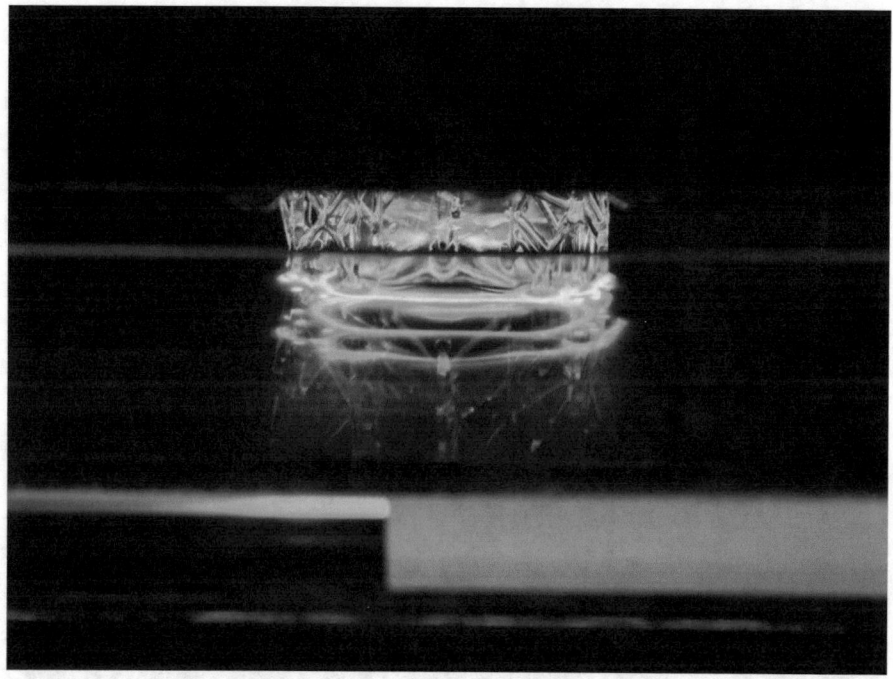

Figure 2-17. *A resin print in progress*

Post-processing

Post-processing is required on SLA prints, and typically involves washing off the print with isopropyl alcohol to remove uncured resin and exposing the print to UV light to ensure that the resin is fully cured. This can be a challenge in environments that are not set up for disposing of chemicals.

Each manufacturer will have a process for its own resins; read the process on the manufacturer's site before purchasing your printer so you are sure you will be set up to handle it. Typically, prints emerge from the printer a little sticky and need to be washed off and light-cured. Figure 2-18 shows a resin print just after it has been washed and cured and is ready to snip off supports. You can also see how much more open support is on a resin printer.

Figure 2-18. *Washing off a resin print*

Notice that this process requires wearing nitrile gloves to keep the resin off your skin. We talk a little more about resin printers in Chapter 4.

Materials

Resin printers use a variety of light-cured resins. Most of them are sensitive to UV light so that you do not have to use them in a dark room, since visible light does not harden them. But because by definition you cannot see UV light, you might be surprised if you do not control the environment around the printer. For example, having a resin printer in direct sunlight can destroy the printer (or at least its resin tank) by hardening a brick of resin into it.

Much of the development in resin 3D printing at the moment is in proprietary resins with special properties. Formlabs, for example, has a high-temperature resin that it says can be used for injection molds. Biocompatible resins for dental work have been an active area of study as well. Because the materials are so crucial, many manufacturers have closed systems with materials cartridges and proprietary software. These may have great properties, but they will be correspondingly expensive.

Some specialty resin applications include the following:

- High-temperature for injection molds

- Biocompatible resins for dental work

- Castable resins for jewelry

- Resins that cure into a flexible material

Formlabs (`www.formlabs.com`) has been an innovator in the materials space. If you want to know more, you can read up on its proprietary materials on the website, which includes case studies.

Other Technologies

The overall field of 3D printing has been expanding in many different directions. There are a few other major categories of printer that are unlikely to come into the classroom in the near term, but given the rate of progress, one never knows!

There are some just-for-fun technologies, like a printer that makes pancakes (`www.pancakebot.com`) and ones that print in chocolate or other foodstuffs. But the industrial market has been moving onward too. In this section, we talk about some of the categories of industrially oriented printers.

SLS

One of the oldest technologies in this space is selective laser sintering (SLS). Typically, a very fine powder is spread on a build platform, and a laser is used to sinter the powder together. More and more powder is added as the print grows. SLS can be used to make very fine, detailed prints. SLS prints do not need support, because the unfused powder acts as a support. However, the powder is very fine and hard to deal with, and SLS has been an expensive technology. Some "desktop" SLS machines are beginning to come on the market, and this may be an area to watch.

Many machines that print metal use a process called direct metal laser sintering (DMLS), which is the SLS process used for metals. Metal powder has to be worked in an inert atmosphere to prevent fires, so DMLS machines are very expensive since they need to be completely enclosed and filled with an inert gas. Other processes like selective laser melting (SLM) and electron beam melting (EBM) use even higher power to more fully fuse metal powder. We discuss metal printing more in Chapter 11.

Binder Jetting and Material Jetting

There are also processes that use a powder bed that do not require a laser (or other highly directed heat source). These processes typically use an inkjet head similar to what you would find in a desktop photo printer. Instead of heating the powder to fuse it, they deposit glue or other binding agents onto the powder. Binder jetting machines typically use gypsum powder and can deposit ink along with the binding agent to create full-color prints.

Binder jetting can also be done with metal, but that requires a second step in which the loosely bound particles are infused with a lower-temperature metal, or a wash and sinter stage to remove the binder. Some machines even sinter nylon powder by using inkjet heads to deposit sensitizing and/or inhibiting agents to the powder before heating it with a more diffuse heat source.

Other processes do away with the powder entirely and use inkjet heads to deposit liquid resin. These printers deposit tiny droplets of UV-sensitive resin and then quickly expose it to UV light to solidify it. This process requires that multiple materials be used—a build and support material at least—and can be used to produce prints with gradients of color and even of material properties like flexibility.

Bioprinting

Printing with biological materials has become fairly mainstream now in lab environments. In some cases, the printer is using some sort of paste to create an object for a biology lab. In others, the printer is very precisely squirting a liquid. The lower-cost "bioprinters" are basically a robotic pipette that can move in three dimensions; there are several competitors in this space already, and there will probably be more. Search for "bioprinter" to see the huge range of capabilities and price ranges.

Organovo (www.organovo.com) has been printing human tissue, as have other researchers. Right now, most people are looking at projects like skin or ear repairs, but there is long-term interest in building entire human organs.

Summary and Questions for Review

This chapter reviewed the different types of 3D printer technology available in the consumer market, with a particular focus on printers that use plastic filament. We also gave a brief introduction to other technologies, particularly printers that use liquid resin. 3D printer evolution is being driven now by inventions of new materials, too, and we discussed some of the wide variety of materials you might want to explore.

Answer the following to test your knowledge of the material in this chapter:

1. What are the relative merits of 3D printers that use filament vs. ones that use liquid resin?

2. What are two commonly used filament materials, and when might you use each?

3. Name three critical components of a filament printer and what they do.

4. How are SLA and DLP resin printers different from each other?

5. What is SLS printing, and what type of material does it use to print?

CHAPTER 3

3D Printer Workflow and Software

People are often startled and intimidated when they discover that a 3D printer is not really the same as a paper printer. Although some consumer 3D printers have a "print" button, there are some steps needed to get to the point of pushing it, not to mention the need to monitor what happens afterward. We prefer to think of 3D printing as more like cooking than printing. Just as you would not expect to cook by just pressing a "bake" button without setting some temperatures and timers first, 3D printing requires some knowledge of your printer, the materials you are using, and the design you are trying to print. If any of those have issues, getting good results is challenging.

As happens with cooking, everyone wants to start out creating a multitier wedding cake. However, it is wise to try for brownies instead, at least for a while. In this chapter, we help you understand what is hard to print vs. what is easy and give you some insight into more sophisticated techniques. Different printers have evolved variations on the basic workflow. Some are the equivalent of an Easy-Bake Oven, whereas others are like equipment in a commercial kitchen, for similar reasons of capability vs. complexity. Your expectations need to match your hardware. Price is not always a guide to capability and quality in the current market; see Chapter 4's discussion on how to buy a printer.

© Joan Horvath, Rich Cameron 2020
J. Horvath and R. Cameron, *Mastering 3D Printing*,
https://doi.org/10.1007/978-1-4842-5842-2_3

As you will see, unlike with cooking, some basic computer skills are necessary to get started. This chapter walks through the steps needed to go from zero to plastic in as generic a way as possible, with some nods to common variations on the theme. 3D printing software is updated often, so the precise options we show here may change by the time you read this. The overall workflow should stay much the same, though. For that reason, we have just a few screenshots and narrate the types of printer settings rather than go step-by-step through any particular program.

Workflow Overview

3D printing typically requires three steps (Figure 3-1) that might be combined into fewer than three pieces of software, might require some scrolling around on a screen on your printer for the last step, or might involve other variations. In all cases, though, you need to create or acquire a 3D *computer-aided design* (CAD) model, slice this model into layers, and generate the commands needed to physically create the model, and, finally, physically create the print.

This chapter is mostly focused on the middle step of slicing the model and creating commands. Some printers use proprietary software that integrates the last two steps. They may automate some of the decisions we describe in this chapter or have hard-coded some compromise settings that will work decently in some common situations but perhaps create bad prints in others. As the market has expanded, printers have fallen into two camps: printers with proprietary ecosystems (typically more expensive) and *open* printers that allow you to use a variety of free software and generic materials. The *closed* printers position themselves as easier to use and the open ones as allowing users more flexibility.

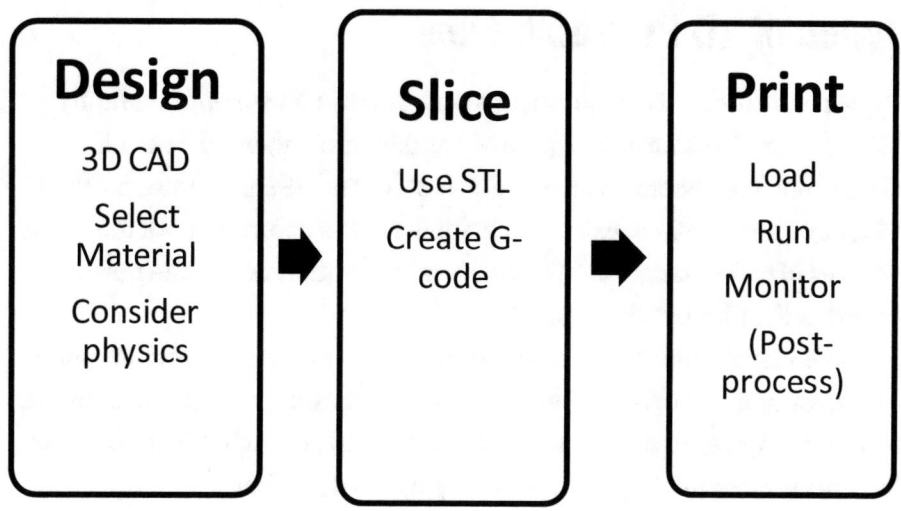

Figure 3-1. *3D printing workflow*

Note   For historical reasons, people sometimes refer to the set of software that runs an automated tool like a 3D printer as its *toolchain.* The word does not imply any physical objects—in the case of a 3D printer, at least. We use the word *workflow* here, which we feel may be more familiar in educational or scientific settings.

Models

The first step in the 3D printing process is developing a 3D model of the design you want to create. This is done in CAD software, which we introduce here and explore in depth in Chapter 6.

Types of 3D Printable Files

Typical consumer 3D printers want a model to be in stereolithography (STL) format. This format is quite old and inefficient, but universal. When software generates an STL file, it converts the surface to a mesh of triangles. An STL file consists of a giant list of the coordinates of the three vertices of each triangle in 3D space, and the orientation of the normal vector to the plane of that triangle.

A similar standard supported by many slicers is an .OBJ file, an open format originally developed by Wavefront Technologies that also supports texture mapping for color and NURBS curvature, though the use of these features is rare and they are ignored by slicers if present.

A superset standard that can be a grouping of multiple STL files is an additive manufacturing (AMF) file, which also supports material definitions required for printing with multiple filaments (for different colors or different material properties). More recently, Microsoft has formed a consortium to introduce the 3D manufacturing (3MF) format, which has similar capabilities (for more, see `https://3mf.io/what-is-3mf/`).

Mesh Repair Programs

Sometimes an STL file comes into the slicing program with issues, and the sliced file does not look the way you expect. STL files define a set of interconnected points and faces that are sometimes called a mesh. Some CAD programs create meshes that are not watertight (the boundary of the shape would not hold water because it has holes in it). Some models are not *manifold*, which means that two parts of the model in the computer are trying to occupy the same physical space. This is not a problem in a computer model, but can have unexpected results when the slicer program tries to reconcile conflicts into something that will work physically. If your model does weird things when you slice it, you might need to repair the mesh.

There are several programs that work well to repair meshes, or to reduce the number of triangles that make up the mesh surface. Sometimes a model can be computationally so big that it can overwhelm the program, and you need to cut down (*decimate*, in the lingo) on the number of triangles. Sometimes, too, you want to cut a model in half to make it easier to print, and then glue it together. Some mesh repair programs let you do that, too.

The venerable MeshLab (`www.meshlab.net`) is an open source, very powerful program. But it is not particularly intuitive, although its 2016 update has a good web page with some instructions. To clean up a mesh, open the program and click File ➤ Import Mesh to bring in your STL file. Then just agree to its cleanup suggestions and use File ➤ Export as to send it back out it again (be sure to select STL, which is not the default).

To use it to decimate a mesh, click Filters ➤ Remeshing, Simplification and Reconstruction ➤ Simplification: Quadric Edge Collapse Decimation, which we are sure you would have guessed on your own. Then you can see how many vertices all the triangles add up to and suggest a smaller number. Or in the box Percentage reduction, type a number between 0 and 1 to reduce it—typing 0.5 drops the number of vertices by 50%. Click the Apply button to have your changes take effect. The program will display what it did. If you like it, you can use File ➤ Export As to save your changes. If not, just abandon the effort and start over.

If the free software is not enough for you, you can look into Simplify3D (described earlier in this chapter) or Netfabb (`www.autodesk.com/products/netfabb/overview`). Chapter 7 also discusses how to create good meshes in the first place.

File Repositories

The other way to get an STL file is to download one that someone else has already created. Many repositories are full of files that people have put out for free, including `www.thingiverse.com`, `www.youmagine.com`, `www.instructables.com`, and `www.pinshape.com`. There are repositories on `www.github.org` that include 3D printable models as well. There are even referencing sites, like `www.yeggi.com`, that reference these other sites.

For better or worse, these repositories are populated by anyone who wants to post something. Although many of the designs are amazing, some of the objects may never have actually been printed, or the designer might be nine years old and posting for fun without any idea of what is printable. Models for education might or might not be accurate. So if you use one, be sure to review it and read the license that spells out how you are allowed to use it.

CREATIVE COMMONS LICENSES

3D printing software and models are often released under a *Creative Commons* license, which you might encounter in the form of notations like "Released under a Creative Commons 4.0 International license, CC-BY-NC-SA," typically including a link to the relevant license text at `www.creativecommons.org`.

These licenses allow you to share your models or software freely while retaining some rights for yourself. The licenses are written in a somewhat modular fashion so you can add on restrictions to a basic license, shown by adding letter codes to the license name. A *CC-BY-NC-SA* license, for instance, allows anyone to do the following:

- Use your material (*CC*, Creative Commons).

- As long as they attribute it to you in a certain way (*BY*).

- And do not use it for commercial purposes (*NC*).

- And anyone who uses your materials must release their materials (including the part you contributed) under the same license (*SA*, for *share alike*).

Deciding how to release and use materials is complex, and you should consult a lawyer versed in software intellectual property if you are embarking on a major project, particularly if money and friendships are involved. The Creative Commons website is a good and lucid place to get some background first, though.

Many 3D printers have heritage to the RepRap project (www.reprap.org), which is an ongoing project to build an *open source* community of Creative Commons hardware and software. These printers are typically referred to as *open source printers*.

Tip   Chapter 5 includes a quick-start guide that talks you through how to create a small cube as a test. You can use that as a first test model and then move on to more complex things. It may be tempting to download something from a repository and try that first, but if you have issues, you will not know if it is a printer problem or a model that has issues.

Scanning

Consumer-priced 3D scanners either require you to take multiple pictures from multiple angles or scan using a device that produces multiple laser beams or some other structured light pattern. Either way, you typically end up a lot of artifacts that have to be cleaned up manually in software, a process that can be tedious and time-consuming. Typically, people use a scan as a starting point for what they are doing or a dimensional reference and then draw over it in a CAD program to correct and clean up the scan. Software is the hard part of 3D scanning, and some professional scanners have software to automate some of this, but as of this writing, these packages tend to cost many thousands of dollars. Figure 3-2 shows a 3D print of Rich, based on a scan made with a DIY scanner.

Tip   If you would like to build your own scanner, there are open source designs out there, like the Ciclop 3D scanner (an open hardware scanner for small objects built with 3D printed parts that uses open source software) and Skanect (a software that allows you to repurpose an Xbox Kinect for human-scale 3D scanning). There are also open source projects like Meshroom for making a 3D model out of a large number of photographs taken from slightly different angles using a process called stereophotogrammetry.

Figure 3-2. *Scanned and 3D printed sculpture*

Slicing Software: Filament Printers

3D printers cannot use a CAD output file (i.e., an STL file) directly. A piece of software known as a *slice engine* has to take the STL file and figure out the commands that the 3D printer will execute a layer at a time. Slice engines might be in freestanding programs or combined with other relevant software in the 3D printing workflow. We call programs containing one or more slice engines *slicing software.*

Tip   If you come into this from a machine-shop environment, slicing software can also be thought of as computer-aided manufacturing (CAM) software.

Slicing programs use different settings to allow for variations in the geometry of the printer, the type of filament you are using, and so on. Resin and other technologies are philosophically similar, but the differences are big enough that we talk about them in a different section of this chapter. In this section, we focus on filament printers.

There are many different slicing engines out there now. In most cases they are freestanding programs or code embedded in programs that are proprietary to a particular printer. Because getting all the settings right for a particular 3D printer can be fiddly, a lot of manufacturers modify one of these open source programs and create a proprietary program just for their machine. However, many printers can still use the basic open source program. We will describe several of those programs here and go over some of the commonest 3D printer settings and what they control.

Some of the more common, freely available programs are Slic3r, Ultimaker Cura, and MatterControl. Printers built around open source standards will often make a file of settings for one of these programs available or create a custom program around one of these slicing engines.

Tip   Most slicing software allows you to simulate what the printer
will do during your print with a graphic to step through the layers, and
in some cases to simulate within a layer. Be sure to use this feature
to walk through every print. It will save you a lot of grief and filament.
We show some examples of this later in the chapter.

Slic3r

Slic3r (pronounced "slicer"—the *3* is silent, or sometimes "slick-three-
arr") has been around for a long time and is maintained by an open
source community led by Alessandro Ranellucci. Its slicing engine has
been incorporated into other programs over time. Slic3r has a reputation
for getting cutting-edge functionality first, which always has pluses and
minuses. You can download it at www.slic3r.org. Prusa Research has also
made a proprietary version called PrusaSlicer for use with their printers.

MatterControl

MatterControl (www.mattercontrol.com) is a free program maintained
by 3D printer retailer MatterHackers. MatterControl 2.0 combines a slicer
as well as a host program that allows users to send single commands to
a printer, jog axes, and change extruder temperature. It also includes a
minimal CAD program as part of the front end.

Ultimaker Cura

Ultimaker Cura is maintained as an open source program by 3D
manufacturer Ultimaker, and can be downloaded from https://software.
ultimaker.com/. Starting in 2016, the launch of Cura 2 initiated a series
of major updates to Cura. These added many different control options to

fine-tune prints. Ultimaker Cura 4 was our baseline while writing, but we attempt to be generic enough for this advice to be valid at least until the next major update. Many manufacturers base their own software on Cura, sometimes on earlier versions than the current Ultimaker version. We will just refer to "Cura," without a version number or company version, specifics in what follows.

Note   In the past, Cura numbered its releases based on the year of release, ending in 2015 (Cura 15.x), and then changed numbering to Cura 2 (as of this writing, Cura 4). Several 3D printer companies based their software on one version or other of Cura 15, so that version will be around for a while. Cura 15 is a lot simpler but very robust. The main point here is that Cura 15 is several years older than Cura 4.

Other Programs

The proliferation of 3D printers has been accompanied by a flurry of slicing programs. Some manufacturers (like MakerBot) have their own proprietary software. There are also printer-agnostic third-party programs out there, like Simplify3D, which is a powerful (but not free) program that also has some editing and mesh repair functions.

Using a Slicing Program

Slicing programs typically require that you give the program information about your 3D printer's geometry, such as the size of the print bed, whether it is heated or not, how tall a print can be, what size filament it uses, and so on. Often this is a file of some sort that your manufacturer will provide. If not, you will have to guesstimate as best you can. Failing that, you can always try the default settings in a slicer. Documentation on the download site for the slicing program you select should walk you through that. Once you have defined your printer, you will be facing the daunting list of settings to select.

Note   Different programs may call similar settings by different names, and may change those names over time. We will not walk through step-by-step screenshots here, since change is a constant in the 3D printing world. Instead, we will talk about the big groups of settings that you will need to think about, and what these settings do.

Example: Ultimaker Cura

We give a general introduction to slicer settings here using Ultimaker Cura. Like most slicing programs it requires you to input some information about your printer, then make some selections that are related to the material you are using, and then finally tweak some settings that might vary model to model. Cura is updated frequently, so we will not show screenshots here and things may be called something else. But we will give the general idea here.

There are dozens of settings in Cura. Hovering over any setting in Custom mode gives you an explanation. In this section we suggest good ways to get started, and get into exceptions and case studies in the later chapters of this book.

In Cura 4, the following process will let you tell the program what type of printer you have. In the menus at the top of the opening screen, click *Settings* ➤ *Printer* ➤ *Add Printer*. Unless you have an Ultimaker, click *Other* to see if your make and model is listed. If not, click *Custom*. A first window labeled *Printer* will come up; input the dimensions (in millimeters) of your printer and whether or not it has a heated platform.

Then click the *Extrude* tab at the top of the window and input nozzle diameter and "compatible material diameter," which most other software would call "filament diameter." Start with either 2.85 for "3 millimeter" filament, or 1.75 for anything else.

To get started, drag an STL file into the window showing an empty platform. You can use the pull-down menu to select a material, and then select a layer height and whether or not to use support. Cura slices a file automatically each time you change something by default, but if that is annoying, you can change it in Preferences.

Tip   We use the names of settings in Ultimaker Cura 4 in this discussion; if you use different software, the names might be a little different. Where similar settings have very different names in different common slicers, we will try to mention the other names you might want to look for. We have case studies scattered throughout the later chapters of this book. In this chapter, we focus on the major slicer settings that you are likely to need to worry about often.

You may fairly rapidly decide you want to play with more of the settings. Select Custom to see more settings. If you know what a setting is called, you can search for it. Alternatively, you can click the gears next to each of the major categories to see more options; many settings are hidden by default, but clicking any gear lets you scroll around all settings. Hover your cursor over a setting to see what it does and what else it affects. You can make a setting permanently visible by selecting what you want to have visible by default.

Simulating Your Print

You can see one of the most important tools in a slicer is the ability to simulate how your print will build up layer by layer. If you switch to Preview mode at the top of the window, you will be able to drag around sliders to move within a single layer, or from one layer to the next. Even if you are an advanced 3D printer user, it is always a good idea to walk quickly through a print to see if you forgot something, or if something does not look remotely like you expected. In particular, look at the very first layer of your object (the first layer beyond the raft, if you are using a raft—see the discussion about rafts that follows) because if pieces are missing, your print will likely fail.

Print Quality and Layer Height

3D printers print each layer in one plane parallel to the build platform and then step up and do the next layer. The extruder head moves upward, away from the platform, after completing each layer. The two axes in the plane of the platform are referred to as x and y, and the vertical axis is the z axis, as we describe in Chapter 2. *Layer height* is defined as the thickness of the material in each step up of the z axis.

Caution   Layer height has to be less than (not equal to!) the nozzle diameter. About 80% of the nozzle diameter is a good maximum value for layer height. Minimum layer height is not really dependent on the nozzle and is determined by other factors. We talk more about ways to improve surface smoothness in Chapter 6.

Shells

In an STL file, the surface is represented by a mesh of triangles. The slicer produces surfaces facing the sides with one or more perimeters around each layer and surfaces facing up or down with solid layers (or solid areas of layers). The space inside this outer surface is then partially filled in to make the object stronger and to create a base for the next layer. The perimeters and solid areas are called the print's *shell*. The material that the slicing software will create for the interior support is called *infill*.

Your slicer will allow you to specify the thickness of the horizontal shell, either as a number of perimeters or in millimeters (which will be rounded to a multiple of your perimeter extrusion width). Two is typically a good number. The width (in the *x-y* plane) of this perimeter is the extrusion width, which must be no smaller than your nozzle diameter, and might be larger.

You can similarly set the thickness of the vertical shell, which your slicer might offer as a setting in millimeters or a number of top/bottom solid layers, or both. You will generally want at least three or four layers to avoid gaps. Setting the thickness in millimeters can be advantageous because it allows you to match your horizontal shell thickness when changing layer heights, and because very thin layers often have more trouble bridging over infill, so they may need the extra layers to smooth themselves out.

Platform Adhesion

One of the challenges with a 3D printer is getting the model to stick to the platform. Sometimes a model has a relatively small contact area with the platform, and when the extruder lays down the next layer, it knocks the model loose. When that happens, the plastic that is intended to make up subsequent layers falls in random places as the structure gets knocked around. The resulting mess is typically called *printing hair* (in polite company, anyway). There are few worse feelings than smugly demonstrating a 3D printer to your friends and then noticing that your model is being merrily dragged around the platform, trailing strands of filament. Techniques to prevent such bad hair days follow.

Brims

A *brim* expands the first layer by creating additional perimeters to increase contact area with the platform, and is intended to be peeled away along the edge of the print's base. A brim usually is specified in terms of width away from the object. A few millimeters usually make a big difference. Figure 3-3 shows a brim stabilizing a print.

Note   Experts often make the first layer of a print a lot thicker than subsequent layers. A thick layer plus a brim can make it a lot more likely a print with a small contact area will survive to the end.

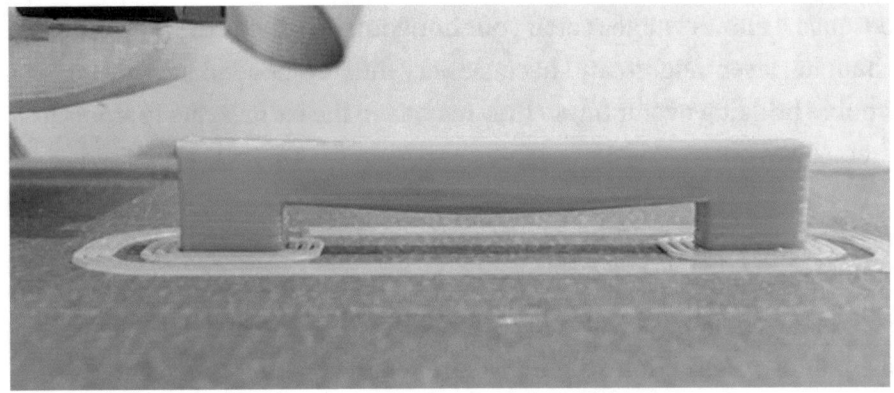

Figure 3-3. *A brim, skirt, and some bridging*

Skirts

A *skirt* is a few loops of filament laid down at the beginning of a print that outline all the objects being printed at a given time and show the maximum size of the first layer of the print. You can see one in Figure 3-3; it is the triple line that does not touch the print. A skirt can solve several problems that might be encountered at the very start of a print.

It is possible to print more than one thing at a time on a 3D printer's platform. The programs for arranging the objects for a print run show you where the prints will be positioned relative to each other. However, it is always possible to create something that would wind up too big to print, since the (virtual) version can be hanging off the platform. When the skirt is drawn around all the objects that you are planning on printing, it allows you to quickly see whether there are any problems so you can stop the print right away.

Also, if you have just switched filaments from one color to another, it is good to print something away from your object first so that any material of a different color that is still in the nozzle is melted out before starting to print the main object. Plastic may also ooze out of the nozzle after a print, or while heating up for the next one, which can leave a void that causes a delay before plastic starts coming out again. Generally, a skirt allows the printer to finish filling the extruder with filament (known as *priming*) before the main object starts printing.

The skirt is usually a few millimeters away from the location on the platform where the first layer of the main object being printed will reside. By the time a few loops are done, any previous filament should also be flushed out of the nozzle. Most programs allow the user to specify both the distance that the skirt is from the main model and the number of loops constituting the skirt.

Tip   Add a few loops to the skirt when you change to a light-colored filament after printing a previous print with a dark filament. Doing so clears out the nozzle so there will not be any mixing of colors and resulting staining of your print.

Rafts

When you look at the lists of settings in a slicing program, you may see options for a raft. A *raft* is a few layers of 3D printed material, a little bigger than your print's first layer, and a few layers thick. It acts as sort of a platform on top of the platform. Because it is made of the same material as your print, the adhesion of the print to it is very consistent. Also, because the printer printed it, the distance between the raft and the first layer is much more predictable than between the print and the bed.

In the early days of 3D printing, when beds were often uneven and there were no heated platforms, rafts could help prints stick better. Rafts were difficult to remove, though, and would often leave pieces behind, so a lot of effort went into raftless printing techniques. The practice of using rafts largely went out of favor for a while, since a good first layer and perhaps a brim are a better combination on a modern printer to make things easier.

Rafts have recently seen a resurgence in popularity, particularly in the default settings of some cheaper printers designed for minimally skilled users. This is because they let you get away with lower-quality surfaces, or ones that have not been aligned precisely. Modern raft algorithms allow the space between the raft and the print to be adjusted to make them stick during printing, but still peel away afterward.

A raft is a good solution if a print does not have many contact points with the bed and you want to be sure it will not fall off—for example, a large object that you do not want to fail midway through a 36-hour print. Rafts are also useful if you need the bottom surface to be dimensionally accurate, since direct contact with an uneven platform can leave it slightly skewed or not entirely flat.

The bottom layer of a raft is printed with extrusion lines that are not only taller than a normal layer, but wider so that they have more contact area with the platform. The larger volume of plastic being pushed out of the nozzle also makes the print less sensitive to being a little too far from the platform surface in some areas, whereas having the nozzle further from the surface reduces the risk of jamming the extruder or even damaging the nozzle or the platform by getting too close in others.

Modern slicers give you the ability to do this without a raft by using a setting called "initial layer line width" or "first layer extrusion width." In conjunction with the initial layer height setting, this allows you to configure the first layer of your print to stick like a raft's base layer, without the added time or wasted plastic. Because you will be putting out a lot more plastic at once, it is a good idea to slow this layer down significantly if you are going to use these features, to prevent jams, and slower printing is good for first layer adhesion anyway. If you are using these features and decide that a print needs a raft, be sure to set them closer to your normal printing settings—otherwise you will be increasing adhesion to the raft, and you may not be able to get it off!

Supporting and Orienting a Model

Consumer 3D printers build up their models from a platform, whether the extruder is fixed and the platform drops away or the extruder head moves up and away from a platform. This means that in some cases, a print head would be laying down material in air. For example, imagine a statue with an outstretched arm. Assuming that the statue is being printed up from its base, the initial bottom layers of the arm would print into the air and fall down unless something was printed into the open space all the way up from the platform. Material printed like this is called *support*. Sometimes this problem can be minimized or eliminated altogether by printing the model in a different orientation. This section talks about these interacting considerations.

Support

In a 3D print, the first layer sticks to the platform. Then the second layer is added above that, and so on, like a brick wall. The printer depends on having something below the nozzle to compress the extrusion against, much like the mortar between bricks. In the case of the wall, if there are no bricks under the second layer (or at least some bricks partially lapped under it), the second layer of brick will fall to the ground. If you want to lay bricks across the top of an opening in the wall, like a window or doorway, you need a scaffolding to support them as you are building. (For exceptions to this, see the section on bridging later in this chapter.)

In 3D printing, the structures that prevent the equivalent problem are called *support*. You can see support structures back in Chapter 2, Figure 2-9. The slicing process generates support automatically in some programs, and with some user control in others. In general, it is best to avoid support if possible because removing it is time-consuming and the process of pulling it off can damage the model. Unless you are using a second soluble print material as support, you will then need to remove the support mechanically. You may need needle-nose pliers, a screwdriver, and ultimately tweezers or other small tool to take off the last bits, as discussed in Chapter 6 (plus some eye protection—those bits can be sharp).

Orientation

A particular model may seem to have a side that is "supposed" to be the bottom of the model. Sometimes, though, turning a model so that it lies on its side or even upside-down can increase the first-layer contact with the platform and decrease the amount of support. Particularly if you are going to be printing the object more than once, spending some time playing with the orientation of a complex model is worthwhile.

A bit of thought can sometimes also eliminate support that the slicing software would automatically create in hard-to-get-at places, like internal narrow spaces. Sometimes turning a complicated object through some arbitrary rotation—for example, 10 degrees about the x axis and 15 degrees about the y axis—will result in the best situation with the least support needed.

Printers that can only use one filament at a time print support in the same material as the rest of the model. Printers that have multiple extruders can lay a dissolvable filament, though this process is often more costly, time-consuming, and error-prone than using your print material.

In addition to not needing supports, surfaces that are close to vertical will have less obvious layer lines than ones that are close to horizontal, because the distance along the surface from one layer line to the next is shorter. This makes the surface appear smoother and allows fine details in the design to show (some of which the slicer might otherwise have to omit because they are less than two extrusions wide), so you should consider this as well when reorienting a model. Figure 3-4 shows a print that was created vertically (gravitational waves, from our 2017 Apress book, *3D Printed Science Projects Volume 2*).

Figure 3-4. *Gravitational wave model, printed vertically*

Avoiding Support by Cutting a Model into Pieces

For an object with a complex surface that requires support, sometimes you can cut the object into two or more pieces, print the pieces cut-side-down, and then glue the parts together later. Some CAD programs have tools to make this sort of cut. If the program you are using does not, there are a few free or open source programs that allow the user to rotate an object around all three axes and then make a cut along a resulting convenient axis. Because this is a rapidly evolving area, search online for "cutting STL files free software." Often printed support can be avoided entirely with one judicious cut. After printing, the halves will have to be glued together. Chapter 6 discusses paint, glue, and finishing.

Managing Internal Open Space

Just as there is open space around the outside of a model (like the statue's outstretched arm mentioned earlier), similar problems arise inside a model or in space enclosed by a model. Imagine a closed box: it would need some sort of support to run between the top and bottom. This support is called *infill*. Sometimes it is not necessary to have infill everywhere, and you can get away with just stringing filament across (usually) small gaps, a process called *bridging*. This section gives you some ideas about the design issues that arise with internal support.

Bridging

It is possible to bridge across open areas in a model without support if the open area is not too wide (say, less than 20–30 mm, depending on your printer's cooling fans and other factors). There are several schools of thought about the best settings to use when bridging across a gap. On the one hand, having the printer move more slowly than usual while trying to increase filament flow rate slightly may result in the bridge sagging a little.

Conversely, having the printer move faster and push out less may mean the filament will not stretch enough to cross the open area and will break. Finding an optimum between the two requires some experimentation with your printer.

Some slicing programs have settings for adjusting speed and flow of plastic specifically for bridging. Defaulting these settings to the rate the slicing program creates is a good place to start.

Another way to get around bridging is to terrace or arc under the bridged area so that the printer is in fact just climbing a 45-degree (or shallower) slope underneath. An overhang climbing at about a 45-degree angle is about the limit that can be consistently printed without support. However, sometimes a steeper slope will work with some combinations of settings; a bit of experimentation is often worthwhile to avoid needing to use support, particularly in a complex structure. If bridges are too long, though, as with the print in Figure 3-3, the bridge may sag a bit or have drooled bits of filament on it.

Prints are often designed with the printer's ability to bridge in mind. Some users have even demonstrated that this bridging ability can be abused by creating a series of thin strands connecting two larger blocks. The printer bridges across the gap between the blocks, and you are left with a series of thin filaments connecting them. Cutting on of the blocks off to free all of the filaments on one end makes a print that resembles a broom or brush (Figure 3-5). Softening the bristles with a heat gun allows them to be reshaped, and others have used this fact to create models with realistic hair.

Figure 3-5. *Deliberately created "hair"*

Other designs take advantage of a printer's failure to bridge by creating thin, level structures that are only supported on one end, knowing that the strands will collapse during printing, to intentionally create random hairlike texture on the sides of a print.

Infill

Users of 3D printers do not usually want to create solid objects, because that uses a lot of filament. However, typically objects cannot be hollow, either, because upper layers would be printed in air. (Exceptions to this are discussed in Chapter 9, where we discuss hollow prints or prints that look like vases.) As a result, most slicing software creates internal support called *infill* inside the solid surfaces of an object to minimize filament use (as well as to make the print faster). Figure 3-6 shows typical infill patterns.

Figure 3-6. *Typical infill patterns*

Another purpose of using infill patterns (as opposed to printing solid plastic), and possibly the most important one for some materials, is to control shrinkage. Infill patterns are sparse enough to stretch axially as they shrink radially so that they do not pull the perimeters inward as they cool and shrink. This can make 3D printed parts maintain dimensional accuracy much better than injection-molded parts, which have to be designed with a significantly different size and shape from the final part in order to turn out the way the designer intends after shrinkage.

Print infill is usually specified in terms of percentage fill. So, 12% infill means that 12% of the interior volume of the object will be occupied by material and 88% will be open. This percentage does not include the outer perimeter of the print or its solid top or bottom layers.

Although infill adds some strength by bracing the interior of the object against collapsing, most of the print's strength comes from the solid surfaces. If you want to make a print stronger, it is usually better to increase the thickness of the skin rather than increasing infill. Compared to printing completely hollow, infill is more important for its ability to act as a support structure for a model's internal overhangs, to prevent sagging or gaps in the top surface of a print. Most slicers have some more exotic options for infill patterns. Unless you are printing with a highly transparent filament, these patterns are unlikely to be visible once the print has finished.

For the best results with top surfaces, you want a pattern that is very regular and not too sparse where it meets that surface, since overly large gaps often result either in sagging or *pillowing* between infill lines (Figure 3-7). *Pillowing* occurs when instead of drooping downward where it is unsupported by infill, the plastic curls upward, and it is an especially common failure mode when printing thinner layers. Adding more solid top layers helps to even these surfaces out, but for very small prints, you may find that this uses more plastic than just using a higher infill density.

Figure 3-7. *Pillowing on a 20 mm cube*

But why do those surfaces need to be solid? If you think of a square filled with a grid of squares, it would be fairly easy to crush that shape by applying force to opposite corners. You can brace it with a triangular grid instead, but filling the front and back faces is even more effective, so strength is rarely a big factor in the choice of infill patterns.

There is such a thing as a print created without top and bottom solid layers. Vase mode prints (Chapter 9) omit the infill and top layers to turn a solid model into a vessel that is open on top. Prints can also be designed to use exposed infill structures for specific effects, like the light grid in Figure 3-8, designed to clip over a bank of LEDs.

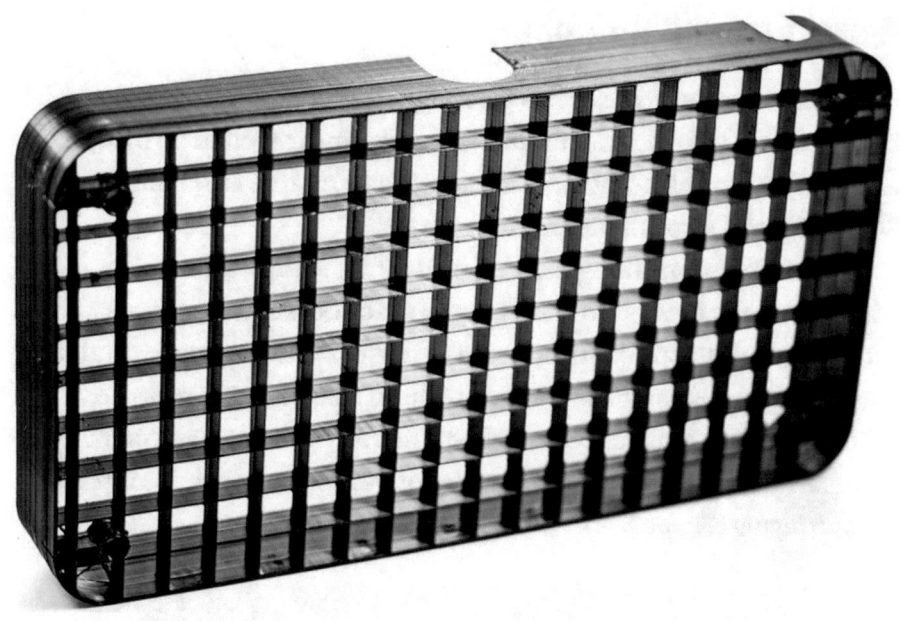

Figure 3-8. *Light grid printed with no top or bottom layers*

While there are now some infill patterns that are designed to create 3D structures within a model, most patterns are the same every layer or print in similar patterns in alternating directions on alternating layers. For example, "grid" infill in Cura prints internal structure like that in Figure 3-8, the same in each layer since the bottom of this print is the side that is facing toward you. The This means that the shape and size of the gaps between lines will be consistent when they intersect with the top and bottom surfaces.

Note   Printing solid (100% infill) is a special case, and we discuss the issues and printer settings relevant to that in Chapter 9.

Retraction and Stringing

One of the big advantages of 3D printing is that complex shapes that might be impossible to create via traditional machining can often be made very easily on a 3D printer. But there are some features that are challenging to 3D print—with a consumer printer, anyway.

For example, one thing that can be difficult to print is an object with two skinny towers. To leave out the space between the towers, the extruder needs to pump out material to make one tower, stop extruding, and start up again on the other tower. This is referred to as *retraction*. When retraction is not adequate, the print may have fine hairs of filament scattered across the spaces that were supposed to be open; this is referred to as *stringing* (Figure 3-9).

Figure 3-9. *Stringing*

Retraction is typically handled as an automatic feature in slicing software with some limited user control. In Cura, there are many settings to fine-tune retraction under the Material heading. In addition, under the Travel heading, you can tick a box to allow *combing*. This is a way to avoid retracting if printing sparse or complex infill might otherwise require it. It does not matter if infill strings a bit, because it will only be visible inside the model when the model is complete. Doing a lot of retraction can wear on the filament in some printer configurations and slows down the printing process, so avoiding it where possible is a big plus.

Temperatures

You may find that you need to tweak settings as you print in different materials. The temperature of your extruder (and your heated build platform, if yours has a heater) will vary with the materials. In Chapter 2 we talked about the requirements for several common materials. The reality is that every time you use a new brand (or even color) of filament, you may need to experiment a bit.

In Ultimaker Cura, temperatures are under the "Material" section. There are a bunch of temperatures you can change, but to start just make them all the same as each other. Filament spools usually suggest a temperature range. In the absence of other information from your experience or manufacturer, just start in the middle of the range. Too hot can result in stringing or blobby prints; too cool can result in poor adhesion between layers and the platform or between two layers.

Be sure that your nozzle and platform can handle the temperature you are asking them to reach. Printers have very limited error checking, and it is possible to damage your printer by telling components to get hotter than they are rated for.

Speeds, Cooling, Extrusion Multipliers

Your slicer will include several settings for speeds of a print. Unless the slicer specifies otherwise, all of its speeds are speeds of linear motion. This is the maximum speed that the printer will move for this portion of the print, but acceleration my not allow it to reach that speed, and cooling settings may also limit it.

Travel speeds control how fast the printer moves when it is moving between parts without extruding. This should generally be set as fast as the machine can handle, since going slower will not only increase print time, it will allow more time for plastic to ooze out of the nozzle in areas where you do not want it.

Most slicers also include several different printing speeds. Perimeters, infill, and solid surfaces all generally have their own printing speeds. You may be tempted to speed up your print by printing the infill quickly and slowing down the outer perimeters to get smoother motion—be careful, because residual pressure in the nozzle might cause a blob where the perimeter starts. The one place it is always good to set a slower speed is for the first layer, because slowing it down helps with platform adhesion and reduces the chances of something bad happening if the platform is not aligned perfectly.

In Cura, the Minimum Layer Time setting tells the slicer to reduce speeds if a layer will take less than the specified time to complete. This is done to allow time for the plastic to cool before printing another layer on top of it. If the plastic does not cool sufficiently, you can get a misshapen blob of plastic instead of the fine features of your model. There are also settings to control the speed of fans pointed down at your print. Depending on the strength of your fans, you may be able to cool the plastic faster, allowing lower values for minimum layer time to be used.

If your print has a single narrow feature at the top, minimum layer time might not be able to do its job because the plastic stays in contact with the hot nozzle and does not have a chance to cool. In this case, printing two of your object at once or adding a cylinder the same height as your print (known as a *cooling tower*) will give the printer something else to do so that it moves away from that feature and allows it to cool properly.

The speed at which plastic is pushed out is controlled by the combination of this speed and the specified layer height and extrusion width according to a calculation of volume. The slicer needs to know the diameter of the filament so it knows how much volume of plastic is in one millimeter of it. If this calculation results in the wrong volume of plastic, usually because the extruder is not properly calibrated, the Flow setting, otherwise known as an Extrusion Multiplier, gives you a fudge factor to tweak this calculation.

More Exotic Settings

Settings often interact with each other, and the details of a particular case matter. We have relegated talking about some of the more exotic options—like printing vases or printing solid, transparent objects—to the case studies in Chapter 9, where we discuss special geometries.

Troubleshooting

Troubleshooting a print that does not look right is a complex subject. In this chapter, we are summarizing some of the big categories of slicer settings. In later chapters, we will go over some case studies and go into more depth for particular types of prints there. Table 3-1 shows a quick guide to where to find solutions to different types of issues.

Tip   Joan and Rich have courses on LinkedIn Learning (formerly Lynda.com) that go into greater detail on these topics. You can find them by going to `https://linkedin.com/learning/` and searching on our names.

Table 3-1. *Quick Guide to Slicer Settings*

Problem	Likely Group of Settings That Will Fix It	Chapter Where Discussed
Print does not stick to bed	Temperature	3
	Bed surface/raft, brim	2 and 3
	Support	3
Gaps in print	Extrusion settings	3
Surface quality	Layer height, speeds, cooling	3 and 9
Blobby prints	Cooling, or print too tall and thin	3 and 9
Stringing	Retraction	3

Printing More Than One Object at a Time

Most slicers will allow you to put multiple objects from different STLs on the platform and print them all at once. Typically, this works by printing all of them in parallel. The first layers of all parts are printed before the second layer of any part starts.

Some slicers offer a sequential printing option as well, which allows you to print one object and then print another on an unused part of the print bed. This requires careful arrangement, though, to ensure that no other part of the printer will collide with the parts that have already been completed. This prevents you from using as much of the space as you can when printing all at once.

Multiple Extruders

A printer with more than one extruder allows you to print in multiple colors or materials. Exactly how this works depends a lot on the multiple-extruder machine in question, but this general guide will give you some ideas on how to get started with your machine. This usually does not mean you can print faster, since only one extruder can be active at once (though as of this writing, there are experimental machines that are designed to work this way, based on Autodesk's Project Escher). Rather, a printer with multiple extruders usually cannot move them entirely independently, so only one can be used at a time.

Some machines have multiple nozzles mounted to a single toolhead so that they move together, and simply offset the toolhead's position when they are using one nozzle or the other. Others use various types of splitter mechanisms to run filament from several different extruder mechanisms through a common nozzle. Still others have somewhat independent motion that allows one extruder to be parked to one side of the machine while the other is working. One company, Mosaic Manufacturing, even sells an add-on device that cuts and splices filament before feeding it to the printer.

Printers that use a single nozzle, like the filament splicing add-ons, are generally only useful for printing multiple colors, since materials with different properties usually need different printing temperatures and may not play well with the switching mechanisms. Though some attempts have been made at color mixing, most of these are only able to switch filaments automatically, so creating a gradient of color usually is not possible. Single-nozzle solutions usually result in a lighter toolhead that can handle high acceleration better than multi-nozzle ones and have the advantage of avoiding ooze from the inactive nozzle and various alignment issues.

Those with multiple extruders, each with their own nozzle, can use the second one to print a soluble support material or a flexible material to have a mixture of print properties. Some of these also have software that allows them to be used in duplication mode, where two identical objects (which must be smaller than the distance between the nozzles) are printed simultaneously.

If the machine is able to move the two extruders independently in one axis (known as independent dual extruder, or IDEX, machines), their duplication mode can usually use half of the platform for each copy. However, multiple nozzles on a single carriage are usually situated as close as possible to one another, leading to much stricter limits on these modes. Some IDEX printers even have a mirror duplication mode, in which the motion of the independent axis is reversed to create copies that are mirror images of one another (like a pair of shoes).

One common use of dual-extruder machines is to use one of the extruders to print support material that can be dissolved away later. To use one of these systems for dissolvable support, you need to configure the slicer to print its support with a different extruder and make sure that extruder has appropriate settings for your support material.

When you are printing models in two colors (or two materials), you need to follow a somewhat different process than printing dissolvable support, or printing in one material. To do this, you need to create two STL files that represent the areas of the print that are to be printed with each color.

You also have to split your model into two STL files so that there are no places with structure created with both colors trying to occupy the space. If something penetrates something else, there must be a hole in the one object to accommodate the second, just as in physical space. These files then need to be interleaved into an .AMF file. Note that any rotation needed when arranging the files for printing has to be done in the STL file generation. We walk through an example in detail in Chapter 7.

Tip   If you are using a dual-extruder 3D printer to print two colors and, on top of that, support is needed, you will need to pick one of the extruders to do the support for both materials.

G-code

Most open source, filament-using 3D printers are controlled with a series of commands, called *G-code*. G-code loads onto the printer from a host computer via USB port, Wi-Fi, or other network connection or is read from an SD card or USB drive, depending on which options a particular machine has. The *firmware* (software running on the printer itself) then interprets the G-code one command at a time and controls the hardware functions needed to execute it. Status information (temperatures and the like) returns to the user's computer through the USB. In some other cases, a G-code interpreter runs on a host computer, and control signals are sent to the printer.

Many open source printers use Marlin firmware, which runs on Arduino-compatible microcontrollers. There is no operating system running on a microcontroller in system architectures like the Arduino. The processing hardware performs minimal command retrieval buffering and interpretation functions and returns requested signals to the user. There are variations on this theme: for example, some printers can read from an SD card rather than needing to use a USB port.

G-code is a very old programming language originally designed to control machine tools with a computer. Its origins are in the 1950s and 1960s and it has survived this long because of its flexibility and ability to run with minimal computing power. G-code is very low level and is typically written such that all the commands are interpreted one at a time sequentially. Typical G-code functions include commanding an extruder to heat up to a particular temperature, instructing the printer to pause until an extruder reaches a certain temperature, moving the extruder to some (x, y, z) position, and conducting similar activities.

G-code for machine tools evolved gradually, with different dialects for each tool manufacturer. A standard of sorts called RS274D stabilized in the mid-1980s. Because the computer numerical control (CNC) market was pretty stable when the first low-cost 3D printers came along, a lot of the early users borrowed firmware and concepts to program those machines, and so a G-code dialect for 3D printers developed.

Each line of G-code commands the printer to do some small task or to set some parameter to a value that will be used for a task later on. For example, the snippet of code in the example that follows first sets the units that the firmware will use for calculation to millimeters (G21). It then tells the firmware to use absolute, not relative, coordinates (G90). The G1(...) command moves the nozzle to position (3.000, 8.111, 4.444). During that move, 0.1234 mm of filament will have extruded, relative to the last time the zero point was reset; resets occur periodically during a print. (Retractions are negative E values.)

```
G21
G90
G1 X3.000 Y8.111 Z4.444 E0.1234
```

The firmware interpolates the movements required to get from one absolute position to the next and similarly determines how to feed the filament to extrude the requested amount before the next step. Millimeters of filament moved is currently the most common unit for the E values, but some machines have begun the switch to units of volume instead.

Not all G-codes begin with G. For example, codes beginning with M are used (with some variation among manufacturers) for most functions that are not directly related to movement of the axes. M104 is commonly used in open source printers to set the extruder temperature to a particular value. M140 sets the temperature of heated build platforms—in the example following this paragraph, to 115 degrees C. M109 waits for the temperature of the extruder to reach the specified level, and M190 waits for the temperature of the heated platform to reach the specified temperature. (Note that though the code is usually written as shown in the example, M109 and M190 do not need to have a temperature specified. If none is given, then the temperature that was set with M140 and M104 commands will be used.)

Tip   Each line of G-code needs to be on one line (no newlines).
A semicolon on the line makes the rest of the line a comment
(see the example that follows).

```
M104 S210 ;comments here
M140 S115
M109 S210
M190 S115
```

Printers with multiple extruders need to address lines of G-code to
the correct extruder. This is done with a *tool change* command, T. For
example, in the case of most open source dual-extruder printers, T0 will
select the first extruder, and T1 will select the second extruder (following
the common computing convention of beginning to count at zero). A T0
code will cause everything that follows to be executed on extruder 1. Some
G-codes allow a Tx to be appended on the same line to show that just that
command is for extruder x.

Tip   A list of 3D printer G-codes and a detailed discussion of their
functions is available at `http://reprap.org/wiki/G-code`.

In Chapter 5 we discuss how it is sometimes useful to be able to type in
these low-level codes to debug possible hardware failures (such as blocked
extruders or lack of connection to the printer) or to change the G-code
built by your slicing program. Sometimes it is convenient to test that the
printer is working correctly with a few simple commands rather than a
complex G-code file.

Host Programs

Programs that give you an interactive interface to control your 3D printer are called *host programs*. They allow you to upload a whole file of G-code commands to create a print, or to send single commands when that is needed. Most 3D printers have a USB port that allows you to connect them to software running on a computer to stream instructions in real time. This is useful for manual control (used for maintenance operations, for instance), but it is not the best way to run a long-running print. If the computer goes to sleep, or you move your laptop and the cable comes out, hours of printing can be wasted.

Today, most printers have an option to store G-code (or whatever format the printer uses for its instructions) on the printer so that it can run untethered. Most often, this is done with an SD card (or microSD), though there are now some printers that use a USB stick or have onboard storage that you can upload to via a Wi-Fi connection. It is possible to upload to an SD card over USB, but for complex prints, that can take several hours because the protocols that 8-bit microcontrollers use for USB and SD card access are much slower than the ones your computer uses to communicate with the SD card directly. If your printer uses an SD card, you will want to take the card out and transfer files to it directly from your computer. Those that have Wi-Fi usually have faster protocols, but it may still be faster to move the SD card.

Most slicing programs have a limited host functionality to allow you to either save a G-code file to an SD card or upload it to a printer. Some allow you to send single-command controls to move an axis and so on, and others are limited to just uploading.

Octoprint

If your printer only has USB, or if you really want Wi-Fi control but your printer did not come with it, there is an option. OctoPrint (`www.octoprint.org`) is a printer host program that is accessed through a web interface, and it also has an API that many desktop host programs now support. It is designed to run on a computer without a keyboard or monitor that is permanently connected to the printer's USB. Although it is possible to run the OctoPrint server on a Mac or Windows PC, it is designed to run on inexpensive single-board computers like the Raspberry Pi.

Resin Printers

There is surprisingly little commonality between printing with filament and with plastic. Within resin printers, too, there are some big differences between the major technologies: SLA cures the resin one small spot at a time. DLP and LCD cure an entire layer at a time. Typically, the light shines in through an optical window at the bottom of a tray of resin, and a layer forms on the window. The window is then mechanically separated from the print by moving the print, the tray, or some combination to separate them.

Support is still necessary with a resin print. However, most print upside-down, so support is needed both to keep the print adhering correctly to the platform and to resist the forces encountered when the print is peeled off the window. One might think that a print should just be printed upside-down from the way you would print it with filament, but it is more complex than that.

The first layer is tricky, because there is very little room between the platform and the optical window. Often people orient their resin prints to rest (upside-down) on top of a bed of thin support with a sacrificial solid layer on the build platform. You can see a cube (like the print in Figure 2-9) in Figure 3-10.

Figure 3-10. *A cube created (upside-down) on a resin printer*

Resin prints are normally printed solid; there is no infill in resin prints. If you want to print something hollow, you need to design it that way and have small holes on the top and bottom to allow air to escape during the print and resin to escape after it is done.

Cups are areas where air will be captured during the print. Bubbles of air can displace the resin that the printer is trying to cure, creating holes in the print. You may need to orient your model manually and add manual supports.

Another issue that makes slicing resin prints tricky is that exposure time and other parameters can depend critically on the characteristics of the resin. This and the fact that creating support is more challenging to think about have resulted in many resin printers having proprietary interfaces. Manufacturer Formlabs has a software package called PreForm, for instance. PreForm allows you to create custom supports too if the defaults are not exactly what you wanted.

When printing in a liquid, you also have to worry about bubbles forming. If any air gets trapped in the print as it forms, that can result in *voids* in the print since nothing will harden there. Prints have to be designed and oriented carefully to allow a way for air to escape.

Printers that use DLP projectors or LCD displays need a more capable processor than filament printers include, because they need to output a video signal. Some older designs have an HDMI port and require software that treats the printer as an external display connected to the host computer. Most newer designs will include a Raspberry Pi or equivalent processor that serves this purpose, making the machine more freestanding. Before buying a resin printer, be sure to check what connections it requires!

Note   Resin prints need significant post-processing. See Chapter 5 for the steps needed to wash and cure a print.

Summary and Questions for Review

This chapter reviewed the overall workflow of 3D printing, with a particular focus on the process of slicing a model into layers. It discussed different software packages that are available for the process and some of the many settings that are available to tweak for the best print. The chapter focused primarily on filament-based 3D printers, with a summary of key difference for resin printers.

Answer the following to test your knowledge of the material in this chapter:

1. If you want to create a 3D print of an object, what are the steps you need to go through from start to end?

2. Pick three objects that would not be sensible to print "right side up." Are there ways to orient each one so it will print without support?

3. Is it always a good idea to use the smallest possible layer height? Why or why not?

4. Give two examples of prints that would most sensibly be printed by a filament-based 3D printer and two more that would most sensibly be printed by a machine that used liquid resin. Why did you make that choice?

5. You are making six-sided dice for a game. What might be a reasonable infill percentage? Would you have the dots recessed or poking out? If you tried these dice and discovered that they were not statistically fair, what would be some of the possible reasons?

CHAPTER 4

Selecting a Printer: Comparing Technologies

There are now hundreds of different models of 3D printer on the market. But how do you even start to think about which one to buy? In this chapter, we will look at what 3D printer features are likely to be important for your intended uses and also discuss how to estimate the long-term cost of ownership.

Because 3D printer models (and even manufacturers) come and go on a pretty regular basis, we will avoid suggesting particular models. Once you know what you are looking for, you can be a more skeptical reader of advertisements. You can also be more confident that you will purchase what you will need.

In Chapter 2, we reviewed different types of 3D printer hardware and, in Chapter 3, of software. Refer back to those chapters if you are not sure about terminology. We cover selected hardware decisions here in the context of deciding what to purchase, but you should read the prior two chapters first for the full details of what part of the printer does what.

© Joan Horvath, Rich Cameron 2020
J. Horvath and R. Cameron, *Mastering 3D Printing*,
https://doi.org/10.1007/978-1-4842-5842-2_4

In Chapter 5, we talk about what happens when you bring the printer into your office, factory, school, or home. That should drive your buying decisions, too. The space your printer will live in, who will maintain it, and how often you intend to move it are things you should think about before settling on a model.

Who Will Use the Printer?

The first thing to consider with a printer purchase is how it will be used. If it is going to be in a home office and used occasionally by one person, it will not need to be as robust as if it is going to be in a room full of people who will be using it 24/7.

Before your purchase, imagine a day in the life of the printer, and have that scenario in mind as you read through this chapter and Chapter 5. Many organizations have huge pulses in use around deadlines or certain times of year, so consider both your routine periods and your peak weeks. Another thing to consider is the sophistication of your users. If you have dedicated staff that will be running a fleet of machines as their main job, you will have different needs than if you have dozens of people who will use one printer with varying degrees of care and patience. In a business environment, it may be wise to make it someone's job to be the first-line keeper of the 3D printer(s).

If you are in a school environment, be aware that most 3D printers are labeled for ages 13 and up, and on average that is probably about when it makes sense to let kids run them. There are a few that are marketed specifically for kids to use directly, but those machines needed to make trade-offs to be able to do that (limiting functionality) that might or might not make sense for your application. Typically, an adult will manage the printer hardware for the younger set because there are hot moving parts involved.

3D Printer Resolution

When you buy a conventional printer to print on paper, you can note a few familiar metrics about how good the image quality will be, often stated in dots per inch (dpi). However, in the case of a 3D printer, it is a little more complicated. You are dealing with somewhat different processes in the cross-layer direction (usually vertically, the z axis) vs. the two dimensions in the plane of the build platform (x and y axes).

3D printers often quote their resolution in the z *axis* (the vertical one) as a number in millimeters (or microns—1 millimeter is 1000 microns); this is equivalent to the thinnest layer the printer can produce. Typically, this number is better (smaller) than the feature size in the x-y plane. It also is a good proxy for how smooth the surface will be. For most filament-based 3D printing technologies, resolution is typically on the order of 0.1 mm, or 100 microns. For practical reasons, such as the fact that smaller layers require a longer print time, going that low can be challenging. Beyond about 0.1 mm, the print time increase is usually much more noticeable than the difference in quality, so even if your printer claims 0.05 mm resolution or better, for practical reasons, you will usually end up using 0.1 mm or larger layers. While 100 microns is usually the minimum practical layer height for filament printers, it is usually the maximum layer height for resin printers, which typically offer options down to around 25 microns.

3D printers that use plastic filament heat the plastic and then squeeze it out of a nozzle that is typically about half a millimeter in diameter. This string of plastic can be compressed between the nozzle and the previous layer down to that 0.1 mm thickness (or even smaller) in the z direction, but it cannot be thinner than the diameter of the nozzle in the x-y plane. The printer's control over the *placement* of these lines is much finer though—usually significantly better than 0.1 mm.

Comparisons of claims about resolution in the x-y plane for these machines are mostly meaningless because of the way the motors are controlled and how that interacts with extrusion on small scales. Most of these machines use open source software that will generate instructions to attempt to print layers as thin as you want, and the printer will attempt to print these extremely thin layers. When this fails, it is usually because the plastic jams due to spending too much time in the nozzle, because it is extruding at such a low flow rate. It may also fail because the z axis is not precise enough, and a layer that would otherwise be just slightly overcompressed instead blocks the nozzle entirely, causing an extrusion failure.

Furthermore, the shape of each layer must be enclosed by a perimeter that is a closed loop, so features need to be at least two extrusion widths thick in that plane, or about 1 mm across. (There are exceptions to this through software that allows you to create single-width sections, but as a practical matter you may not want to.) So, you may find that your "50 micron" printer really is limited to features about 20 times that big, just because that resolution does not really apply in all three dimensions!

Figure 4-1 shows how thick layers (in the foreground) might not be able to fill a curved surface completely compared to thinner ones. The real benefit of higher resolution (of thinner layers) is that the deviations from a smooth surface where one layer transitions to the next are smaller. All other things being equal, this means that a higher resolution print has smoother surfaces with sharper edges. Corners in the x-y plane still will not have a radius smaller than half the nozzle diameter, though. Thus, whether a finer resolution actually makes smaller features visible depends on the print's orientation with respect to the x-y plane, as you can see in Figure 4-1.

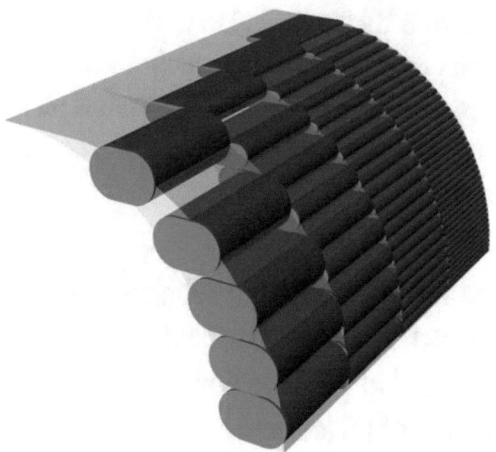

Figure 4-1. *Resolution showing effects of layer thickness*

Selecting a Printer

Two of the most critical questions when you are thinking about buying a 3D printer are who is going to use it and what they are going to use it for. How computer-sophisticated the user is will matter, too. In later chapters, we go into this in some depth for different types of users, but here we will summarize the aspects that affect a purchasing decision. We have organized this section around the choices of features that you need to make when buying a 3D printer.

Filament vs. Resin

The main choice facing most users considering consumer-level 3D printers is whether to buy one that uses spools of plastic as a raw material or one that uses liquid resin. Filament printers are still far more prevalent and diverse, so we focus on them more here. A filament printer will be more practical for most users because the raw material is relatively easy to store and transport, and there is very little waste. The main drawback with a filament printer is that, as noted in the discussion of resolution, the smallest feature you can print is about twice your nozzle diameter—about a millimeter for typical 0.35–0.5 mm nozzles. That is plenty fine enough resolution for many things, but it is usually a little too coarse for jewelry or other delicate structures.

Note   If you need to get even more sophisticated (and have a budget to match), you can consider powder printers. These printers create objects in a bed of very fine powder. Most systems are based on variations on either SLS (selective laser sintering) or binder jetting. We have them in their own section later in this chapter since they step you up into a very different range of costs and facility requirements than the filament and liquid resin printers. Powder-based techniques are at the root of most metal 3D printing, and we have a discussion of powder printing using metal in Chapter 11.

Resin printers (which come in several types, as discussed in Chapter 2) can create prints with smaller feature sizes, since they are only really limited by the spot size of a laser or the pixel size of a projector. Print volume, though, also tends to be correspondingly small, and except for exotic, very expensive technologies, resin printing is significantly slower than filament printing (individual layers might be faster, but those layers are usually thinner, requiring more of them to print a given part).

The resin and the cleanup chemicals are messy and will have to be managed and disposed of. If you can handle that and you are looking at doing sophisticated projects that require fine detail, you may want to explore resin printers. If in doubt, buy a low-cost filament printer and get some experience there first.

For this chapter, we are going to assume that if you want to go to the more sophisticated technologies described in Chapter 2, you will have good reasons and a specialized problem to solve. 3D printing with metal is explored in Chapter 11.

Time to Print

3D printers build up objects one layer at time. Typically, this layer is about as thick as one or two sheets of paper. This means that 3D prints take a long time. Often 3D printers are purchased by people with little or no exposure to traditional manufacturing, and the expectation is that the print will pop off the platform in the time it takes to print a page with ink. Making anything with a subtractive tool takes surprisingly long, too; precise manufacture of physical things is just inherently slow. Think how long it takes to build a brick wall, or for that matter, paint a mural on one.

Tip   Print times will drive a lot of your workflow and probably narrow the types of projects that will be feasible. A fist-sized print may take from several hours to a day to print, depending on a lot of things. As we note later in this section, smaller printers are often faster, if the thing you want to make will fit in the smaller build volume.

Selecting a Filament-Based 3D Printer

For most educational users, the basic decision will be which filament-based 3D printer to purchase, so we will focus most of our analysis on that topic in the following sections. For a discussion of the different types of resin printers on the market as of this writing, see Chapter 2.

Platforms and Nozzles

Whether or not your printer has a heated platform will determine what types of materials you can print. To determine what materials you want to print, consider the intended uses of your 3D prints. The first question is whether you want to create *functional* parts—parts that will be under some sort of load, like a motor mount on a robot.

Almost every printer that uses filament can print in polylactic acid (PLA), the biodegradable corn-based plastic we talk about in Chapter 2. However, PLA deforms at relatively low temperatures, by plastic-melting standards (like that of a car dashboard in summer), and so is of limited use anyplace it will both be under load and warm. If a constant load is acting on it, it will deform slowly over time (known as *creeping*) even at room temperature. Many low-cost printers (and some pricier ones, too) are not designed to handle any materials other than PLA.

If your printers will mostly be used for small, decorative student projects like keychains, you should be able to stick with the simplicity of printing in PLA, which is by and large pretty forgiving to print with and relatively cheap. Figure 4-2 shows how good a PLA part can look—there are many different kinds now, and some have very good finishes.

Figure 4-2. *A PLA vase*

If you are making parts that have to withstand some banging around or do something useful, you will probably need a printer that can print in a wider range of materials. This in turn means that the printer needs to handle a bigger temperature range. For that, it will probably need to have an all-metal hot end (as opposed to one lined with polytetrafluoroethylene, PTFE, a high-temperature plastic commonly known as Teflon) and possibly a heated print bed. Some of these materials need to be used in an area that is ventilated well; see Chapter 5's discussion of ventilation. People often make parts that need to stand up to some repeated motion out of nylon, like Figure 4-3's extruder mount from a Bukito 3D printer (the white part).

Note   Some filaments are very abrasive and will quickly wear out a nozzle. The "filled filaments," which consist of a PLA or other base polymer mixed with metal or composite materials like chopped carbon fiber, fall into this category, as do glow-in-the-dark filaments. Hardened-steel or ruby-tipped replacement nozzles are intended to withstand abrasive filaments.

Figure 4-3. *Nylon functional part*

Some 3D printers can handle more exotic materials like polycarbonate, but these materials can require specialized hot ends, a platform that can be heated to a very high temperature, and a platform surface material that is compatible with the material being printed (see the discussion of filament materials in Chapter 2).

Higher-temperature materials tend to shrink as they cool if they are not kept continuously warm, hence the need for a heated platform. If the build platform is cold, each layer will shrink as it cools. The hot layer on top will misalign, and over time the corners of a print will warp and peel up from the platform. Having a heated platform mitigates this. There are exceptions. Nylon can be printed on a printer without a heated platform (the piece shown in Figure 4-3 was printed that way), but the platform material needs to be one that nylon will stick to, like Garolite LE.

An intermediate choice is polyethylene terephthalate glycol-modified (PETG), which can be printed on a printer without a heated bed. The material is usually a little more expensive than PLA, but tends to creep less than PLA. Figure 4-4 shows a hollow cube 20 mm on a side, printed in translucent PETG.

Figure 4-4. *Hollow cube printed in PETG*

Thus the bottom line is: if you want to make 3D prints that do something mechanical, you are probably going to need a heated platform and an all-metal hot end. Table 4-1 summarizes this information. Note that you can use a heated bed with some of the materials listed here as not necessarily needing one, but you will need to use a platform surface other than blue painter's tape, because that tape's adhesive cannot handle heated bed temperatures.

Note that not every material can be printed with every surface. Some materials stick not at all to some platform materials, and some stick so well that it is impossible to get the print off. Be sure and read what your manufacturer says about your print bed and what is and is not compatible.

In some cases you will need to add a bit of glue stick. Polyvinyl acetate (PVA), sometimes known as Elmer's glue, is appropriate. Some printers have a removable bed of a flexible material which can help with removing prints.

Table 4-1. *Material Effects on Printer Requirements*

Material	Platform Surface (Unheated)	Platform Surface (Heated)	Nozzle
PLA	Blue tape	PEI, PET tape, PVA glue (60–70 C)	PTFE-lined or all-metal
ABS	None	PEI, PET tape, PVA glue (100–120 C)	All-metal
Nylon	Garolite LE	Some formulations, PVA glue (55–75 C)	All-metal
PETG	Blue tape	PET tape, PVA glue (70–90 C)	All-metal
Filled PLA	Blue tape	PEI, PET tape, PVA glue (60–70 C)	Requires hardened nozzle

Tip There are a few published papers and dissertations on the strength of 3D printed ABS and PLA parts. They have found rather inconsistent results. Joshua Pearce's lab at Michigan Technical University has done some systematic studies in this sphere—for example, a paper by Nagendra G. Tanikella, Ben Wittbrodt, and Joshua M. Pearce: "Tensile Strength of Commercial Polymer Materials for Fused Filament Fabrication 3-D Printing." *Additive Manufacturing* 15: pp. 40–47 (2017). DOI: 10.1016/j.addma.2017.03.005.

Multiple Extruders

Some printers come with two extruders. The purpose of the second one is to let you create prints with two colors or two materials. The best reason to use one of these is to use dissolvable support material. As we discuss in Chapter 2, because prints are created a layer at a time on the platform, anything with a steep enough overhang will require support material. Support material on a single-extruder printer requires that you snap off the material with pliers or other tools.

Dissolvable support is one solution to this, although the material tends to clog nozzles, and when you dissolve it, you then need to get rid of the water with the dissolved material. Polyvinyl alcohol (PVA), the commonest material, is a relative of Elmer's glue, and it is not a great idea to put much Elmer's glue into your plumbing (and might not be legal). Talk to your waste-management person before creating a lot of gluey water.

High-impact polystyrene (HIPS) is another material used for dissolvable support. It dissolves in limonene, a cleaning solvent made from oranges. Here too you will need to check on local restrictions on getting rid of solvents. See Chapter 2 for more about materials, including these.

Caution   A two-extruder printer will not use both extruders to print something in half the time, although a few two-extruder printers have a limited ability to print two copies of the same object at once, and some offer more ambitious experimentation. Typically, printers will print a lot more slowly in two-material mode because they have to pause on each layer and execute commands to wipe off each nozzle so that it does not drool onto the print while the other extruder is laying down material. In other words, do not buy a dual-extruder printer thinking that the second print head will allow you to print twice as fast. There is no way to do that with printers on the market as of this writing, because you might bang into one object with the opposite extruder.

There are new systems appearing that will analyze your model and in effect print in two colors from one nozzle. As of this writing, they are still a little experimental for most consumer use but are something to watch in the future. There is also at least one 3D printer on the market with a limited ability to create full-color filament prints by using an inkjet head on an ink-absorbent PLA, somewhat analogous to how powder full-color printers work (discussed later in this chapter).

One Big Printer or Several Small Ones?

People often have the impulse to buy the biggest printer their budget will allow. However, 3D prints take a long time. If you have three small printers, they can all be chugging away creating different projects. If you only have one, then you will have a queue.

You can print more than one thing at a time on a print bed, but that has its own issues. First, you need to start them all at once. Second, if one print out of five on the bed has an issue that makes it fall off or fall over, most likely you will need to stop the entire print. It is usually better to have beginner prints run in isolation, one per printer, so that you can kill a print that has problems and send the student back to the drawing board.

Except in the case of tall, thin prints that would require extra cooling time, usually not much time is saved when you try to print multiple things on the same printer plate rather than print one after the other. These longer-running prints are more prone to failure. So this, too, argues that spreading prints across several small printers is often a better idea than plating them all at once on a big printer.

Small printers are easier to move around. Although it is not a good idea to move a printer if you can help it, if you are going to move it much, you are better off with something that is, well, moveable. On the flip side, if you are concerned about theft (e.g., in a library public room), a big printer is harder to steal, but also more awkward to move and lock up in a closet when a room is unattended. We have run a bicycle cable lock through the metal handle of our portable printer when we needed to leave it unattended at a show, but obviously you need to be sure any locking mechanism does not get in the way when the printer is moving.

There are exceptions, but by and large smaller printers are faster than bigger ones if they are printing something that will fit on either printer. 3D printers have to move the build platform and/or a carriage that is big enough to get to all parts of the print. Whipping around bigger carriages and platforms makes precise movement more challenging, and often you can print at better resolution in less time on a smaller printer. Smaller frames can also be stiffer, with similar positive results.

There are cases when it is nice to have a bigger printer. Obviously, if you want to print something substantial frequently, and you think it would be a bad idea for strength or cosmetic reasons to glue several smaller pieces together, you may want a bigger printer.

Also, if you often print tall, skinny things, remember that printers can only put down material for a new layer when the previous one has cooled enough to hold its shape. This does not take very long, but tall, skinny prints will be limited by this minimum layer time. For these, it may take the same amount of time to print two or three things as it does to print just one (and the quality may be better, since the plastic cools better if the hot nozzle does not remain in contact with it). Of course, if something is tall and skinny, you can probably fit a few on your small print bed, as long as the print area is big enough.

We usually recommend buying a few small printers rather than one large one, unless there is a specific use case that requires a large printer.

Note   We are reserving a discussion of metal printing to Chapter 11, since there are some complex trade-offs peculiar to printing a plastic mold for metal vs. directly printing in metal. There are also halfway steps where you print with filament or something like it that is mostly metal with a plastic binder. After printing, you use heat and/or chemical processes to melt or dissolve the plastic out, and then use a high-temperature furnace to sinter the remaining metal into a solid part. This is a rapidly expanding field, which we contrast to traditional metal manufacturing in Chapter 11.

Printer Connectivity

In Chapter 3, we talk about the types of software involved in using a 3D printer. Regardless of the printer, one way or another a set of commands to print a model has to get to the printer from a computer somewhere. Printers handle that in one of several ways: they require a USB cable to be connected to the computer that created the file of commands; they accept those commands wirelessly; or they read a file off an SD card or USB flash drive. Depending on your environment, each one of these has advantages.

Printers that require a hard USB connection the entire time they are running are somewhat unusual now. That is a disadvantage, because if the computer sleeps or is otherwise interrupted, the print can fail (not to mention that it ties up a computer). One way around this is to use OctoPrint on a Raspberry Pi to control your printer (see Chapter 3's discussion of OctoPrint).

Printers that receive files over Wi-Fi work well if you are in a stable Wi-Fi environment, but it obviously causes problems if you are not. We are partial ourselves to printers that hold their models on SD cards or other outside storage, since this works everywhere and does not tie up a computer. However, SD cards are small and easily misplaced. Printers often have an LCD screen to choose among the files on an SD card or files transmitted wirelessly.

Open Source Materials vs. Cartridges

Some printer manufacturers require (or at least encourage) you to use their proprietary materials. In some cases, a computer chip in the cartridge will take care of software settings for you automatically. The catch is that these materials will be vastly more expensive than their generic equivalents— sometimes vastly more expensive for specialty materials. It also may mean you will not be able to try new materials that come along.

Particularly if you are in a cost-conscious environment, it is best to avoid being locked in to one manufacturer for your raw material. If nothing else, if your manufacturer goes out of business or stops supporting your printer, you will not be stuck if you can use open source materials.

That said, if you use generic (often called *open* or *open source*) filament, read reviews on Amazon and other popular retail websites. Very cheap filament sometimes has impurities that clog printers or varies in diameter enough that it can cause printers to jam. Low-cost printers have, in a way, outsourced their precision to their filament, and if it varies more than a few percent in diameter or composition, you may not be able to use it at all. People become very brand loyal after a time. If you are starting out, you might consider getting recommendations for one or two brands and buy a small amount to be sure that it works well for your printer before stocking up.

Filament Size

Printer filament comes in two standard diameters: 1.75 mm and what is called (for historical reasons) "3 mm" filament but is usually close to 2.85. When you first buy your printer, you will typically buy two or three spools of filament with it. Over time, you will want to try a different color or material, and you will build up a pile of partial spools. It gets very irritating to have a mix of the two kinds, both because of the double storage space and, if you are moving your printers around, the possibility that the filament spool and printer will not match. As of this writing, LulzBot and Ultimaker were the major printer brands using 3 mm filament; most others use 1.75.

Tip   Filament should be kept in its original sealed package until first use and then if at all possible in an airtight container to keep out moisture. Materials that absorb moisture (especially PVA, polycarbonate, and nylon) will tend to outgas and pop when heated, which can make pits in the print or jam the extruder and can weaken the prints. Five-gallon buckets with tight lids are a common solution. Resist the temptation to open and display every colorful spool as it arrives, unless you are in an extremely dry climate.

Enclosed or Open

Some 3D printers have open gantries (like a miniature construction crane), whereas others are completely sealed boxes. If you are printing acrylonitrile butadiene styrene (ABS), there are advantages to an enclosed box to keep the temperature more even. If young kids are around, a closed box will keep their hands away. An enclosure limits the visibility into what is going on, of course. This decision is closely related to the issue of where you are going to put it, discussed in Chapter 5. Some printers also have the option of built-in air filtration, which only makes sense with a closed printer.

Buy Within a Brand

If you are starting out and supplying a new makerspace, you may be tempted to try out several different brands of 3D printer. We recommend against that, because every 3D printer has quirks. If you stick to a particular brand, you will be able to learn and anticipate the issues a little better. It may also make training staff a little easier.

Should You Buy a Kit?

A lot of printers still come as kits. If you are confident in your ability to put together an electronic device, building a kit is a good way to really know how the printer works. However, if you have not tried anything like this before, and if there are no hackerspaces around that could help you, it might not be a good idea. Sometimes a high school robotics team is the early adopter and buys the first printer. If coaches and students are up for it, it might be a good off-season project. In a business environment, unless you want your employees to intimately understand how the printer works, it is unlikely to be cost-effective to buy a kit that requires more than minimal assembly.

Initial Costs, Filament Printing

We are often asked, "What will it cost for us to start a 3D printing lab?" As with everything to do with 3D printing, the answer is that it depends on what you are doing. If you want to buy, say, two small printers and one bigger one and run five to ten smallish projects a day, the cost of just the equipment breaks down something like this:

- *Smaller printers*: About $200–$1000 each

- *Bigger printer*: $1500–$5000 each

- *Tools*: Initial purchase of incidental tools such as pliers, spatulas, tape, and glue: $200

- *Filament*: 4–8 kg PLA per month at $30/kg, or $120–$240/month

- *Miscellaneous supplies*: $20/month

Some printer manufacturers provide support contracts, but most assume you will be on your own. Chapter 5 talks about living with your 3D printer and discusses facilities, ongoing costs such as training and maintenance, and similar staffing issues that affect lifecycle costs.

Selecting a Resin Printer

Some of the earliest 3D printers used a process called stereolithography (SLA). These machines used a laser directed by a pair of rotating mirrors to trace out a path to draw each layer, rather than moving a nozzle around the way filament printers do. Some of the larger manufacturers still use variations on this process today, particularly for resin printers designed for printing larger things.

An alternative that has been becoming more popular adapts technology used by visual display systems to expose a layer. This usually involves using a Digital Light Processing (DLP) projector, though in an effort to get the price down, some newer designs are using liquid-crystal display (LCD) masking to selectively illuminate the resin. In either case, the light intensity is much lower than with a laser, but these technologies have the advantage that they can illuminate an entire layer at once. The terminology of resin printers is in flux and is used somewhat inconsistently in the marketplace.

Some DLP printers have a built-in projector, and sometimes you have to provide an external one. If you see a suspiciously cheap DLP printer, you probably will have to buy a projector, too. These printers are coming down in price, but are still expensive to purchase and to run relative to filament printers.

LCD-based printers have recently been entering the market at much lower price points. The technology is cheaper because it uses commodity phone displays, but these displays are not intended to be used this way and will likely need to be replaced periodically. Before buying, you will want to find out how involved this task is for the printer you are considering and how much the replacements cost.

Fundamentally, resin printers use a source of light to harden a light-sensitive resin. Some sort of solvent has to be used when the print comes out of the printer to wash off excess resin. The operational trade-off comes down to whether you have a space that can handle a device that is more at home in a chemistry lab than a computer lab. Of course, if you have a chemistry lab, that is a pretty good place to keep it.

Caution   For a while, crowdfunding sites offered printers that used a cell phone as a source of light. Although this makes the "printer" incredibly cheap, there are several fundamental issues. First, your phone will be tied up for many hours for the print, and if you get a call or text during that time, it will probably ruin the print. Second, curing resin using the phone screen's backlight as the light source requires much more sensitive resin, which is more prone to curing when you do not want it to. Finally, we will just say that we would not want to put one of our phones under a vat of resin that will harden when exposed to light from the phone. The rise of very low-cost LCD printers with a proper UV light source has largely obsoleted these printers.

Cleaning and Curing

Resin prints require cleaning and curing. *Cleaning* usually means washing them off with alcohol, which leaves you with a solution of alcohol and dissolved resin to dispose of. *Curing* can mean putting the prints out in the sun or exposing them to some source of UV light.

The resin in the vat must be kept extremely clean. Any stray bits of cured resin floating around can damage a print in progress or even the printer itself.

Resin Printer Technologies

DLP (and LCD) printers, as discussed in Chapter 2, illuminate an entire layer at a time and can generate very fine detail. SLA printers move a laser spot. DLP theoretically can produce smaller features, but will also show pixelation artifacts in all directions. SLA printers, on the other hand, should show smoother outlines within a layer, but have a minimum spot size bigger than a DLP pixel. Relative speed of the technologies depends more on brand and the formulation of the resin being used than on the difference between the technologies. The technique used to peel each layer off the base of the vat makes an even bigger difference.

Common Types of Resins

As with filament printers, there are printers that require you to buy a proprietary resin (or at least highly encourage it) and there are those that allow you to use resins that are not proprietary to their printer alone. However, the trade-offs are a little different here. One advantage of resin printing is that it can create parts requiring specialized materials, for applications in dentistry, for example.

If you want to do something that requires a specialty material, you might want a printer that uses resin cartridges that communicate with the printer to optimize its settings. But if you do not have a specialized technical objective in mind, you may want to buy a printer that can use resins from other manufacturers. As with filament printing, not every printer can support every resin. Which printer will support which resin though is not as easily determined as it is for filament printers, where nozzle temperature and whether or not you have a heated bed are the drivers.

For resin, there are generally fewer settings to adjust compared to similar filament printers. If you have a printer designed for proprietary resin, it might still have an "open mode" to allow you to use other resins. If the resin is intended for your printer, it may specify a recommended exposure time and a few other parameters, which in turn depend on features specific to your hardware. But if there are no recommendations for your printer, you may be reduced to trial and error with expensive resin.

Since the hardening process is a photochemical one and not a thermal one (as it is with filament printers), resins exist that melt at low and high temperatures. A resin intended for creating injection molds, for example, can withstand high temperatures. On the other end of the spectrum, wax-like resins are commonly available that are designed to be easy to melt out of a mold for metal casting. There are also resins for parts that need to be sterilized, and that can be used in the mouth.

Most standard resins use a brittle material similar to acrylic plexiglass, which can produce fine details and good clarity, but can be fragile. Resins typically described as "tough" or "durable" may create parts that are less so. Flexible, rubberlike resins have also come along. You need to put some thought into part design so that each layer will peel properly.

Caution   Proper curing has a strong effect on the properties of resin prints. If you are using trial and error with a printer not designed for a particular resin, do not count on published mechanical or thermal properties for the finished part.

Initial Costs, Resin Printing

Resin printing costs are pretty variable right now, but for rough comparison with our earlier estimates for filament printers (assuming several printers, averaging one or two runs of small parts per day), here are some rough numbers as of this writing (in late 2019):

- *SLA system*: $1300–$5000 each

- *DLP system (with integrated projector)*: $3000–$5000 each

- *LCD system*: $200–$2000 each (plus ongoing cost of replacement LCDs)

- *Resin*: 4–8 liters per month at $60–$150/liter

- *Drying/cleaning devices*: Not essential but might save solvent and other materials—around $1000

- *Replacement trays/vats*: Replace every 5–10 liters for low end, more than that for higher end: $50–$100 each

- *Solvents (IPA, most commonly)*: Varies—consider disposal costs in your jurisdiction

Printing with Powder

We have focused here on technologies available to a consumer or small business that do not require industrial facilities. Both filament and resin printers do come in larger formats with more features for industrial users, but philosophically they are pretty much the same as their smaller consumer cousins.

3D printers that use powder as a medium, however, are larger investments. These printers create objects in a bed of very fine powder, typically with variations on techniques called SLS (selective laser sintering) or binder jetting. A layer of powder, usually around 100 microns thick, is spread over a platform. Then, either a laser will sinter the powder, called selective laser sintering (SLS), or a binder is sprayed on the powder to make it adhere (binder jetting). The process is repeated one layer at a time. The powder builds up on the bed so that at the end there is a solid block of powder the size of the bed and as high at the highest point on the model.

These machines have the virtue that you can print very complex and delicate structures without support, since the powder supports the print in progress. At the end of the printing process, the part or parts have to be dug out of the powder. Prints are often post-processed in one way or another to make them less porous and more robust.

This process is messy and requires varying degrees of protection for the user depending on what the powder is. Most of the powder left in the printer usually can be recycled for the next print, depending again on the details of the print.

Full-color prints are also possible with binder-jetting machines. These use gypsum powder to produce sandstone-like prints. The binder is mixed with colored inks as it is sprayed. The models can be fairly fragile, but for art applications very impressive resolution can be achieved. Usually they are infused after the fact with a substance like superglue to seal them and to make the colors more vivid. Figurines (about 10 cm tall) created in this way by CoKreeate in Alhambra, California, can be seen in Figure 4-5.

Figure 4-5. *Example of full-color binder jet print. Model courtesy of CoKreeate/Will and Jewelyn Co*

Nylon powder is the most common material used for laser sintering. There are several efforts underway to create "benchtop" powder 3D printers to bring the cost into the range between $10,000 and $100,000, including necessary accessories like a device to contain the block of powder while the user is digging the part out of it and sieves to clean the support powder you want to reuse. Materials are expensive, and facility issues with handling powder will add significantly to overall operating costs. If you are considering powder printers, you should get some bids from manufacturers and good advice for setting up the facility.

In particular, when pricing systems, be sure to note how much of the support powder can be reused from print to print. On a per-liter basis, it may appear cheaper than liquid resin, but you need a lot of it for each print if you need to add a high percentage of fresh powder each time.

Since the whole bed fills with powder to the height of the tallest print, these printers are more efficient if each run nearly occupies the printer's entire build volume, or at least the horizontal footprint to a consistent depth. This means that you want to print many small objects (that need not be identical) at once and work small objects into the empty spaces around larger ones. Resin may be a better choice if you do not print very much at a given time and you need the high resolution.

Powder-based techniques are at the root of most metal 3D printing, and we have a discussion of powder printing using metal in Chapter 11.

Using a Service Bureau Instead

If you want to design objects and have them 3D printed, but all these choices sound overwhelming, you can always use a service bureau. That will be far more expensive, of course, than printing yourself. You may be hesitant to pay for printing a student project, for example, or a personal project. However, as a business decision when your employee time is valuable, a service bureau might be the cheapest.

The cheapest bureau is likely to be a shared service, where people who have printers bid on jobs. Two of the big ones are www.3dhubs.com and www.makexyz.com. These sites were established as "Uber for 3D printers."

Like Uber itself, they have evolved from their initial roots. Where initially many of the providers were teenagers earning money to pay for more filament, these sites are now mostly used as aggregators for independent professional service providers.

You may want to have some small test part printed as a data point to see the cost, quality, and turnaround time. Remember, though, that some of these providers are one-person shops with a few printers, so if you throw a mission-critical order at them, they may not be up for handling a sudden large order. If confidentiality of your print is a concern, you will probably need to use one of the larger (and thus more expensive) service bureaus.

Summary and Questions for Review

This chapter discussed some of the major hardware choices that you have to make in selecting a 3D printer, particularly a filament printer. We went over the different types of materials you might want to use to create objects and the requirements for common filament types. We also gave some rough estimates of startup costs. In the next chapter, we talk about what happens once your printers arrive and what the facilities and staff issues might be.

Answer the following to test your knowledge of the material in this chapter:

1. What type of printer would you buy if your budget was about $2000 and you wanted to make prints that had details at the 100 micron level?

2. If your application required making one fist-sized print every few days, without a lot of fine detail, what type of printer would you most likely buy?

3. Consider the 3D application(s) you have or are thinking about having. Give the key points that you would consider about making the parts in-house vs. outsourcing them.

4. What are two advantages of filament-based printing over resin printing? What are two relative disadvantages?

5. When would you use one of the powder-based 3D printing technologies?

CHAPTER 5

Operating and Troubleshooting your 3D Printer

In Chapter 4, we talk about how to buy a 3D printer. In this chapter, we discuss what to anticipate when you bring it into its new home and unpack it. You do not need an expensive, special space for it, but knowing a few things about what a 3D printer really does *not* like might save you a lot of grief.

We cover the environment which makes a printer less prone to fail, what it takes to train typical nontechnical staff users, and maintenance requirements. We also talk you through how to create and print a small cube, a 3D printing equivalent of printing "hello world" when learning a new programming language.

Note   The bulk of this chapter focuses on filament-based printers. Then we have a shorter section at the end of this chapter summarizing the differences between that baseline and printing with resin. Powder printing is more manufacturer-dependent, and if you buy one of these pricier machines, it is likely that there will be training bundled with it.

© Joan Horvath, Rich Cameron 2020
J. Horvath and R. Cameron, *Mastering 3D Printing,*
https://doi.org/10.1007/978-1-4842-5842-2_5

Getting Started with a Filament Printer

When you look at many consumer-level filament-based 3D printers, it is easy to forget that you are looking at a little precision factory. The temperature, airflow, vibration environment, and ambient dust in the room all matter to the quality of your print (and to the lifetime of your printer).

Bigger, enclosed printers are less vulnerable to some of these things, but for the price of one of those, you may be able to get several smaller ones that can live tucked into suitable corners. In this chapter, we give you some background you can use to trade off those costs.

Where to Put It

Very often, people do not ask this question until the box arrives. Filament-based 3D printers should be in a room as free of dust as possible. Yet you want them in a ventilated area (particularly if you plan to use ABS). We will go through some of the common options here and talk about pluses and minuses.

A first impulse with a 3D printer in an educational environment is to think about making up a nice cart with the printers on top and the filament spools in the bottom part. However, doing this has many issues:

- 3D prints take a long time. Typical print times will range from an hour or two to several days. Most consumer printers cannot be reliably stopped and restarted, but features that allow a printer to recover from a power failure (with varying degrees of reliability) are becoming more common. Without this ability, you cannot unplug it and move it while printing, and even for printers that do have the capability, it is not intended to be used routinely (and will likely leave a visible artifact in the print).

- Carts are wobbly and often pretty flimsy and do not provide a very stable base for the printer. You might have to recalibrate the printer every time you move around if you are jouncing over thresholds and other obstacles when you move the cart.

- Many printers, especially smaller ones, do not have frames that enclose their full range of motion. If you have more than one printer running on a cart, that can end badly if they move around and you neglect to check that they are clear of each other for the whole range of their motion.

- Carts can get jounced around during a print, also causing artifacts.

- Filament needs to be protected from heat and moisture, which can be hard to do consistently rolling around on a cart.

- It can be challenging to think through ventilation issues if the cart will be going many arbitrary places.

In our experience, 3D printers that start off moving on a cart fairly quickly wind up in a permanent home instead. Or the cart gets tucked solidly in some corner and never moved, which defeats the purpose.

Tip   Although it is good for students to see their creations being made, one option is to do some short in-class demonstration prints and then print from an SD card, cloud storage, or whatever your printer supports thereafter. A science room or art room that students pass through on some regular basis can be a home for printers, if there is no "makerspace" per se.

That then brings us back to the question: where should I put it? For most printers, a sturdy table or shelf in a reasonably clean room with good ventilation is the best bet. A printer should never be in direct sunlight, and all printers should not be too close to a heat vent or area that gets very hot when the air conditioning is off. One particular early printer of our acquaintance (that had 3D printed parts) turned into a Dali version of itself when left in a sunny window with the air conditioner off on a particularly hot summer weekend.

Caution   If you do have to move a printer frequently, be sure you are picking it up by its frame and not it up by one of its precision parts, like one of the axes, or (worse) by a belt. Printers intended to be portable sometimes have a handle. If yours does not, stop and think about whether you might be bending or otherwise putting unusual stress on a critical part when you pick it up.

Ventilation and Drafts

3D printers are melting plastic, which means it is always prudent to make sure you have adequate ventilation. If you are printing ABS or one of the more exotic filaments in particular, it is wise to have active ventilation (a fan) pulling air away from the printer. A lab or art space that is designed with similar issues in mind can be a good home for a printer for those reasons as well. Some spaces use freestanding filters in addition, and some printers come enclosed with filtration.

One person's "ventilation" can be another's "draft." Drafts can either be a plus or minus, depending on the material. Air flowing across the printer may make the bed struggle to maintain temperature, particularly if the ambient air is chilly. The exception to this is that having a fan blowing on a PLA print can improve print quality, particularly if you are printing on blue tape at ambient temperature (and thus not affecting heated bed temperature).

There are aftermarket "safety enclosures" for some printers that you can consider, and filtration is available for some enclosed printers.

Noise

3D printers vary widely in how much noise they make when running. Your best bet is to see if you can be around whatever one you are going to buy to assess whether it can live in a particular room without bothering the occupants. On the other hand, a 3D printer wants to live in a reasonably low-vibration environment, so you probably do not want to banish it to a loading dock either.

In noisy trade show environments, it is often difficult to hear the noise a printer makes at all. The same printer may be annoyingly loud in an otherwise silent room. Some tables, lightweight wooden ones in particular, may resonate in a way that more than doubles the apparent volume of the noise the printer makes. If your printer sounds significantly quieter when lifted just above the table while printing, you might want to consider special vibration-dampening feet or other means of isolating the printer from the table.

Dust

3D printers are precision machines. Nozzles on filament machines are typically less than half a millimeter in diameter, and it does not take much to clog them. For a filament printer, the little kludge in Figure 5-1 works quite well. Take a piece of microfiber fabric (like a Swiffer) or just a paper towel, and binder-clip it loosely onto the filament ahead of the extruder gear so that the filament slides freely through it. Be sure it is well clear of any moving part. Swap it out once in a while and judge whether or not it is necessary by how dirty it is when you take it off.

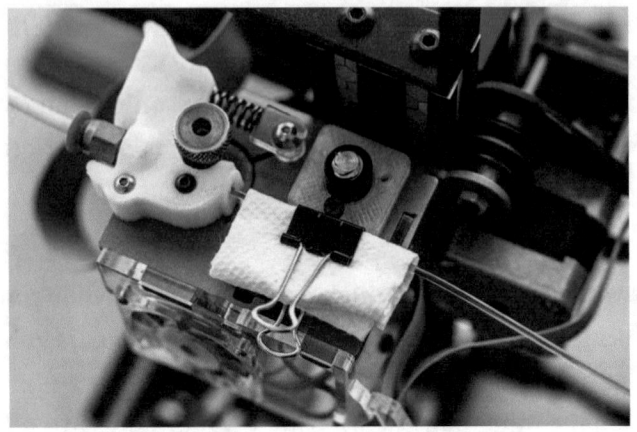

Figure 5-1. *A DIY dust catcher*

If you search on "filament cleaner," you will get other gadgets and folklore on ways to deal with this issue. Some of these advise using a cotton ball or sponge, but a cotton ball can be a source of particles that will cause an even worse clog. Sponges can dry out and lose contact with the filament. We do not recommend either of these methods.

There are also aftermarket enclosures and covers that you can buy to manage these issues. Joan leaves an upside-down large fabric shopping bag (handles down) over her open-frame printer if she is not going to use it for a while.

If, despite all your best efforts, your nozzle clogs, see the section on unclogging a nozzle later in this chapter.

Caution   Do not keep a 3D printer or store materials for one in a room with woodworking, pottery, or other activities that create fine dust.

Storing Filament

Filament should be stored in a cool, dry place without big temperature swings. Keep them in their original packaging until you are ready to use them. Consumer 3D printers have, in some ways, outsourced their precision to their filament manufacturers. Filament can absorb water from the air, and this is a bigger problem for some materials than others. For ones that absorb it very easily (notably nylon and PVA), the water will pop and boil off when the filament is heated, which can cause pitting on the surface and poor layer-to-layer adhesion.

If you live in a humid climate, keep your filament tightly sealed in a plastic bag with desiccant when you are not using it. Avoid leaving your printer and filament outside overnight or allowing water to condense on them. There are also filament-drying devices, but because we live in a mostly arid climate, we have not tried them personally.

PLA filament is the most forgiving of conditions except excessive heat. Do not leave a spool of PLA filament in a hot car on a summer day. Other than that, most reasonably sealed filament will be useable for years.

Tip   Tightly sealed 5-gallon paint containers work well to keep several rolls of filament sealed up. Stacking plastic boxes with tight lids work well too. You can place a renewable dehumidifier in the container with filament to keep its environment dry. These plastic modules contain a desiccant and a heating element that you can use to remove the absorbed moisture from it by plugging it in once it has been saturated.

Your First Print

In Chapter 3, we discuss all the many and varied software settings that come up in the general case of creating a 3D print. Here we give you a short summary of how to print something to get started. Resist the beginner temptation to download something complicated for your first print. Instead, create a small cube. The classic test cube is 20 mm on a side—a little under an inch. (3D printing is a metric world.)

The simplest way to do that is to use the free software package Tinkercad (`www.tinkercad.com`). Tinkercad is web based and recommends using a Chrome browser, or Firefox in a pinch. You will need to set up an Autodesk account. Then open Tinkercad. It has tutorials, but if you just want to make a simple cube, click Create New Design and drag the cube from the menu of shapes on the side to the workplane.

The default cube is, as it happens, 20 mm on a side. You do not have to do anything now except save the file. Figure 5-2 is a picture of a 20 mm 3D printed cube, with the bottom of the cube in the foreground so that you can see the pattern on the bottom as well as the layers. A happy print should look like this—nice clean bottom layer, and regular layering up from it.

Figure 5-2. *A 20 mm cube*

To save it, click Export ➤ Download for 3D Printing. You should now have a file with a name ending in .stl.

The next step is to load this STL file into software that will turn this model into commands for your printer, usually called a *host program* or *slicing software*. Hopefully your manufacturer pointed you to either its own program or one of the open source free options. If not, MatterControl (`www.mattercontrol.com`), Ultimaker Cura (`https://software.ultimaker.com`), and Slic3r (`www.slic3r.org`) are all commonly used. Chapter 3 details how to use these programs to create a file that can control your printer, called a *G-code file* on most printers (but a proprietary format on others).

Calibrating Your Printer

A critical requirement for good 3D prints is having the printer's parts align correctly *to each other*. This requires that the printer be both *square* and *tram*. *Squaring* refers to ensuring that the axes are at right angles to one another, whereas *tram* and *tramming* are used specifically to refer to adjustment of the *build platform* to ensure that it is parallel to the *x/y* motion of the machine.

A 3D printer that is square but not tram will have the axes at right angles, but the nozzle will not maintain the same distance from the platform as the *x* and *y* axes move. A machine that is tram but not square will usually print fine, but the angles will be wrong so that rectangles will become parallelograms and circles will become ovals.

If you suspect that your machine's axes are out of alignment because prints that should be rectangles are skewed, first check that the axes are square relative to each other (use a carpenter's square or, in a pinch, any other stiff, accurate rectangular object). If they are not, use whatever adjustments your printer manufacturer provides.

Depending on how your printer is constructed, this may require loosening several screws, nudging parts into alignment, and retightening the screws to lock them in place. Other designs may make this more difficult if the misalignment is due to bad manufacturing tolerances. These issues can be more difficult to fix, but can often be solved with strategic use of shims. If the error is in a part that can be printed and you feel competent to modify your printer, consider making a new one without the error as a more permanent fix (but save the old one, just in case).

If the width of an extruded line is inconsistent from one end of the platform to the other, check the alignment of the build platform relative to the axes, hereafter referred to as *tramming the platform*. Always check your squareness first, though, because if you have to make any adjustment to your frame, you will need to tram the platform all over again.

Caution   Some manufacturers refer to "leveling" a platform, but we try to avoid this terminology because it often leads to confusion about how to go about dealing with a platform that is not "level." Do *not* use a bubble level to align your platform. If you have your printer on a table that is not level, but your printer is otherwise square, changing any printer adjustment based on a bubble level would most likely not fix the problem. We use the word *tram* to draw this distinction about internally consistent alignment of the printer axes relative to the platform vs. level relative to gravity. Note that the axes are imaginary lines in space; normally, the printer's linear motion components will be lined up with the axes, but in principle software can compensate if they are not. Be sure you understand what your printer does and does not compensate for before attempting to fix problems.

If the build platform gets out of tram, you can wind up either printing in air in places where the platform is lower than expected or mashing the first few layers on parts of the platform that are too close to the nozzle.

Prints that do not stick in one corner and are a bit overcompressed (with wider-than-normal extrusion lines) on another part of the platform are symptoms of this problem.

A typical way to fix this for most printers is to home the axes manually using your printer's host software (Chapter 3) or perhaps an item in an onboard menu. Then take a piece of paper (we like to use a sticky note by sticking it to our fingers and placing it sticky-side-up on the platform) and move your extruder in x and y near each of the adjustment screws for your platform. For most printers, the piece of paper should be able to get between the platform and the nozzle, but there should be a bit of resistance. There is a device called a *feeler gauge* that does the same thing, but do not use one—a feeler gauge is made of a metal that is harder than your nozzle and might damage it.

As a quick test, you can print a small item with a big skirt (a skirt that is near the edges of the platform) to check platform tram. A skirt is made up of several lines that surround the print. If you see gaps between adjacent lines of the skirt, the nozzle is too far from the platform in those areas. If the nozzle is too close, the lines may fail to extrude because the nozzle is blocked. Alternatively, they may be pressed wider than they are supposed to be, so that they overlap and mound up around the nozzle. On an ideal platform, these lines will just touch one another, and will do so consistently on any part of the platform.

Some machines have "auto-leveling" features. These features use some kind of sensor to probe the height of the platform in various locations to ascertain how it is (mis)aligned and then apply a transformation matrix in software to align the printer's coordinate system to the platform, rather than vice versa. This can make it a lot easier for a beginner to set up a printer, but it is better not to rely on these features if you can avoid it. In some cases, rounding errors in these calculations can cause unsightly lines in the surfaces of prints, especially if your logical axes end up very close to, but not quite perfectly aligned to, the physical axes of a Cartesian printer.

This is less of an issue for delta-style 3D printers and some other non-Cartesian printers, because their physical axes are not straight. They are already doing similar math to translate Cartesian coordinates.

When a Print Starts

When you have successfully sliced a part to create G-code and used a host program to send it to the printer (both of which are described in Chapter 3), what happens next depends on what is in the G-code and also on the printer's firmware. If your manufacturer gave you standard settings files, it is likely that there are some G-codes that are added to the beginning of every print to *home* one or more of the axes (to bring the nozzle to some known point relative to the platform). Homing involves moving the extruder to a predetermined starting point, usually with each of the printer's physical axes at one of its two extremes, and touching a switch or triggering some other feedback mechanism to let the controller know that it is there. Aside from homing, most printers run their axes open-loop, moving the motors in discrete steps and counting steps to determine their location relative to home. The printer will also need to wait for the extruder and the platform heater (if there is one) to reach the specified temperature(s) and may do this before or after homing, depending on the order of commands in the start code.

Once the extruder and platform reach the right temperature, the extruder will usually drool a little to get some filament melted before the print proper starts. Then the printer will start to print a skirt (if you specified one) and then your print.

The first time you see a 3D printer making an object, it is mesmerizing. There is an in-joke in the community that the second item people print out is a chin rest so that they can watch their prints in comfort.

Tip   Slicing programs give estimates of build times, but the actual build times may vary. This is because the firmware does not move at exactly the speeds specified in the G-code, but rather accelerates and decelerates each time it changes direction, making its average speed lower. These calculations occur in the firmware, so the host program does not know how much this will affect the print time; some hosts offer better estimates than others.

During a Print

Once a print starts successfully, there is not a lot to do except to keep an eye on it in case something goes wrong. It is not a good idea to leave a 3D printer unattended, just as you would not go too far from a turned-on stove or oven. After a while, you will be able to tell from the sounds your printer makes if all is well. 3D prints can take a long time (many hours is common), and in the beginning we recommend small tests of new techniques and materials so you can watch the proceedings actively and intervene if the print does not go as planned.

The commonest failure is having the print come loose and slosh around. The only thing to do in that case is to kill the job (from the host program, or by resetting the printer) and change some of the design to have a bigger footprint on the build platform, or perhaps print at a bit higher temperature. If a print just does not look right, go back to Chapter 3 and consider changing some of the slicing settings; look at Chapter 2 to see if the filament properties might be the problem; and consider troubleshooting ideas in this chapter if you suspect your printer. The platform may not have been adequately aligned and prepared.

When a Print Finishes Normally

When your part finishes printing, ideally the result will be a part sitting on the build platform looking just like you imagined it would. However, you still need to get the piece off the platform without breaking it. How do you get any support, brims, and so on off the part? And what should you do to be sure the printer is ready either to be turned off for the day or to print the next job?

Caution   If your printer has a heated build platform, wait for it to cool down somewhat before you remove the part. Otherwise, the part (which is still a little soft) may bend or warp as you take it off or if it cools too quickly off the platform.

Getting a Part Off the Build Platform

Once the print has cooled down (see the preceding "Caution"), sometimes you can just grasp a part firmly and snap it off the platform. Depending on the combination of platform surface and print material you use, you may find that a print releases almost on its own as the platform cools. Some printers also use removable platform surfaces made of metal or plastic that can be flexed to separate from the print. Usually, though, you need a little leverage to get it started. You may also find that there is some intermediate temperature at which the print is easier to pry loose, but that it is more difficult once the print and platform have fully cooled. Keeping a part firmly attached while printing but allowing it to be easily removed afterward is one of the more difficult issues in 3D printing. If a print breaks loose too early, it can ruin a print, but sometimes the pieces adhere a little too well.

Unless your manufacturer recommends another implement, a common tool to pry pieces off the build platform is one of the tools used by artists: a paint knife (shown in Figure 5-3), an artist's spatula, or a palette knife. These work well on most types of platform surface. Get one that is fairly stiff so that it is strong enough to move a substantial part. The exact form factor is a matter of taste and experience, but the shape in Figure 5-3 works well.

Figure 5-3. *A painting knife is a good tool to remove a part from a tape-covered platform.*

Any art supply house should carry these tools (for example, Blick's, at www.dickblick.com). Very sharp edges should not be necessary, and you particularly want to avoid sharp corners like those of a razor blade that will scrape your platform, as these can damage the surface and force you to replace it more often. Once you get your tool under a corner, try twisting it to lift that corner rather than sliding the tool further under where it may scrape the platform surface.

While we are talking about small, handy tools to have in your kit, you should also get a good pair of tweezers, which are useful for plucking bits of drooled filament out of places they should not be.

Picking Off Support and Cleaning Up the Print

If your part needed support, you now have to pick it off. This can be a painstaking process, and the precise procedure you use will depend on the shape of your print and the tools you have available. Be careful because the plastic can be sharp; protect your eyes with safety glasses from the possibility of small, flying, sharp bits.

Grasping the support with needle-nose pliers and twisting it sometimes works well for sparse support; experiment and see what works for you. As discussed in Chapter 8, it is best to design your model in the first place to avoid big areas of support because they are very hard to remove. Chapter 6 discusses finishing techniques.

Restarting or Shutting Off the Printer

When you take your print off the build platform, you can either turn off the printer or create your next print. If your manufacturer gave you slicing settings, it is likely that there are some shutdown lines of G-code in the standard setting, or the firmware may take care of some activities.

For example, a printer without a heated build platform might add a few lines to every G-code file like those in the following example. The first line turns off the extruder heater (sets the temperature to zero); the second line sends the x axis to its home (zero) position; and the last command disables all motors:

```
M104 S0
G28 X0
M84
```

In general, if a print finished normally, you probably can create or load in another G-code and just run the next job. If you are not planning on using the printer again right away, it is best to turn it off and possibly unplug it.

Manually Controlling Your Printer

From time to time, you may suspect that your printer has a problem, or you may need to manually back out of an awkward failure that left a part skewered on the extruder. In those cases, you will want to use the Print or Control window in one of the host programs to send a G-code single line or two, or use the other manual controls that most host programs provide.

There are measures you may want to take as part of routine printing. For example, what do you do if you want to change filament colors, but you forgot to pull out the previous filament when you turned off the printer (and now it has cooled down and gotten stuck in the nozzle)?

Note   Some printers allow you to perform some or all of the functions we describe here from an LCD interface on the printer rather than in software. Check your manufacturer's directions for the precise steps to take to solve these common issues.

All the procedures that follow use the printer control mode in the host program you are using, as described in Chapter 3's discussion of host programs. There are variations among the hosting programs, but all of them allow sending a single line of G-code at a time, as well as moving the extruder in any axis, heating the extruder, and heating the platform.

Tip   By default, most printers use degrees Celsius (C) for temperature and millimeters (mm) for length measurements. If you are having trouble thinking in metric, keep in mind that there are exactly 25.4 mm in an inch, 210 degrees C equals 410 Fahrenheit, 115 C is 239 F, and 230 C is 446 F (to pick some commonly encountered temperatures).

Stopping a Print

Sometimes a print does not stick to the platform and starts to slosh around, or the print you thought would be fine without support is not going to work after all, or you just look at what is building and scratch your head about how your lovely computer image could have turned out like that. When a problem like this becomes obvious, the best thing to do is to click the "Kill Job" or "Stop" button, as the case may be in your host program.

However, the printer buffers commands so that it can plan acceleration for the next few moves. Especially if the printer is printing long continuous lines or waiting for a temperature to be reached, these commands may result in the printer not stopping immediately. If you need to stop the printer immediately, perhaps because it has gotten into a state where it might hurt itself (or you), you should go for the reset button or power switch instead.

If the print got jammed under the extruder somehow, you may want to move the extruder away manually (see "Backing Out of a Bad Situation" later in this chapter) and then retract the filament. Once you get the failed print off the build platform, turn off the printer if you are not going to try again. Note that G-code to turn off heaters and other shutdown activities will not be executed if the job was killed partway through. Your host program's stop function may shut down the heaters for you, but probably will not do any of those other things.

Typically, it is a good idea to cycle (turn off, wait, then turn back on) power to the printer just in case the partial print left it in some strange mode. If the failure rammed anything into the extruder, you might want to check that the build platform was not thrown out of alignment. Check your manufacturer's alignment instructions.

Changing Filament

When you finish printing a part, it is a good practice to retract the filament out of the nozzle before it cools completely, so that you will not have to heat it up again to remove it if you want to print with a different one next time. To retract the filament, as soon as the print job finishes, open the printer control panel and type in 10 mm of retraction. You can click the button to extrude 10 mm a few times; the filament should pop out of the input device after an appropriate number.

If you have a Bowden extruder (see Chapter 2), you only really need to get it out of the hot end to have the option of pulling it out easily later. Some printers also add commands to retract after every print job so you do not have to think about it. Even these printers, though, normally do not retract if you kill a job mid-print for some reason.

Suppose you forgot to retract the filament last time. You have bright pink ABS filament in the nozzle and you want to make an object in white in PLA. If your printer does not have a touchscreen option to facilitate this process, you will need to use one of the host programs described in Chapter 3. The steps will be something along these lines, with details dependent on which software package you elect to use:

- Type in the temperature appropriate to the *filament that is in the nozzle* (in this case, ABS, so about 230 degrees; see Chapter 2).

- Turn on the extruder heater (typically by clicking a button).

- Look at the monitoring display in the host software and wait until the temperature is near the right level (but not all the way there, because then you will just melt more filament into the nozzle).

- Retract 10 mm at a time until the filament springs out (or until you can pull it out the rest of the way, for printers that have a release).

- Then change the extruder temperature to the level appropriate *for the new filament* (in this case, PLA, so about 210 degrees). If there is plastic left in the nozzle, purge it by pushing it out with the new filament. This has to be done at the higher of the two extrusion temperatures (in this case, 230 C). If there is a big temperature difference between the two filaments, you may have to use an intermediate filament to purge out the old one, or use the "cold-pull" technique described later in this chapter to clean it out.

- Start the new filament into the extruder in whatever way is appropriate for your printer once the extruder is at the appropriate temperature (look at the temperature status graph).

- Once it is nearly in, type in 40 mm or so and extrude.

- Keep extruding an additional 10 mm or so at a time until the filament stops coming out the old color. Using a skirt on your next print will take some of that away too.

- You can then run your next print with the new color and material.

Tip   You could, in principle, use the preceding process to change out filament midrun to have a multicolor or multimaterial print with one extruder. Experts can and do try this (by using "pause"). It is very tricky, though, and results may be unpredictable.

Changing Temperatures During a Print

If a print looks like it may be having trouble sticking to a heated platform, you might want to raise the platform temperature just a few degrees. Your printer might have a way to do this through a touchscreen or other controls on the printer itself. Assuming you are not so lucky but that you have a computer connected while the printer is running, you will need to type a new temperature in a host program (but not a slicing program) under Heated bed. There will be a Set or similar button to click to confirm changing the settings. You can change your extrusion temperature on the fly this way too if you decide you should be running a little hotter or cooler.

Basic Hardware Troubleshooting

Sometimes you will want to determine whether a printer is having hardware issues of some type, so it is good to be able to try some basic commands to debug what is going on.

Checking the Motion of One Axis at a Time

If you want to check the motion of one axis in a controlled fashion to see whether something is broken or loose, the printer control panel in the host programs (see Chapter 3) allows you to move the axis in a positive or negative direction by typing in a positive or negative number (or in some cases by clicking buttons with fixed positive and negative increments). In Chapter 2, you saw that the z axis is the vertical axis; x and y are in the plane of the build platform.

If nothing happens when you enter a value, you may be at an endstop. Try entering a small value to move in the opposite direction. (For example, if nothing happens when you input -10 mm in x, then try +10 mm). Use small values—a few millimeters—if you are trying to debug a problem. Some machines are also configured with software endstops. It is not uncommon for machines to refuse to move in the negative direction past the point where they were when the machine started up until it has been homed, because it thinks that that position is zero.

If no axis will run, you may have a connection problem; be sure your USB connector is firmly attached and that your printer hardware settings are correct for your printer. Some printers may be able to power up their controllers and communicate with a host program using USB power, even if the printer's power supply is not plugged into the wall or its switch is off. Power to drive the motors and heaters can only come from the printer's power supply, though, so these functions will not work without it.

Backing Out of a Bad Situation

If you forget to take a previous print off the platform, or otherwise do something you are not supposed to do, you may find the extruder jammed into a print or blocked somehow. Because it is hard to figure out which way is $+x$ and which way is $-y$ under battle conditions, you might want to familiarize yourself now with how your printer is set up in case you need to walk your way out of a problem with the manual controls.

Extruder Not Extruding

If the extruder is moving around but no material is coming out, there are a few possible problems. The extruder nozzle might be jammed, or the extruder motor might not be pushing out filament. To debug this problem, you may have to trick the printer a little to get the information you need.

Most printers are set up so that the drive system does not try to push filament through a cold extruder. However, for printers with a visible filament drive gear, it is helpful to see whether the gears are turning even though nothing is coming out. A drive gear and its relationship to filament are shown in Figure 5-4. You may not be able to see anything if the filament is stuck in the nozzle. But if no filament is in the extruder drive, you might be able to send an M302 G-code command to the printer to tell it to override the need to heat up the extruder. Then tell the gear to extrude a few tens of millimeters of filament. See if the gears are turning. If not, you have some other failure.

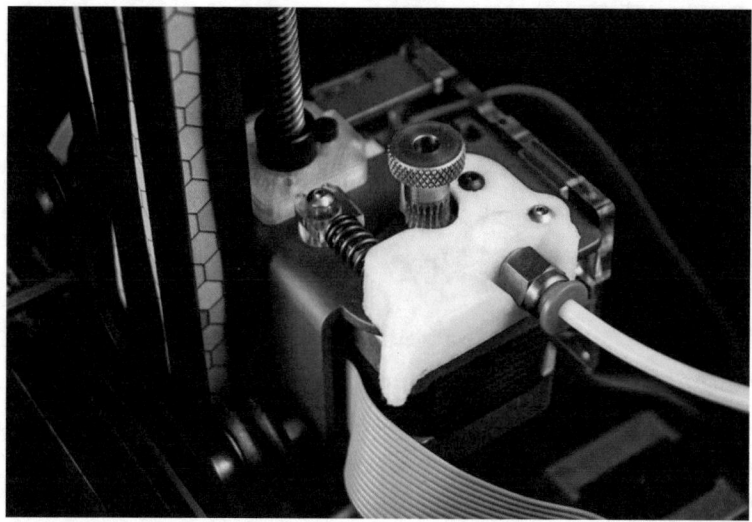

Figure 5-4. *A visible (Bowden extruder) filament drive gear*

If the gears do turn, then your nozzle is probably clogged. To unclog a nozzle, follow your manufacturer's instructions. If your manufacturer did not provide any suggestions, you can try the following:

- Heat the extruder a little above what you used for your last print and try manually extruding, as we did for the filament-changing process earlier this chapter. If you have input an M302 command, be careful not to try to extrude any filament until the head is at the appropriate temperature.

- If nothing comes out, manually retract the filament.
  Take a look at the end of it—is there anything burned or
  strange on it?

- If not, try breaking off the end cleanly and extruding
  again.

- If all that fails, try the "cold-pull" procedure described
  in this chapter.

- You might also try searching online using the phrase
  "Unclog extruder *<your printer name here>*."

Clearing a Clogged Nozzle

One of the more common problems with a 3D printer is that the printer
stops extruding plastic because the extruder nozzle is clogged. The
nozzle hole is small and it can fairly easily be blocked with debris that
was embedded in the filament, dust, or plastic that got too hot and
scorched or burned.

Caution   If your nozzle is not rated to 240 degrees C, you should not
try to use nylon for this procedure.

Cold Pull

In the past, the only way to get a clog out of a nozzle was to take the entire
hot end (nozzle, barrel, and heater block) apart or take it off and put it in a
solvent. Because that is not very convenient, and taking the hot end apart
can damage it, the *cold-pull* technique was developed. Somewhere along
the line, it also developed the name *atomic pull*, but we call it by its older
name here. A cold pull starts with inserting filament in the nozzle just as if
you were going to print with the filament.

Instead of using the usual extrusion temperature, though, which would melt the filament, a cold pull involves pulling the plastic out at a lower temperature. The temperature is warm enough to allow the plastic to stretch enough to pull away from the sides of the barrel so that it does not seize up entirely, but cold enough so that the filament remains solid enough to stay in one piece. Usually, any debris in the nozzle will then come out with the filament. We estimate the best *cold-pull temperature* in the following description.

The cold-pull technique works best with printers that have polished-smooth stainless steel nozzle barrels. It also works for nozzles that have a polytetrafluoroethylene (PTFE) internal coating if they are rated to 240 C. The cold-pull technique has been successfully done with ABS (cold-pull temperature of about 160–180 C). PLA is much more difficult to work with, but a cold-pull temperature of 80–100 C will sometimes work. Nylon filament (cold-pull temperature of 140 C) is far easier and more reliable to use for this purpose due to its strength, flexibility, and low friction.

The cold-pull technique works as follows: To begin, remove as much of the plastic that you have been using as possible. To do this, you can attempt a cold pull with ABS or PLA with the temperatures listed previously. For the rest of the instructions, we will assume that this failed to fully remove the filament.

Next, heat your nozzle to 240 C so that it can thoroughly melt the nylon and push the nylon filament in. If your printer has a Bowden tube, you may find it easier to remove it so that you can push and pull the filament by hand. Attempt to extrude the nylon slowly. Most clogs (especially those caused by accumulated dust) will not actually block the nozzle entirely, but will be pushed into the nozzle and stop it when the nozzle pressure increases and then float up out of the way when left to sit.

If you do not have a hard clog (usually a solid foreign particle lodged in the nozzle), a slow, pausing extrusion should allow you to purge the old printing material.

Once the nylon starts coming out of the tip, you can begin cooling your nozzle. See Chapter 3 for information on manually controlling your printer to see how to extrude some filament. If your extruder has a release mechanism, you may also be able to apply pressure to the filament by hand, but be sure to support the extruder while doing so to avoid transmitting force to the motion components. You want to keep trying to push the filament slowly into the nozzle as it cools to prevent voids from plastic oozing out.

When your extruder temperature is well below the pull temperature, start heating it again to the specified temperature. When it gets close, start pulling on the filament manually if your printer mechanism allows it, or by retracting it using a host program (this requires the M302 command). Pulling as the temperature is rising allows you to ensure that it releases at the lowest possible temperature, which will make the filament more solid. Nylon should come out solid and nozzle-shaped, which is why it works best. Other materials often will not release until they are soft enough that they will stretch significantly. If this happens, you may still be able to get a successful pull if you are careful not to let the long, thin strand of plastic break.

Note   The temperatures specified in the preceding directions are maximum temperatures—temperatures above which the plastic is unlikely to come out solid. For best results, you should always pull the plastic at the lowest possible temperature.

Figure 5-5 shows some examples of cold pulls. If you pull the nylon out and the surface is rough, dark, discolored, or has black spots around the sides, this indicates that there is residue of overheated or carbonized, burned plastic in the nozzle. If you see this, you should clip off the end and repeat the process until the nylon comes out smooth, clean, and mostly white. Figure 5-6 shows similar examples from with a nozzle that was clogged with overheated plastic, rather than burned plastic.

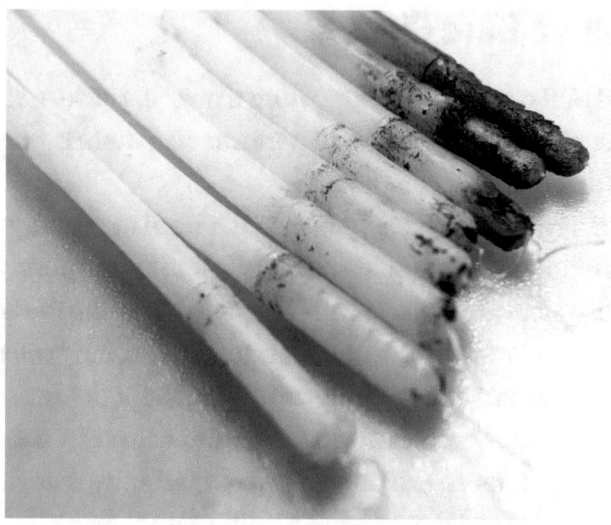

Figure 5-5. *Burned residue on cold-pulled filament*

Tip   You might want to do cold pulls from time to time as a preventative measure if your print quality seems to be degrading.

Figure 5-6. *Nylon with residue of overheated plastic*

Dealing with a Hard Clog

Usually a cold pull can remove debris from a nozzle. However, if you cannot get the plastic all the way in to perform one, there is probably a hard bit of debris blocking your nozzle.

To clear this type of blockage, you will first need to dislodge it. There are two types of tools that are sold specifically for this purpose. Some sellers advertise small drill bits for this purpose, but using these is a bad idea. Drill bits are made of hardened tool steel so that they will not bend and can maintain sharp edges. These are designed for cutting softer metals like the brass that most nozzles are made of, and will easily damage the orifice, resulting in uneven extrusion. More importantly though, these thin pieces of hardened metal are extremely brittle, and they can easily break off inside the nozzle and block it permanently.

You can also buy nozzle cleaning kits that have smooth springy needles in metric sizes. These have little handles on the ends, distinguishing them further from drill bits. They are also much cheaper than the drill bits. When selecting them, be sure to choose a size that is at least 0.05 mm smaller than your nozzle.

It is a good idea to have these on hand in case you need them, but what if you do not? Sewing needles are not recommended, since they are generally harder (and thus more brittle), and they do not typically come in sizes that are long enough and thin enough to use easily. Piano wire can be used if it is a thin enough gauge. Smaller gauge numbers mean larger diameters; 28 gauge or smaller should fit a typical 0.4 mm nozzle. However, cutting the wire is likely to leave sharp edges that can scratch the nozzle. Another solution is to pluck a bristle from a small wire brush and push it into the nozzle using needle-nose pliers. Figure 5-7 shows some of these implements.

Once you have poked your chosen implement through the nozzle, try a cold pull as described earlier in the chapter to see if you can pull the debris out. Note that the nozzle has to be hot for this maneuver to work, because otherwise the nozzle will be clogged with solid plastic. Be careful not to get your fingers near the hot nozzle. Figure 5-8 shows one way to keep your fingers out of harm's way.

Using one of these tools does not usually remove the blockage from the nozzle entirely. It only dislodges the clog so that hot plastic can flow past it and then harden around it so that it can be pulled out, though occasionally it will break up the clog enough to allow it to be pushed out of the nozzle in smaller pieces.

Figure 5-7. *Good (and bad) tools for clearing nozzle clogs*

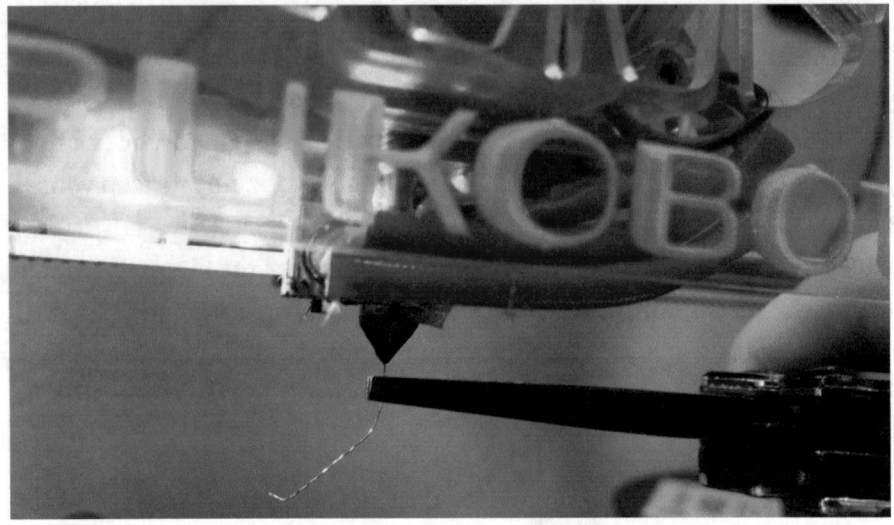

Figure 5-8. *Using a wire brush bristle to clean a nozzle*

Clicking or Grinding Noises

One of the first signs of trouble with a 3D printer is an unfamiliar noise. You will know you are an experienced 3D printer user when certain noises make you immediately execute a high-speed dive across the room toward your printer. Because prints can take many hours, listening to your printer is often the best way to monitor it (with an occasional glance, of course).

Tip   In addition to being sensitive to abnormal noises, be aware of what a "normal" print run smells like. A burning smell is never a good thing around electronics. Be able to distinguish problems from, say, the smell of ABS printing.

A filament-based printer has to drive the filament into the extruder somehow. Clicking noises usually mean that the filament is not going into the nozzle smoothly (or at all). Here are some possible causes:

- The filament might be hung up on the spool or catching on something.

- The nozzle might be clogged, as just discussed.

- The filament might not have been seated correctly when it was inserted. (This applies at the beginning of a print; if the ticking starts mid-print, this is unlikely.)

- The filament might be too wide to go into the nozzle (check it with calipers as discussed in Chapter 2).

- Something might be hitting one of the fans on your printer. Check that the fans are clear.

- If your nozzle is too close to the platform, you may have trouble extruding in the early layers because the plastic coming out of the nozzle does not have anywhere to go.

Sudden grinding noises usually mean that the print came loose and is jammed under the nozzle. This warrants a sprint across the room to turn off the printer, because the jammed part can exert some unexpected forces on the platform and its supports. Get your printer into a safe condition by stopping the print job. Then manually walk the extruder back out using the techniques in the section "Backing Out of a Bad Situation." You may have to readjust the build platform as described earlier in this chapter.

Note   If you have been trying to extrude filament into a clogged nozzle, the drive gear may have been digging into the filament and clogging up the gears with ground-up filament. Check this too if you had to clear the nozzle. Otherwise, the filament may not feed well, and you might think that the nozzle is still clogged. Pick and/ or blow it off carefully and be sure you are not blowing plastic dust someplace where it will cause other problems.

Post-processing Tools and Space

Depending on what you are doing with your 3D prints, you may need some additional tools to use to clean up or otherwise post-process prints. In Chapter 6, we talk surface finish considerations, which may require gluing, sanding, painting, and similar operations (and thus a facility that can handle those things). Earlier in this chapter, we discuss printers needing to be in a clean environment; this may mean that you will want the post-processing to happen away from the printers.

Removing support can be a little messy and result in lots of small bits of plastic everywhere. Doing this over thick carpet is a bad idea since you will be picking the bits out forever. If the 3D printers are in a computer lab–type environment with carpets and nice tables, you may want to designate a "messy room" for the post-processing activities.

Chapters 10, 12, 13, and 14 address applications of 3D printers in various situations. If you are outfitting a makerspace or industrial facility, you may want to skim through those chapters to get an idea of what types of materials you might want to keep in stock, beyond filament.

Recycling Prints

People ask us all the time if you can recycle your 3D prints into filament. Many people are working on that. The challenge, though, if the filament diameter is off even a few hundredths of a millimeter, it can cause you problems. So, any local machine would need to produce very high-quality and high-volume extrusion of plastic.

Parts you make yourself are not currently appropriate to put into recycling streams, because the filament typically is not clearly labeled with an appropriate recycling number, nor are the resulting prints. PLA composts in commercial composting facilities (but will not break down at the temperatures of a typical home compost bin). Whereas bottles made from PET plastics are commonly recycled, PET filaments are different formulations and are not appropriate for the same recycling stream.

Getting Started with Resin Printers

To this point, most of what we have been talking about is specific to the care and feeding of filament-based 3D printers. Resin printers magnify some of these issues. The printers need to be in a very dust-free environment since they can be damaged by small bits of debris in the wrong place at the wrong time. Treat those as you would treat an equivalently priced microscope in terms of clean and stable environment. Do not ever move a resin printer in mid-print.

Before and During a Print

The front end of the resin 3D printing process (creating a model) is the same as for filament-based printers. Consumer resin printers, however, are more likely to have their own proprietary slicing program than their filament-based counterparts. This software usually does not have very many user-settable parameters for creating a resin print, compared to creating a filament print.

Some resin printers use proprietary resin, and the exposure time and other parameters will be set by the manufacturer to be optimum for the resin. See Chapter 3 for a discussion of slicing software for resin printers and Chapter 8 for a discussion of the design issues for resin prints.

Most resin prints need support—sometimes more support than a comparable filament print. You might think that floating in resin would support the print, but it does not. Most resin printers have a platform on the top and their illumination window at the bottom. This means a print is created upside-down, which means that supports work a little differently. During printing, the print will be hanging from where it attaches to the platform. The supports need to keep pieces from falling off and floating away in the resin, but they also need to withstand the force of peeling the print off the bottom of the tank. Thus support is working against forces that are not the same as just a filament print upside-down.

Resin prints are typically solid. If they are hollow, then the print has to be oriented so that no air is trapped in it. If a bubble of air is captured in a hollow or bowl-shaped area of the print when it lifts out of the resin during the peel step, the trapped air may displace resin that is needed for the next layer. Strategic holes might need to be placed to allow air to escape during the printing process, as well as to let any captured resin drain out after printing.

The resin curing process essentially glues the print to the print platform. This adhesion is often much stronger than you would want for a filament print. Removing the print often requires prying and scraping the platform, which can damage the base of the print.

It is difficult to print an accurate base anyway, because with such thin layers, it is often necessary to overcure the initial layers to ensure proper adhesion. For this reason, the software will often print entirely on top of supports. It creates a base layer on the platform that widens to create a lip, so that you can get a tool under it. These structures will need to be broken or cut away after printing.

If a print does fail and start floating around the tank, you will need to very carefully clean off the platform and be sure you strain any loose bits out of the resin tank before trying again.

Post-processing

Post-processing for resin printers further complicates matters. Different resins and printers require processes that will vary in detail, but go something like this: the print will be created in a tray of resin. When it is done, the platform (on which it has been created upside-down) will be removed from the machine. The print will still be tacky, and the surface may be marred if touched. Figure 5-9 shows a small print on a resin platform. The person doing the post-processing needs to wear chemical-resistant (not latex) gloves, like nitrile ones.

Next, the print needs to be washed and cured. Typically, the wash is done with isopropyl alcohol (various concentrations are advised by manufacturers). The wash alcohol with resin in it needs to be captured for disposal along the way (Figure 5-10).

Finally, the print needs to be UV cured, either in a special box or in the sun. Figure 5-11 shows the print after it has been UV cured and then the supports snipped off. Supports for resin prints tend to be spindly and usually are snipped off with flush cutters or other small cutting tools.

Figure 5-9. *A resin print just out of the printer*

Figure 5-10. *A resin print being washed with alcohol in a Formlabs wash station*

Figure 5-11. *The completed print (and its cut-off supports)*

Working with Resins

Unlike filament, which pretty much you just have to keep reasonably cool and dry, resins usually have a shelf life. Resin that has been poured out also has to be kept away from any source of light that can harden them. Direct sunlight into a printer can result in a printer with a solid block of resin in its tray, which would destroy at least the tray.

Resins are typically more expensive than filament, so you will want to avoid failed prints and perhaps create small subscale experiments when in doubt about whether something will work. It does not help that most resin prints are solid, so you may go through more resin than you might expect if you are used to filament printing.

On the plus side, usually the resin remaining in the tray after a print is completed can be reused. Most manufacturers will suggest that it be strained through a paint filter after a failed print to be sure there are no stray bits floating around. If a piece broke loose, it may end up stuck to the window at the bottom of the vat. Your printer may have a wiper built in to clear anything like this away. If not, the manufacturer likely will instruct you to use a smooth plastic scraper (not a metal tool or bare hand) to gently check the bottom between prints. Most resin printers have a glass window under the vat, and any stray bits of hardened material between the window and the print surface when the next print starts can break the glass.

The platform also needs to be carefully scraped clean after each print. We suggest running a (gloved) finger over it to check for remaining bumps.

After the prints are done, the alcohol (or other solvent suggested for your resin) with dissolved resin needs to be appropriately disposed of, which varies from jurisdiction to jurisdiction. In an industrial setting, check with your facilities manager on whether they can handle however much material you will generate, and take a careful look at your manufacturer's instructions. Many solvents are flammable, so bear that in mind when figuring out where to locate your printer.

There are other maintenance issues involving keeping the tray clean and being sure that it is not in need of replacement. Some printers have a film that needs to be replaced, rather than replacing the tray per se. The details of this vary from machine to machines; follow your manufacturer's recommendations. Also review your manufacturer's requirements for storing resin and disposing of any unused and expired materials.

Staff and User Training

As should be obvious by now, it is challenging to learn how to use a 3D printer on your own. We hope that our books are a good solution if there are no other options, but it is helpful to most people to take a course. We find that two sessions of two hours each work well.

Learning to use a basic consumer-level filament printer with PLA or other nonexotic filaments typically takes a day or two of fiddling around to get to the printing out a cube stage described earlier in this chapter. If CAD is new as well, then the learning curve can take a little longer. Then it usually takes a while (a few weeks) of experimentation and a mix of successes and failures to get to a point where your prints are repeatable. Printers with proprietary filament might shorten this learning curve, but typically at far higher materials costs in the long run.

If possible, we would suggest learning on a filament printer first and then moving to resin or powder afterward. There are some significant differences in design issues for each one (see Chapter 8) but your mistakes will be cheaper on a filament printer, and you can develop intuition more simply there. Printers that use powder or are in the industrial price range likely will be bundled with training and/or facility setup consulting, and obviously, you should take advantage of that.

For a consumer-level 3D printer, we have found that someone with no exposure does well in a two-hour or so session that gets them to the point of making a cube or other simple thing. We then leave them to play for a week or two. Then we come back and cover the material in Chapter 3, see what has happened in the interim, and get them started with applicable material for what they want to do.

Summary and Questions for Review

This chapter covered the day-to-day issues of supplying and housing a 3D printer and its supplies and associated tools, with a particular emphasis on 3D printers that use filament. We went over basic calibration, facilities issues, and solutions to common problems. We concluded with a review of the basics of resin printers and touched on staff and user training issues.

Answer the following to test your knowledge of the material in this chapter:

1. In the middle of a print, your model comes loose and starts moving around. What should you do if this happens on a filament printer? What about with a resin printer?

2. Your filament printer starts making a clicking or grinding noise. What, if anything, should you do about it?

3. Describe what things you would try to do to clear a clogged nozzle.

4. Why is it a bad idea to use a small drill bit to clean out a nozzle?

5. What are the additional post-processing steps required for a resin print vs. a filament one?

CHAPTER 6

Surface Finishing Filament Prints

Some like the texture of layer lines, while others consider them a nonstarter. In this chapter, we talk about what you can do to get the surface finish you want for prints created from filament, which usually have visible layer lines.

Post-processing a resin print, discussed in Chapter 5, is not (primarily) about smoothing the surface, but rather about stabilizing the print and finishing the curing process. Fortunately, their surfaces are created quite smooth to begin with. We will have a few notes about sanding a resin print later in this chapter. The composition of "resin" is varied and proprietary to different printers, so for the most part, you will need to depend on suggestions from your manufacturer.

Similarly, powder prints made with gypsum or nylon powder typically need to be infused with something like superglue to keep them together. Again, the printer materials tend to be proprietary, and you should get finishing advice from your manufacturer of the printer and materials.

Specialty Materials

One way to get desired effects in your prints is to use a novel material. In Chapter 2 we review many types of materials. Here we will focus on some that have particular surface effects. However, not every printer can use

© Joan Horvath, Rich Cameron 2020
J. Horvath and R. Cameron, *Mastering 3D Printing*,
https://doi.org/10.1007/978-1-4842-5842-2_6

every filament or resin. Check that the temperature range and required print bed surface are compatible with your printer.

In the case of filament printers, one way to get interesting surface effects is to use a *filled filament*. These are typically PLA-based filaments with metal or wood particles mixed in. The filaments can be challenging to use, with a tendency to clog the nozzle, and the metal or fiber ones can abrade a nozzle. But the effects can give the appearance of wood or metal.

Figure 6-1 shows four pieces that were printed and then sanded with many progressively finer grits of sandpaper. The top-left and lower-right pieces are plain PLA. The upper right is steel-filled PLA, and the lower left is wood-filled. Filled PLA can be printed on blue tape at PLA temperatures.

Figure 6-1. *Sanded PLA pieces*

Another option to create surprisingly smooth and shiny prints is to print with *silk* PLA. Silk PLA does not contain silk; it is regular PLA which has some lignin plant fiber as an additive. These fibers make a print shiny, and the extrusion of the plastic through the nozzle aligns the fibers in a way that makes the surface very smooth and regular (Figure 6-2). Pieces look like anodized aluminum without any post-processing. The filament can be a little tricky to use, though, since it can be blobby while printing. Avoid any tall, spindly structures or use a cooling tower (Chapter 3).

Figure 6-2. *Silk PLA piece*

Flexible filaments made of various elastomers also are readily available. They can be challenging to print, though, because they can tend to jam (particularly in machines that use 1.75 mm filament and Bowden tubes). However, if you can get past that, you can make some pretty interesting flexible objects.

We talk about creating transparent prints in Chapter 9. Prints that are translucent (as opposed to fully transparent) can be created in a variety of materials, notably PETG or translucent PLA. The print in Figure 6-3 is printed in blue PETG. The print is a model of the gravity well of the Earth and Moon from our 2016 Apress book, *3D Printed Science Projects*.

Prints made with materials that are only a little translucent (especially in white and other light colors) can look much smoother than those made with more-opaque ones, because subsurface light diffusion prevents layers from casting hard shadows on one another. In Figure 6-4, the part on the left was created with opaque filament and, that on the right, with slightly translucent filament.

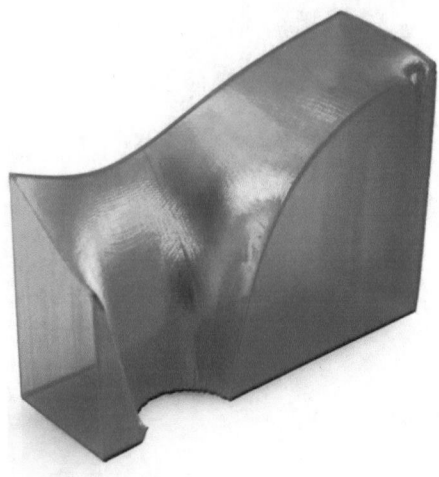

Figure 6-3. *PETG vase-printed piece*

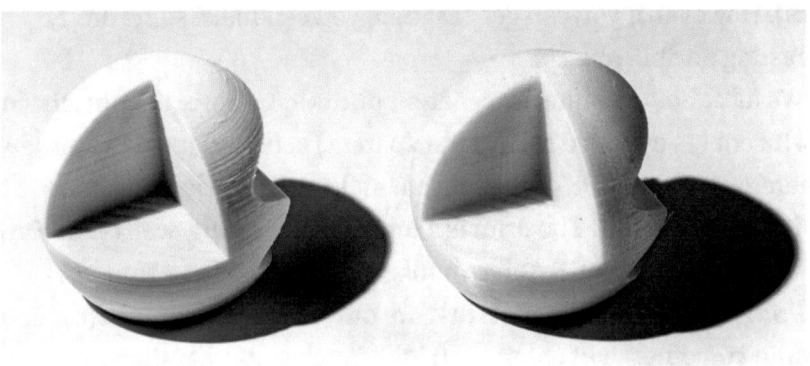

Figure 6-4. *Opaque(left) vs. lightly translucent piece (right)*

More transparent materials usually look best when vase-printed or printed hollow (both also addressed in Chapter 9), since otherwise infill will show through, as shown in Figure 6-5.

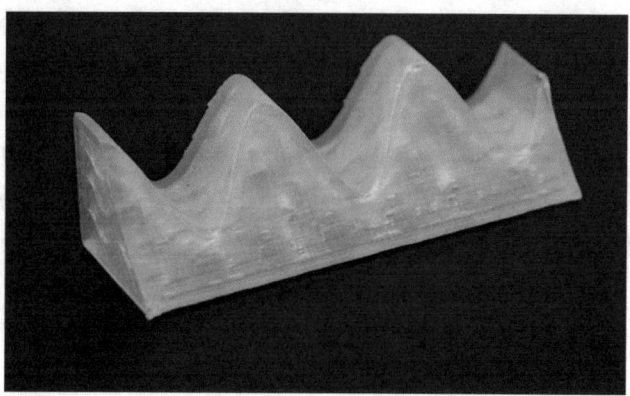

Figure 6-5. *Infill showing through on transparent piece*

You can also get some interesting effects by filling a transparent piece with something else (that will not leak out). For example, Rich designed the chess pieces in Figure 6-6 to print hollow in PETG. To make them heavy enough to use, he filled them with metal ball chain, and put a small dab of hot glue to keep the filler from falling out.

Figure 6-6. *Chess pieces printed transparent and filled*

In the case of resin printers, it is difficult to generalize because a lot of the differentiation from manufacturer to manufacturer is in development of specialty resins. Resins exist that are flexible, particularly durable, suitable for high-temperature applications like making injection molds, and more. Your choice of a resin printer is likely to be driven in part by what type of material you want to use.

Gluing Pieces Together

Once you have printed the pieces, use glue that works on plastics. Cyanoacrylate adhesives ("superglues") work pretty well on PLA and ABS, though you will likely want to use the thicker gel style varieties to fill the gaps between layers if you want to glue to the side of a print (and especially if you want to glue to a surface that was slanted in the printing orientation). Nylon is difficult to glue with any adhesive appropriate for home use.

PETG is somewhat difficult to glue, but not as much so as nylon. For any of these plastics, you can get better adhesion by roughly sanding the surfaces on which you will be applying glue. Roughing up the surface creates fine scratches that give the glue more to hold onto. Of course, if the surface you want to glue to is printed in contact with the platform, you may be able to select a build surface like blue painter's tape that will impart some texture to serve this purpose.

Caution   Before using any glue, read the manufacturer's instructions. Always use glues in well-ventilated areas. You may want to try out a particular glue on a few scrap pieces first to be sure that it does not discolor your material. Some glues may dissolve pieces a bit, which allows the "welding" process described later in this chapter.

Using an Acetone Slurry

If you are printing in ABS, there is another alternative for adhering pieces to one another (but see the "Caution" that follows). Acetone will melt ABS, so it can be used to weld one piece of ABS to another. Some people put a little bit of acetone in the type of bottle used for nail polish (ones with a small brush) and add the skirt, support material, or other scrap from the print.

The acetone will dissolve the scrap into a slurry that will weld the pieces together and fill the gaps created by layer lines without melting the edges of the print too much. Or, if precision edges are not important and your mating surfaces are sufficiently smooth, you can use a drop of acetone to bond the parts together. We talk about using acetone to smooth a print later in this chapter.

Caution   Acetone is flammable and volatile. Its vapor is invisible and heavier than air. The vapor can pool if you are in an unventilated area and cause a fire or explosion. Follow the cautions on the manufacturer's label.

Acetone welding only works for acetone-soluble plastics, such as ABS, MABS, or HIPS. Even with these materials, results may vary from one supplier to another due to differences in formulations and additives.

Caution   When you paint acetone on a part, the acetone evaporates, and you will get a bit of condensation from the air. This can make the surface of the object a bit cloudy.

Most other 3D printing filament materials (such as PLA, nylon, and PET/PETG) are not acetone-soluble. Some PLA formulations (depending on additives) may partially melt, whereas others have been known to warp and crack when exposed to acetone.

Welding with a 3D Pen

One alternative to using chemicals and glues to weld parts together is to use a 3D pen; see the sidebar about them in Chapter 2. Use the same filament as your print, and weld prints together that way. It may not look very smooth, but it should be serviceable. Welded seams can be sanded once the plastic has cooled. Many people buy those pens just for this purpose.

Sanding, Painting, and Dyeing

All types of 3D printers will produce fine layer lines in printed objects, but the physics of filament-based printing tends to accentuate these lines more than other methods. You can think of them in one of two ways: as inherent in the medium (like brush marks on an oil painting) or as a problem that needs to be resolved.

If your application falls into the latter category, this section suggests some ways to get rid of those lines and to color your printed part other than by choosing colored filament. We talk about issues with chemical smoothing and then discuss sanding, painting, and dyeing finished prints.

Most common materials can be sanded and painted, except for nylon which must be dyed instead. Be careful to manage the dust created during sanding, to protect both you and your printer.

Chemical Smoothing

There are various smoothing techniques described online that use acetone vapor to smooth ABS, along with do-it-yourself devices to create and handle the vapor. Many of these are unwise and/or too hazardous to use without significant protective measures, and we do not go into these here. As of this writing, available solvents that can smooth most plastics other than ABS are too toxic to be used in a home or school environment, for example.

Although we have not personally tried it, if you want to do a lot of vapor smoothing, you may want to look into PolySmooth's line of PLA-like filaments that are formulated to be smoothed with isopropyl alcohol vapor (using the Polysher vapor smoothing device, which the company also sells). As always, be sure you are set up for the chemical handling the manufacturer suggests.

Sanding

With enough time and a range of grits, sanding can make prints incredibly smooth. Powered sanding can easily generate enough friction to melt most printable plastics, though. There are rotary tools (like the one made by Dremel) that rotate a tube covered with sandpaper that you might be tempted to use for this. However, it can easily catch on the softened plastic and bite in, ruining a print in less than a second.

Wet sanding helps to keep the plastic cool during sanding and has the added benefit of helping to control the dust produced by the process. A rotating power tool will spin water away from itself. Tools that oscillate rather than spinning can often be used for wet sanding, and they are less likely to bite into a print. You may also find it easier to avoid removing too much material if you use a bench-mounted power-sanding device and move the print into it, rather than using a handheld tool.

Depending on the shape of your print and how much sanding you intend to do, you will likely need to do some manual sanding. Powered sanding starting around 80 grit is useful to initially remove the layer lines, but this will leave a fairly rough surface. Multiple steps through progressively finer grits (higher grit numbers) are required to get very smooth surfaces, and grits above a few hundred are not likely to be available for these tools. The pieces in Figure 6-1 were sanded (in approximately 20 stages) down to a 1 micron-particle-size sandpaper, which is roughly equivalent to 16,000 grit. Creating surfaces that are not only smooth but also flat is best achieved by laying sandpaper down on a hard, smooth, flat surface like glass and rubbing the print against it. Sanding internal features is trickier, but can be made easier by using tools like needle files and sanding sticks that are designed to fit into small spaces.

It may not be necessary to take sanding this far, though. You may want to sand to initially remove layer lines, but once that is done, you might want to switch to one of the other techniques in this section to continue the smoothing process.

Sanding before vapor smoothing, for example, would allow you to smooth out the layer lines and get a glossy surface with less rounding of edges and loss of detail than trying to remove the lines with vapor smoothing alone. Also, as with glue, the roughened surface left by the initial passes with a course sandpaper will give paints and clear coats more to hold onto.

Some plastics, particularly ABS, tend to whiten a bit when sanded, particularly those that bruise when bent. Wet sanding and continuing to sand with progressively finer grits may reduce this effect. For plastics that can be vapor smoothed, this chemical smoothing may reverse the discoloration, so sanding can be used in conjunction with vapor smoothing to reduce layer lines while maintaining sharper features that would be rounded off using vapor smoothing alone to remove the layer lines (though see the "Caution" earlier in this chapter about acetone).

Note   Some resin prints will sand well. Many resins are brittle, though, so you need to be careful that you do not shatter the print in the process of trying to sand it. Use protective equipment any time you are raising lots of dust.

Painting and Clear Coats

You can paint ABS and PLA parts with acrylic paint, like that available in a typical hobby store. If you need a multicolor print and you have a one-extruder printer, painting the object after the fact is a good workaround to produce the colors you need.

Some clear coat products like XTC-3D are formulated to be thick and self-leveling. They can be an alternative to sanding, since they smooth a model by filling in the gaps between layer lines. You can think of this as additive smoothing, as opposed to the subtractive smoothing you would get from sanding.

Smoothing with more traditional fillers like Bondo, wood filler, and high-build primer may also work well for some print materials if you intend to paint afterward. When applied properly, high-gloss paints can do some self-leveling as well. This avoids extreme levels of sanding, and the paints may adhere better to a slightly coarser surface. Layer lines can also be hidden by using textured paints to cover up the print texture. Before attempting to use any of these products, be sure to carefully read the manufacturer's instructions and follow all recommended safety procedures.

Post-processing like this can lead to some spectacular results. *The Butterfrog* (Figure 6-7) by Vermont artist Rodney Batschelet was printed in four pieces. The wings were printed on their edges vertically and then glued to the body.

The frog is attached to the base using an old airbrush needle. Rodney tells us that the piece took about two hours of hands-on work: five minutes to coat all parts except the rock base with XTC-3D epoxy coating, an hour to prime all parts for final painting, thirty minutes to hand-paint basic colors with a brush, and about ten minutes to add shading and rock color to the base with an airbrush.

Figure 6-7. *Butterfrog by Rodney Batschelet (courtesy of the artist)*

The drying times during the process were also significant:

- *XTC-3D*: two hours

- *Primer*: thirty minutes

- *Hand-painted acrylic*: thirty minutes

- *Airbrush painting*: Dries immediately on contact

- *Goop glue*: About thirty minutes for each wing

Batschelet teaches at Benson Village School in Vermont and feels strongly that his students' 3D printed work needs to be finished (sanded, painted, and so on). He says that raw, unfinished prints look like toys, and he does not want his students to think of them that way in an art class.

Dyeing Nylon

Although 3D printed nylon may not look the same as it does in fabric form, it will take up dye in a similar way. Nylon filament typically is white, which makes it easy to dye. People have had good luck with household cloth dyes when dyeing a printed nylon object. Check the label on the dye package to be sure it works on nylon. The pieces in Figure 6-8 were printed in white nylon and then dyed. Uptake is better if hot water is used, but you will need to be careful not to have the dye so hot that the print warps.

Figure 6-8. *Nylon pieces, dyed (three to the left) and undyed (right)*

Summary and Questions for Review

In this chapter, we discussed ways to improve the surface quality of 3D prints. We covered mechanical means like sanding and various chemical ways to smooth prints. Painting is also an option to hide layer lines, if that is desired, and different materials can give various effects.

Answer the following to test your knowledge of the material in this chapter:

1. If you have printed something in standard PLA, what are some ways to smooth out the layer lines?

2. If you sand off out the layer lines in a print, what does that imply for any fine surface features or small protruding features?

3. If you wanted to change the color of a nylon print, how would you do it?

4. What are some things to consider if you are thinking about painting a print?

PART II

Designing for 3D Printing

3D printing requires a 3D model, which might come from a CAD model or might be a scan of an existing object. This section looks at various aspects of creating a 3D printable model that will fabricate well and do the desired job. Chapter 7 reviews common computer-aided design (CAD) software and their strengths and weaknesses. Chapter 8 gives you some design rules for creating a part. Finally, Chapter 9 describes part geometries that require special handling.

CHAPTER 7

3D Models

Your first step in using a 3D printer will be to create a 3D computer model. You do that by scanning an existing object, downloading a model from the web, or creating a model yourself. In each case, there are a lot of options to choose from. There is more to design than picking a software package, though, and there are design decisions you can make that can simplify the printing process.

This chapter first covers the basic file requirements for a 3D printer. Then it reviews options for scanning and downloading 3D models. Finally, the chapter looks at 3D computer-aided design (CAD) and CAD-related programs that you can use to make a 3D model. By the end of the chapter, you should have a computer model that is ready to go on to the next stage of processing. Models can be made from scratch using a 3D CAD program. Some 3D CAD programs are intended for simple beginner projects, but others are more capable (and complex).

Note If starting from zero seems daunting, you might consider downloading a preexisting model from a database. However, models from these databases often have problems or will not print at all. In Chapter 5, we give the workflow for creating a cube measuring 20 mm on a side. We recommend trying out something like that first before getting into a situation where you do not know if problems are being caused by the model, the slicing settings (Chapter 3), or the printer hardware.

© Joan Horvath, Rich Cameron 2020
J. Horvath and R. Cameron, *Mastering 3D Printing*,
https://doi.org/10.1007/978-1-4842-5842-2_7

3D Model File Formats

The term *3D computer model* is used in many different contexts, which can cause confusion when someone wants to print something using a 3D printer. In this book, *3D computer model* means a computer file that contains enough information about the surface of an object to allow the object to be printed. In the open source consumer 3D printer world, the most common file format is the STL file. This acronym is sometimes said to stand for *STereoLithography* and sometimes for *Standard Tessellation Language.*

STL is something of a lowest-common-denominator file format, consisting essentially of a long list of triangles that collectively cover the surface of the object. This is not a terribly efficient format (particularly in its ASCII version, which is a text file), but it has the virtue of being relatively simple to generate and deal with, and therefore has become a de facto standard. STL standards exist for both ASCII and binary file versions.

On some Windows computers, you may get an error when saving or moving around an STL file. On Windows, the STL filename extension is presumed to mean Certificate Trust List, and STL files will show up that way in directory listings. STL files will work with 3D printing programs on Windows machines, but sometimes opening the file or saving them will result in an error message complaining about Certificate Trust Lists.

There are newer formats like AMF (Additive Manufacturing Format) and 3MF (3D Manufacturing Format) designed specifically for 3D printing, but they are not as widely supported yet by CAD software as of this writing.

Tip   The open source program MeshLab (discussed under "Mesh Repair Programs" in Chapter 3) is able to translate many different types of files into STL. It can also fix the problems that sometimes occur during translation or as a result of printing incompatibilities in the original model itself.

Scanning

We introduced the issues with scanning a model in Chapter 3 and discussed scanners a little. In this section, we talk more about consumer, off-the-shelf scanners and stitching software you can buy and more or less use out of the box. We also introduce specialized medical scanning.

Off-the-Shelf Scanning

Like many things in 3D printing, the ability to get a good scan is dependent on your software. As of this writing, there are several different scanning technologies. The two most common can loosely be broken into two categories: structured light and stereophotogrammetry.

Structured light scanning uses a laser (typically projected through a lens to create a thin line, or sometimes several lines) or a sequence of patterns from a projector. These scanners calculate depth by measuring the distortions in the image of a projected pattern, which are caused by a known offset between the camera lens and the illumination source. This requires specialized hardware with matching software, though open source versions like the BQ Ciclop exist.

These scanners can create a depth map from a single view, but multiple overlapping scans from different angles need to be stitched together to recreate the entire surface of an object. Some scanners include a turntable to take multiple scans automatically, but additional angles may be required to reach inside concave spaces, or to capture features that are occluded from several angles. Hollow internal spaces are unlikely to be visible from any angle. Projector-based systems capture data more quickly than those using lasers, but work best in a darkened room, whereas laser light is more likely to be intense enough to achieve sufficient contrast in bright environments.

Stereophotogrammetry creates a digital 3D surface based on many ambient-light photographs. Software identifies features that appear in multiple photographs taken from different angles and, by analyzing the changes in the apparent distance between these points from one picture to the next, calculates their relative locations in 3D space. This software generally requires consistent lighting in all of the photographs, and that the optical qualities of the camera do not change. This means that you need to move the camera around the subject, rather than turning the subject to get different angles. It also means that collections of photos that were not taken with stereophotogrammetry in mind usually will not work, or will at least give inferior results. Some software can work with frames pulled from a video taken while walking around an object. Video resolution is typically much lower than still photographs, which gives the software less detail to work with.

Both of these technologies rely on using software to identify features in images from a camera. Transparent or reflective surfaces are a problem, because the light's behavior is harder to predict. Calculations are much simpler for matte, opaque surfaces, and this is what the software assumes. Surfaces like metal, glass, or even plastic with a polished finish may not be scannable without first applying powder or a coat of matte paint to make the light's interaction with the surface closer to what the software expects.

Some structured light scanners get around this limitation by using infrared light, since subjects are less likely to be reflective to those wavelengths. This technology can also be found in depth cameras like the Xbox Kinect and the face unlock sensors used by some smartphones. Some of these depth cameras can be used as 3D scanners by pairing them with special software, but they generally do not have enough resolution for a high-quality scan.

The key thing to consider is how much work it is to assemble a clean 3D scan with either a scanner plus software package or with freestanding photogrammetric software. Scanning software creates a point cloud (which is what it sounds like—a cloud of points) which then needs to be edited and cleaned up to get a 3D model. Loosely speaking, the more you pay for your system, the less manual work you will need to do. This area is changing fast, so read reviews carefully and try to see a system in action before you buy it if you can.

Caution   It is still very challenging to get a scan of an engineering part and to use that scan to print a duplicate. Scanning will introduce uncertainties and artifacts and is particularly questionable if you have something with a concave part that needs to fit precisely with a convex one. If you need precision, it is better to think of a scanned model as a reference and to rebuild at least the important parts of the model in CAD. Lots of people are working on this, and this may change over time, but do some diligence on how well a system addresses this before committing to one.

Dentists are becoming heavy users of 3D printing to create models of patient's teeth or appliances. Dental scanners correspondingly are becoming a big market. Some manufacturer sell tightly integrated systems of scanner, printer, and material to minimize the variables and improve reliability of the end-to-end process. But of course this comes at the cost of more-expensive devices.

CT Scans

We introduce the issues with scanning a model in Chapter 3 and discuss commercial scanners. Here we will add a bit to that for scientific users. A scientist may need detailed, high-resolution information about biological structures. Medical professionals and those with access to computerized tomography (CT) scanners have been using CT scans as a starting point for 3D printing. CT scans can capture internal and complex, concave structures. CT scanners are not consumer items, but if you are a scientist or researcher, you might see whether a local hospital or research center offers scans on a fee-for-service basis. Different CT scanners can handle different densities and sizes of objects.

There are also "micro-CT" scanners with smaller beam sizes. University imaging centers and labs buy these smaller scanners for research projects, but often they are not used full-time, and the facilities will do a scan as a fee-for-service arrangement. Facilities with micro-CT scanners are not cheap, and thus neither are these scans. But if you are solving a real problem, micro-CT scanning may be a powerful way to get the information you need to create 3D models of structures of interest.

CT scanners usually output a DICOM (Digital Imaging and Communications in Medicine) file. A web search will reveal various free and proprietary tools to convert DICOM files to STL files, depending on the specific application at hand. One readily available conversion package is InVesalius. Do a web search for their download page, because the software is available in various versions and you may want to hunt around for one that is right for you.

Downloading and Modifying Models

Sometimes a model of something that you would like to print already exists. In that case, you may be able to download it from one of a growing number of model databases. Some databases contain fun items and household objects. Some of the existing models in databases are of complex, specialized objects that might be very useful to you professionally.

Models of Everyday Things

Many databases of 3D printable objects are available online. The Thingiverse (www.thingiverse.com), YouMagine (www.youmagine.com), and Pinshape (www.pinshape.com) websites all feature a wide range of objects, from sci-fi figurines to parts for enhancing 3D printers. These models have been contributed by users and as such vary widely in the quality of their design both for printing and for their intended purposes. Yeggi.com provides a search engine for searching across these various 3D printing–specific databases. The Instructables (`www.instructables.com`) site is not, strictly speaking, a repository, but many of its projects also point to models.

Sometimes model creators will upload both the STL file for printing and the file in the original format of the software that created the model. That means if you happen to be conversant in the original program, you can start with an object and modify it. For example, in Thingiverse, when you click the Download This Thing! button, you get both a list of the available files and the type of license under which each is being made available. Sometimes the developer just wants you to credit them if you use it. Sometimes commercial use is not allowed. If you obtain something from one of these databases, be sure to look carefully at the requirements, particularly if you are going to modify the object or sell something based on it. See Chapter 3's notes on Creative Commons licenses.

Specialized Databases

Chemists and biologists visualize complex molecules and analyze how these molecules will interact. The Research Collaboratory for Structural Bioinformatics (RCSB) manages the Protein Data Bank (PDB) at `www.rcsb.org/pdb/`. Anyone can search this databank to find collections of published data about nearly 100,000 protein structures (as of early 2014). These structures are identified by a PDB ID, which is a four-character alphanumeric code. Once you find the PDB ID, you can use a program that can then take the ID and generate an STL file for printing. The following are two such programs:

- Chimera, from the University of California, San Francisco (`www.cgl.ucsf.edu/chimera/`)

- Visual Molecular Dynamics (VMD), from the University of Illinois at Urbana-Champaign (`www.ks.uiuc.edu/Research/vmd/`)

Both programs have extensive documentation. They are freely available, but have some restrictions on commercial use.

The National Institutes of Health (NIH) in the United States maintains a repository of medicine-related models (`https://3dprint.nih.gov`). The Smithsonian (`https://3d.si.edu`) and other institutions are increasingly putting together "greatest hits" downloadable sets from their collections. Often, though, these files are huge and may have other issues. You will probably want to repair and decimate them (make them have fewer triangles)—see the section "Mesh Repair Programs" in Chapter 3.

Tip   Do not assume that an STL file you download from a site is perfect or that it will work on your printer. It is usually wise to run files through MeshLab (see "Tip" earlier in this chapter) or a similar program to see if they are watertight and manifold (see Chapter 3). On download sites that allow comments or that have an "I made one!" contribution area, see whether anyone besides the author *has* made one. If not, that might be a bad sign.

Some repositories also offer G-code for download. This can be more convenient if you have the exact same printer and a similar enough material, especially if the print requires special settings, or if you suspect that you do not know how to use that machine as well as the designer does. On the other hand, there is some risk in trusting G-code provided by other users. G-code is a language of machine instructions, and malicious users can craft sequences of commands that would cause a printer to damage itself.

Creating a New Model

If you want to print out something that does not exist anywhere, you will need to use software yourself to develop a new model. Fortunately, many software packages are available that make developing particular types of models as simple as possible. This section helps you think about which CAD software package you may want to learn about, if you do not already use one. In Chapter 8, we will get into how to design a model to print well on different types of machines.

Using a CAD Program

Most CAD programs will either save a file as STL directly or offer an option to "export to" STL. Which CAD program is the right one for the job? This section describes commonly used programs ranging in price from open source and/or free to quite expensive. The programs also vary in the steepness of their learning curves. In general, the more powerful the program, the longer it takes to be reasonably proficient in its use. As a side note, some slicing software will also accept a .OBJ file, but often these files are created by programs that are not really designed for creating 3D printable models.

Some software packages are geared toward creating models meant to be viewed on a computer or theater screen (called *3D rendering*). A "3D" movie normally does not contain the parts of the model that are not on the screen at that moment. Various tricks exploit the way your eyes perceive 3D and fool you into thinking you are seeing a 3D image when really all you are seeing is two offset versions of a 2D image.

If you are at a 3D movie looking at a 3D stereo image of the north side of a tree, that side was generated in a computer. The south side of the tree, the underside of the trunk, and some of the top, east, and west sides are not needed for the movie viewer to see the tree in 3D. However, all of that *is* needed for printing an object. Be sure the software you are looking into can export an STL file or a format that can be converted into STL.

Some programs have the user write computer code–like instructions, whereas others require a lot of mouse use and more of an artistic bent. This is a quick overview of some of the available options; for the most part, the open source programs offer extensive documentation available for free download. The proprietary software programs typically offer training or have help available.

Options for Getting Started Quickly

If you want to go from "zero to plastic" as soon as possible, you might try Tinkercad (`www.tinkercad.com`) and OpenSCAD (`www.openscad.org`), both of which are free. Tinkercad requires registration; OpenSCAD is open source. Both have example files available that you can play with and use as guidelines for your own first project.

Tinkercad: Drag and Drop

If you want to use something simple that requires no programming knowledge at all, you will like Tinkercad. Tinkercad is a member of Autodesk's suite of 3D printing productivity tools. The program is free as of this writing, although it requires the user to register. Tinkercad is a purely drag-and-drop program that supplies a lot of simple shapes such as rectangular solids, spheres, cylinders, three-dimensional letters of the alphabet, numbers, and so on. Printable objects are created by assembling them out of these standard virtual pieces.

Tinkercad requires a good Internet connection because the program is entirely cloud based and frequently saves incrementally. If several people are using it on one Wi-Fi node, the result can be frozen screens and frustration. However, it is a great way to develop something quickly just to test the end-to-end process of creating a model, slicing it, and printing it. Figure 7-1 shows a simple "star and Saturn" pendant designed by Joan in Tinkercad.

Tinkercad has extensive tutorials that are arranged into bite-sized brief walkthroughs of the key features, and there are a lot of examples that others have designed and put out there for you to play with and build upon. The classic project to try first on a 3D printer is a small keychain fob decorated with 3D initials or a few hearts. Most people can do a project of that scale in an hour or so starting from zero with Tinkercad. In Chapter 5, we suggest just printing a cube from Tinkercad as an end-to-end plastic "hello world."

To get started in Tinkercad, follow the process at the Tinkercad home page, www.tinkercad.com. Autodesk also has special accounts for teachers to register their students; click the Learn tab for details. First, you will need to create an account (with Autodesk) to use the program. There are good tutorials on the site that appear by default when you go in for the first time.

When you feel comfortable, you can close the tutorial and click "Create new design" to open a new open build plate. You can drag the preexisting shapes onto the build plate, select two or more of them, and use the group icon to merge them into more complex building blocks. You can make any shape a hole (negative space) by selecting the shape you want to use as a hole and then clicking the "hole" graphic. By adding and subtracting shapes, you can build up fairly complex models.

Tinkercad also has features that are new as of this writing—scribble and a coding capability. We describe those in some detail in Chapter 13.

Figure 7-1. *Saturn and star pendant*

Save your model by clicking the Export button and selecting the option to download for 3D printing. Laser cutting is an option too, for models that can be made as a flat cutout.

You should now have an STL file in your downloads folder that you can import into your slicer of choice (see Chapter 3) and ultimately print. Tinkercad makes up weird, pseudo-Swedish names for models. You can make them something more memorable by clicking the name it made up and typing in what you would like to call it. Alternatively, you can take one of the public Tinkercad models and alter it a bit, if the model creator allows that, and then save it to STL. Remember to start small and simple—see the "3D Printing Design Rules" section at the end of this chapter about what makes a model "simple."

Tinkercad also has the ability to model basic circuits and create enclosures for some electronic components in your 3D print. See www.tinkercad.com/circuits for details.

Note   There are a variety of other low-cost, school-oriented CAD programs, and more pop up all the time. Morphi (www.morphiapp. com) has a small cost per seat, but does not require a live Wi-Fi connection (which Tinkercad does). People sometimes try to use Inkscape (https://inkscape.org) for 3D printing, but it is not designed for it, and you will need to export your drawing to another program to extrude it into the third dimension. The result after all that will be better suited for a laser cutter.

OpenSCAD: A CAD Programming Environment

OpenSCAD follows the opposite philosophy from Tinkercad in that it is not drag and drop at all, except for adjusting how you view the model you have developed. OpenSCAD uses a programming language very similar to C to define geometrical shapes, translations, rotations, and so on.

The program has built-in functions for most common shapes, although the names can be a little misleading. For example, all the rectangular solids are called "cubes." A simple bridge shape with three overlapping "cubes" is assembled by moving (*translating*) the horizontal top upward from the zero point, and one of two identical vertical side pieces horizontally to support the other end; the numbers given are *x*, *y*, and *z* coordinates. The following OpenSCAD model would create the print in Figure 7-2:

```
cube([10,10,30]);
translate([40,0,0]) cube([10,10,30]);
translate([0,0,20]) cube([50,10,10]);
```

Note that the cubes were designed to be slightly overlapping—because shapes with purely coincident faces may not have created a manifold STL.

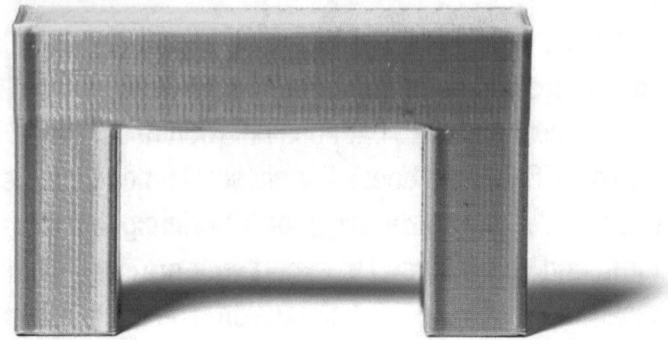

Figure 7-2. *OpenSCAD simple demonstration*

To try out a simple model in OpenSCAD, first either click File ➤ New to start a new model or pick an example from the Example submenu. You can also type in this little example; the three lines shown are all you need for the model shown. As with any program, saving frequently is a good idea, which you do from the File menu. This will save the program in OpenSCAD format, not STL.

If you want to see what your model will look like, select Design ➤ Preview. This creates a quick visualization of your model without taking the time to calculate all the geometry.

Click and drag with your mouse in the preview pane to roll your model around and see it from different angles. This is also useful to give you a better idea of what the shape actually looks like in 3D.

If you like the looks of what you see in the 3D preview, you will want to render the model and create an STL. Go back to Design ➤ Render. This may take longer than the preview step (especially if your model is very complex or uses certain computationally intensive elements), which is why the preview is available.

When rendering has finished, the preview pane will update. If you had used colors or certain other features, you may notice that they disappear, because they are not supported by STL and thus are only usable for previewing. Roll your model around in the 3D view again and make sure it still looks like you expect. If it does, go to File ➤ Export and then choose STL as the file format.

You can then take the STL file and run it through a slicing program (see Chapter 3), and you will be ready to print. OpenSCAD is particularly suited to modeling objects that can be built up out of geometric shapes. Complex objects are possible by starting with these basic shapes and rotating them. You can make impressive geometries with a little programming experience and the OpenSCAD manual.

We have two books of 3D printed science and math models, all of which were created in OpenSCAD (*3D Printed Science Models* (Apress, 2016) and *3D Printed Science Models Volume 2* (Apress, 2017)). Figure 7-3 shows a botanical model created in OpenSCAD from the "Plants and Their Ecosystems" chapter of the 2016 book.

Figure 7-3. *Botanical model (agave plant) from 3D Printed Science Models (Apress, 2016)*

Programs for Specific Applications

Tinkercad and OpenSCAD are great for beginners. If you are using your printer mostly as a hobbyist, in a classroom, or to make fun objects around the house, you can probably be happy for a long time with these programs. However, if you need to create professional-level sculptural models, or if you need dimensioned drawings, then these programs probably are not enough. Many, many design programs can either produce an STL file or a file that can be translated into STL. Most of these programs deserve (and in some cases have) their own book-length tutorials.

Generally speaking, you need to consider a few key attributes when selecting a design program. First, think about your own strengths: Are you good at programming, or are you better at drawing with a mouse? Do you have decent hand-eye coordination and drawing skills? How much time do you have to devote to becoming proficient, and how much design are you really going to do? A program with a short learning curve but limited capability may be okay if you are only going to make a few complicated objects, but learning a more-capable program may be worth it if those features will vastly enhance your productivity.

Some software only runs on either Mac or Windows, not both. If you only have access to one or the other operating system, that may force a choice.

Next, consider budget. Free and open source software varies in quality; documentation can be uneven or incomplete for open source software. However, it *is* free. For pricey software, research whether demonstration versions of the software are available, and if so, try before you buy. If you are a student, check with your school to see whether any discounts are available to you.

With all that said, programs to create models for 3D printing need to serve various constituencies. Engineers, architects, industrial designers, mathematicians, and similar professionals need drawings with each part's dimensions shown and great precision. Often, they will need to integrate 3D printed parts with traditionally manufactured ones and thus will need both the ability to create a file for printing and a traditionally dimensioned, human-readable drawing. Artists may want good drawing tools that allow them to sketch freely but not require as much precision. Different tools have evolved for these respective communities, as we will see next.

Engineering and Architecture Programs

Engineers, industrial designers, and architects use 3D modeling programs oriented toward applications that require precision. A relatively new arrival on the engineering CAD scene is Onshape (`www.onshape.com`). Onshape is cloud based and free for many educational uses. It has a growing suite of plug-ins for modeling and analysis. It runs in a browser, so it runs on Chromebooks, Macs, and Windows and Linux machines, and it also has apps for iOS and Android devices.

Fusion 360 (`www.autodesk.com/products/fusion-360`) is Autodesk's entry in this category. Autodesk used to have a line of CAD programs called "123D…". The simpler end of these applications has been rolled into Tinkercad and, the more sophisticated, into Fusion 360. Fusion 360 has some CAM (computer-aided manufacturing) capability included. It also has (confusingly) a "slicer" function, but it slices models into pieces suitable for laser cutting as interlocking pieces. As of this writing, its integrated CAM abilities were limited to CNC machines, and not 3D printers. The program is free for many educational and personal applications at the moment; see the website for terms and conditions, or to purchase it.

A common (but expensive) engineering tool is SolidWorks, from Dassault Systèmes (`www.solidworks.com`). SolidWorks is designed to create real engineering projects and, as such, is a good end-to-end program to go from concept to final dimensioned parts. It does take a while to become proficient in SolidWorks, though, and cost can be a barrier once one is beyond the reach of educational discounts. SolidWorks is only available for Windows (although there is a free viewer called eDrawings that works on Macs).

SketchUp (www.sketchup.com) is a program focused on making it easy to lay out an architectural project, including a large library of many common home fixtures from various manufacturers. SketchUp can be used more broadly, but it focuses mostly on assembling geometrical and precise models, and the resulting models may require format conversion and have problems with 3D printing.

Mathematica (www.wolfram.com/mathematica/) is a programming system that allows users to model complicated mathematical functions. Mathematica creates STL files based on user-generated mathematical models. That means it is possible to develop sophisticated mathematical models and then visualize them in physical form. This possibility has many implications, particularly for people who teach courses that use Mathematica. A natural spectrum of mathematics visualization options starts with OpenSCAD and moves up to Mathematica.

Visual-Effects and Sculptural Programs

Visual-effects developers, animators, and similar artists develop 3D models in computer programs that are good for complex, curved, organic objects such as characters in animated films. Most of these either can export an STL file directly or employ translation utilities and procedures to take their output and turn it into STL. The commercial program Rhino, for example, exports directly into STL.

ZBrush (www.zbrush.com) is another commercial program for artists. It is a complex but very capable program that allows the user to sculpt in virtual clay. Users often abandon the mouse and draw instead on a graphic tablet with a stylus to create very sophisticated, realistic designs of animated characters and the like.

Blender is an open source visual-effects development program, available from www.blender.org. It is extremely powerful—you can make an entire animated film with it—but has a correspondingly steep learning curve. If you are very fast with a mouse, this may be the program for you, but the program is notorious for "thinking" differently from all other programs. It is, however, free.

Tip   If you are interested in creating 3D models with Blender, you might try to locate a class or, even better, a local Blender community or Meetup group. LinkedIn Learning (formerly Lynda.com) has online Blender courses.

Maya (`www.autodesk.com/products/maya`), an animation program, exports OBJ files that some slicing programs, including Ultimaker Cura, can read. However, Maya is a mesh-based modeler. That means when you draw something, you are creating a "mesh" that defines surfaces rather than working with geometric solids and letting the software generate their surfaces.

For example, if you model a ball and cut it in half, you are creating a cup-shaped hemispherical surface, facing outward, but it does not have an inward-facing surface and does not enclose any volume. The software later in the 3D printing workflow will do unpredictable things with this. You need to use the solidify functions of the modeling software to give your mesh some thickness or add faces to the open sides to create a half sphere. Once you are sure your mesh has no holes connecting the inside to the outside, and that the surface does not intersect itself, you can safely export it as an OBJ file.

Because programs like Maya or Blender are intended only for creating models that will look right when rendered as 2D images, the user has to do some extra work to ensure that the models it produces will be manifold. You will have to make sure that your meshes are all closed and have no unnecessary internal geometry or self-intersections, or your slicing program and printer might both do unpredictable things.

If you want to turn a 2D surface into a printable mesh, you will need to *extrude* or "solidify" it so that it has a thickness of at least a millimeter or two. Be sure you are working in millimeters first or you might make inch- or centimeter-thick walls!

Tip   As of this writing, Maya comes with a plug-in that generates OBJ files, but the plug-in by default is not enabled. Use Maya's Plug-in Manager to enable the OBJexport plug-in so you can then export Maya's native format to OBJ files.

Creating Multiple-Extruder Files

A printer with dual extruders allows you to print in two colors or, in some cases, two materials. Exactly how this works depends a lot on the dual-extruder machine in question, but this general guide will give you some ideas on how to get started with your machine. You can use a dual-extruder machine in a couple of different ways. First, you can use a different color of the same material in each extruder. You can also load one extruder with a dissolvable support material so that you can just wash off support. You may also be able to combine different materials with different properties, or your printer may have the ability to use the second extruder in parallel to make two identical objects. There are now several different types of multi-extruder setups, each with its own capabilities and caveats.

Using One Extruder for Support Material

If you are printing something with significant amounts of support material, you may want to simplify the removal of that support. Dissolvable support is made for this purpose. In this case, no extra steps are necessary prior to sending an STL file to your slicing program (Chapter 3). You will need to tell the slicer which extruder is using the support material.

Water-soluble support filament is usually relatively expensive and may come in smaller quantities (both for cost reasons and because it can be ruined by leaving it out to absorb moisture from the air). For this reason, it can be advantageous to minimize how much of it you use. Most slicers now have the ability to configure the extruder used for the support interface separately from the rest of the support structures, which allows you to print the bulk of the supports with the cheaper print material and only use the soluble material for the interface between the supports and the part. Depending on the geometry and orientation of your part and of its support structures, this may allow the supports to just fall off, or some breaking of the supports might still be required to remove them, but it makes support removal easier and less likely to mar the surface of your part than using breakaway supports.

If your printer has multiple extruders that share a single nozzle, you may find there is no way to use them for materials with different properties, or if you can, that it requires significant purging of the extruder to switch back and forth. Using a support material that is formulated to have similar printing temperatures to your print material will help.

Two-Color or Two-Material Prints

As mentioned, dual-extruder printers allow you to print objects in two colors or materials. It is still a little complicated, though. First, you need to create the STL files for each of the extruders separately, so that you can assign each one to an extruder. In the example here, we will be printing a red heart pendant with a light blue star and exclamation point. This entire object was created in Tinkercad, with the exclamation point, star, and heart all in the same file.

To create a two-color object, we needed to create two separate STL files. To create the first one, we turned the heart/pendant hook into a "hole" in Tinkercad and subtracted it from the merged item to ensure that the two shapes would not overlap. We then saved that much into what we will call STL number 1.

Then, to make the second STL, we undid the merging, turned the heart/pendant back into a regular object, and deleted the star and exclamation point so that we could export just that part as STL number 2. Remember to undo the deletion (or better yet, work with a copy of your original file) so that you do not lose the ability to edit your file and try again.

These two STLs are shown in Ultimaker Cura (Figures 7-4 and 7-5) as they look when they are dragged in separately. Note that some of the model in Figure 7-4 is just hanging in air, because the models need to have the same coordinate system as each other to begin with.

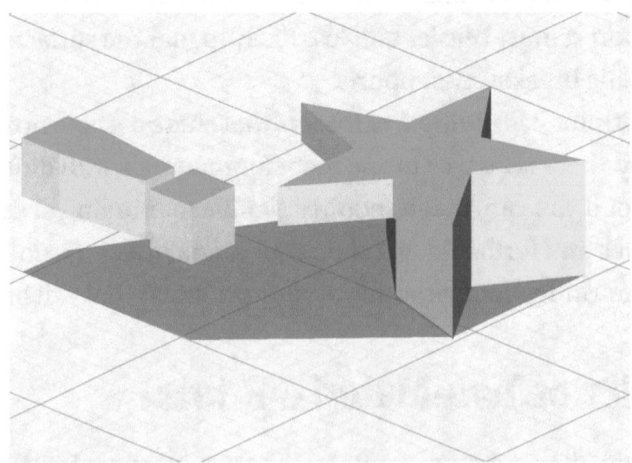

Figure 7-4. *The first of two models to be merged in a dual-extruder print*

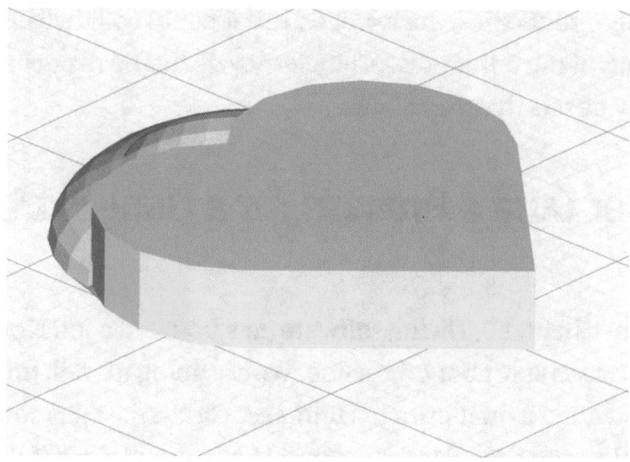

Figure 7-5. *The second model*

While making these two files, we were careful not to move anything around during this process so that the STL files would line up properly when we remerged them.

The following directions assume you have two STL files that were created with a process similar to what we just described for our heart pendant—that is, two STLs created in a way that maintains the same coordinate system across the two files and avoids overlaps. If your printer has multiple nozzles, check your documentation for determining the offset between them and making sure that they are at the correct relative heights. For some printers, you will need to enter the correct offset values in the slicer; others carry this information in the firmware, and should have values of zero set in the slicer. The offset is the distance between the two extruder heads in the x and y directions.

Your manufacturer should provide default values based on the printer's design, and possibly a test print for fine-tuning them to account for manufacturing tolerances. In a pinch, you could measure from the center of one nozzle to the center of the other nozzle, but this is difficult to do precisely. Unless your printer has some method of moving the inactive nozzle out of the way, height adjustments will need to be made mechanically—otherwise, the lower extruder could collide with the plastic that came out of the other nozzle. Single-nozzle dual-extruder systems do not have any offsets to worry about.

Ultimaker Cura's Process for a Dual-Extruder Print

As we note in Chapter 3, slicing software gets updated a lot. However, the general processes stay about the same. We are going to walk through the process of creating a dual print in Ultimaker Cura, since it is so tightly tied to the model generation. For the example here, we used a MAKEiT Pro 3D printer, which automatically handles the extruder offsets in firmware.

First, we brought both STLs into Cura and selected the MAKEiT Pro M, which has two extruders. We selected each STL in turn and chose an extruder for it (Figure 7-6). Then we right-clicked one of the models and selected Select All Models and then Merge Models. The result is Figure 7-7.

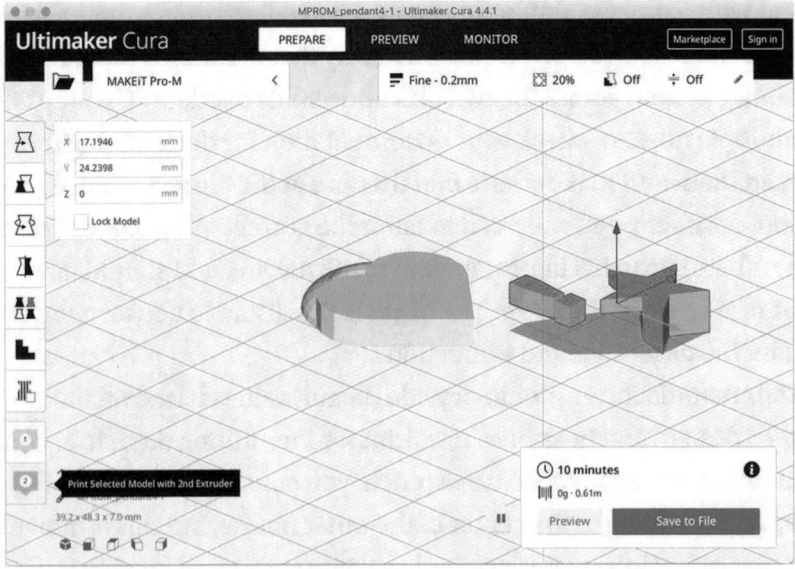

Figure 7-6. *Assigning an extruder to an STL in Ultimaker Cura*

Finally, under the Dual Extrusion settings (visible in Figures 7-7 and 7-8), we added a prime tower and an ooze shield. This figure highlights a single-layer simulation in Ultimaker Cura, with the tower and shield (you have to select "show helpers" to see these) and the travel among them shown in light purple.

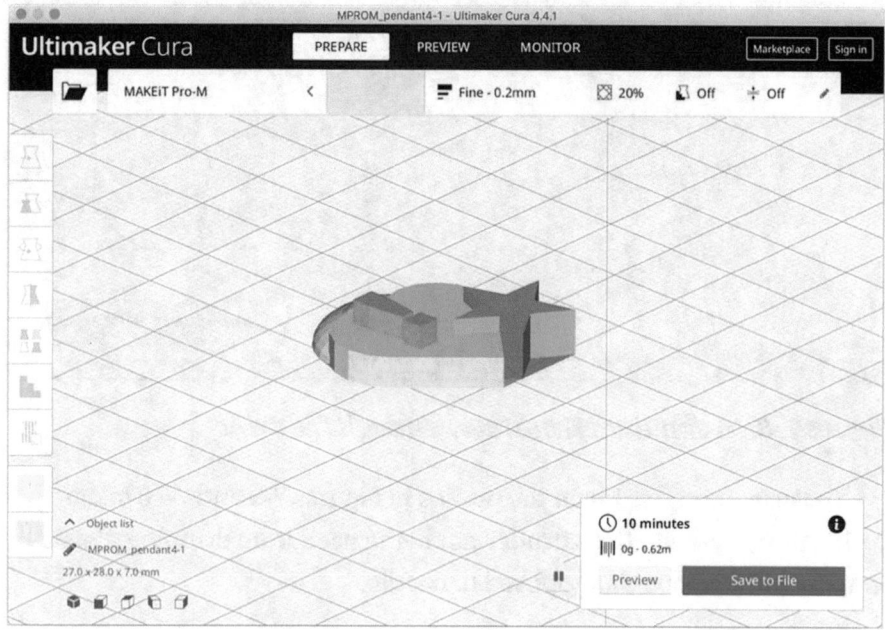

Figure 7-7. *The merged STLs*

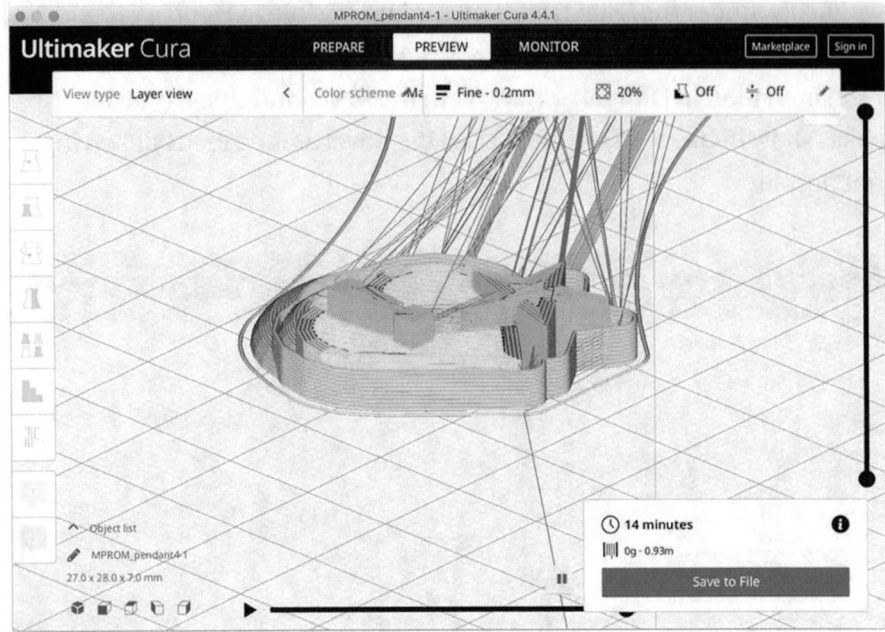

Figure 7-8. *A simulation partway through the print*

These features, visible in the photos in Figures 7-9 and 7-10 taken during printing, keep the extruder not being used from dripping plastic onto the print when it is supposed to be idle.

Figure 7-9. *The dual-extruder print in process*

The prime tower can get a little uneven and get knocked off near the end; if that happens near the end of a long print, you can let the print finish just drooling over where the prime tower was as long as the prime tower wound up somewhere out of the way. The geometry used for the prime tower changes from time to time with software updates, so yours may look different from the one here.

Note that the wipe shield curves around the print and does not go straight up. Figure 7-11 shows the print after it has been removed from the platform and separated from the wipe shield.

Figure 7-10. *The completed print on the printer*

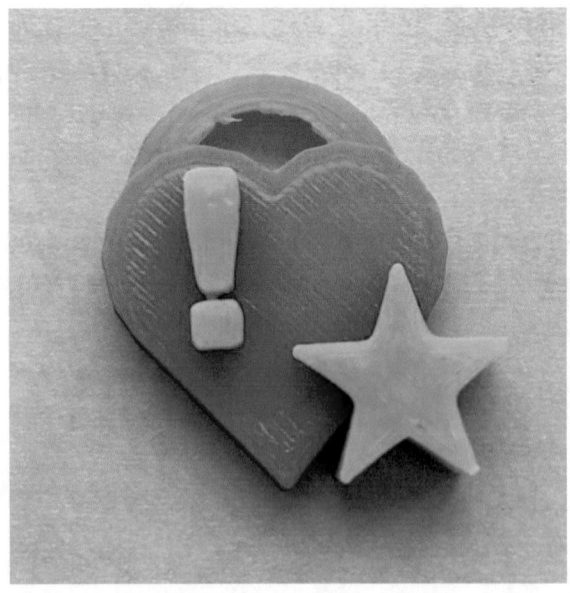

Figure 7-11. *The final print*

Caution   Most CAD programs and 3D printers use millimeters as a default. Be careful that you do not accidentally save a file in inches, since the printer software will interpret it as a very tiny print in millimeters instead.

Complexity Is Free: Hardware as a Service

One of the mantras of the 3D printer community is that *complexity is free*. Because 3D printed parts are built up one layer at a time, it really does not matter whether that layer is one unbroken sheet or an intricate design. There are models that would be essentially impossible to machine, but people who know what they are doing can print them on a low-cost consumer printer.

Consumer-level printers have one more strong advantage: the opportunity to iteratively design something, see how it came out, and then change the design if necessary. When that became possible in the 1980s for computing (vs. overnight batch jobs), there was a real change to the nature of creating software. We all hope the same thing is about to happen for making physical things!

This phenomenon is starting to be called *hardware as a service* (an analogy to *software as a service*), and the business models are still unclear. Resolution and materials are likely to continue improving, and all the pictures in this book will probably look primitive to anyone reading this a few years down the road. Chapter 14 speculates on how 3D printing businesses may evolve toward short-run manufacturing or mass customization.

Speed vs. Customization

Complexity is not entirely free because the amount of material used (and the time it takes to print) is more proportional to surface area than to volume of the part. Complexity may matter less in 3D printing than in conventional fabrication, but complex prints may take a long time. Consumer 3D printers take a while to print anything out—it is rare for a print of any size to take less than a few hours, and prints that take a day are routine. If you are making one of something or a prototype for a mold, such a length of time may be competitive. The other option is a machinist or other professional making a prototype in a way that involves a lot of labor. But if the part is simple or you want a lot of them, a 3D printed part is probably not the way to go. If you are happily creating injection-molded parts for something now, then 3D printing that part is *definitely* not the way to go.

To narrow it down a bit more, consumer 3D printers may not be the best fit for your project if everything you do will require a lot of hand finishing after the fact. You might consider using a service bureau to do one of the more industrial processes. To put it another way, only the right kind of complexity is free.

3D printing has a role for items that are by their nature one-of-a-kind (or a-few-of-a-kind) and that work well with the technology. Time will tell what the best applications are. Our sense is that one key role for 3D printing is that it makes the front of the product-development process faster. People who would have made a computer model and then created a foam-core physical mockup as two separate chores are obviously better off with a 3D printer.

Other promising markets exist in industries that make custom parts for one-of-a-kind applications (or, even better, industries that *should* operate that way but cannot do so economically at the moment). The biggest market now, though, is a somewhat intangible one: allowing people to make stuff again just because they want to and can.

Summary and Questions for Review

In this chapter, you learned about how to create a model to start the 3D printing process. The first step is creating or finding a 3D digital model of your object, which requires you to visit a website with objects available for download, 3D scan something that already exists, or learn one of the many available 3D modeling software packages. The chapter went over the various types of software packages available for the engineer vs. the artist to generate a standard (STL) 3D printing file and some rules of thumb about best design practices for 3D printing. Answer the following questions to test your understanding of the chapter:

1. If you are an absolute beginner and just want to make some simple test objects, what would be a good software package for you to start with?

2. What are some options if you wanted 3D modeling software to create complex parts for an engineering project?

3. How likely are you to get a perfect scan of a complex object with a lot of concave details?

4. What is the process for printing in two colors, for a printer that has two extruders?

CHAPTER 8

Design Rules for 3D Printing

Sometimes minor design changes can make a big difference in how well your print will come out. Chapter 7 discusses software options for creating a 3D printable model, and Chapter 3 discusses the software used to create commands for a printer given an STL model. This chapter offers considerations around the design of a part and how to orient it on a printer's platform for best results. Chapter 9 will discuss some geometries that require special treatment (like tall, thin prints) or have their own slicer software options (prints that are shaped like vases).

Note It is often said that "complexity is free" in 3D printing. That is true to a point, but some features can cause issues in some technologies or materials. It is true though that the time to create a 3D print is more or less proportional to how much material you are laying down, whether that is a fine latticework or a solid cube using the same amount of material. (Tall, delicate structures are an exception we talk about in Chapter 9.)

One complication is that printing with materials in filament, liquid resin, or powder form imposes somewhat different constraints, and materials play a role too. We will discuss filament-based printing first and then compare with liquid resin and powder.

© Joan Horvath, Rich Cameron 2020
J. Horvath and R. Cameron, *Mastering 3D Printing*,
https://doi.org/10.1007/978-1-4842-5842-2_8

Filament-Based Printing

When you are creating a print with a filament-based printer, the first thing you need to do is to be sure your print will be anchored solidly to the print bed. Typically, when you orient a print, you will be trading off having as big a platform contact area as possible while minimizing or eliminating support.

On the other hand, if you are creating a print with a material that sticks a little too well to your platform material (as is the case with some PEI platforms), you may want to avoid having too large a contact area with the bed, or you might want to print on support, at an angle with a raft, so that you can remove the print in one piece and then wrestle the support and raft off the bed separately.

Minimize support by reorienting your part while maximizing contact with the build platform. Overhangs of up to about 45 degrees can generally be handled without support. If you have a part that is very thin or delicate, you probably need to avoid support completely because the part will break when you want to break off the support. If you are willing to tolerate some drooping or other issues on the underside of the print, you might get away with more than 45 degrees. Active print cooling generally increases your ability to print overhangs, but can reduce layer adhesion with some materials. Different combinations of settings like layer height, extrusion width, printing speed, and temperature may interact with different materials in complicated ways that increase or decrease the angles of overhangs that can be printed without support. As something of a last resort, you can also break your part into pieces (in your CAD software or other software tools) and then glue the parts together after printing.

A 3D print can bridge over a gap (Figure 8-1). How long a gap and how good the bridge will look will depend on the material and on the printer's characteristics. An inch or two should work in any material on any printer; larger than that might require some experimentation.

When you design a part, know your printer's minimum feature size. For most printers, this will be around 1 mm, or twice the line width the printer is laying down. Anything smaller will be marginal to print, particularly in the plane of the platform. If you have really fine detail, you will want to print it on a flat vertical surface if possible. Figures 8-2 and 8-3 show a comparison of printing Braille dots and raised and engraved details on a top surface or on the side of a print. In Figure 8-2, the prints in the top row were printed flat on the platform, and the prints on the bottom row were printed vertically. You can also see the difference between the raised and engraved (negative space) details.

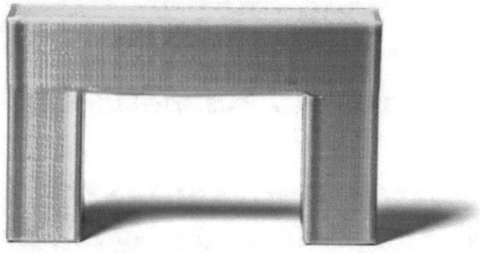

Figure 8-1. *Bridging over a gap*

Printing fine details on the side of a print can give better detail than printing on top of a print since detail on the side can be created without retraction as the nozzle goes around one layer's worth of the detail. Details on top might require a lot of retraction, which can lead to stringing and features that are not as smooth as they could be on a vertical surface. Features with very thin lines like letters also work better if they are inset into the surface rather than a raised, for similar reasons. Figure 8-2 shows a comparison of raised vs. inset letters with a variety of typefaces when printing in two different orientations.

Figure 8-2. *Details printed in various orientations*

Figure 8-3. *Prints in Figure 8-2 on the printer*

Part tolerance is an issue, too. A hole 10 mm in diameter is too small for a 10 mm part to fit inside. Leave at least 0.1 mm tolerance as a general rule. You may need more or less depending on your printer, the layer height you are using, the facet size of your model, and how much resistance you want between the two parts, to name a few factors.

You do not need to add draft to a 3D print or explicitly chamfer corners, but you should be aware that external corners might not be perfectly crisp because of the width of each extruded layer, which is after all a rounded bead. While internal corners can, in principle, be very sharp, the behavior of the molten plastic often results in some rounding of those corners as well. In general, if you design with slightly rounded corners, you are more likely to get a print that is faithful to your CAD. If you are planning on using your print as a mold, however, as we will discuss more in Chapter 10, then you will need to take the ability to release the product from its printed mold (or a mold made from your print) in your design process.

Prints can be hollow (as long as the internal overhangs can be bridged), or they can have any infill percentage up to and including solid (100%). To make a print sturdier, first up the number of perimeters before increasing the percentage infill.

If the print is functional and will be stressed, orient it so that loads are in the plane of the platform, not stressing the layer-to-layer bond. We will talk more about functional parts and orienting them for strength in Chapter 10.

If you are going to be sanding or otherwise finishing a print in a way that will remove material, or if you will be adding a filler to the surface to smooth it out, allow for that in the print.

Bear in mind the heat, UV light, and chemical sensitivity of your print if it will be used in environments where those things matter. PLA will warp in a hot window in summer, and will deform over time even at room temperature if there is a constant load on it.

Print tall, skinny parts with a cooling tower (Chapter 9) so that you do not get a blobby semblance of your print. You can either print a cylinder a little taller than the highest part of your print, or sometimes it just makes sense to print two or more copies of a tall skinny print at once, which acts as the cooling tower.

If a model has a thin part (such as a fin), try to add perimeters until the thin part is solid and work out the thickness so that an even number of perimeters fits, if you have flexibility on sizes. Otherwise infill might be spotty and uneven and distort the surface. Figure 8-4 shows an Ultimaker Cura simulation of how *not* to do this. A fin that is just a little thicker than its bounding perimeters will have a sputter of infill that might show through or cause surface irregularities. Figure 8-5, on the other hand, shows a print that was designed to have exactly the same dimension as two perimeters so that this fine feature is solid throughout.

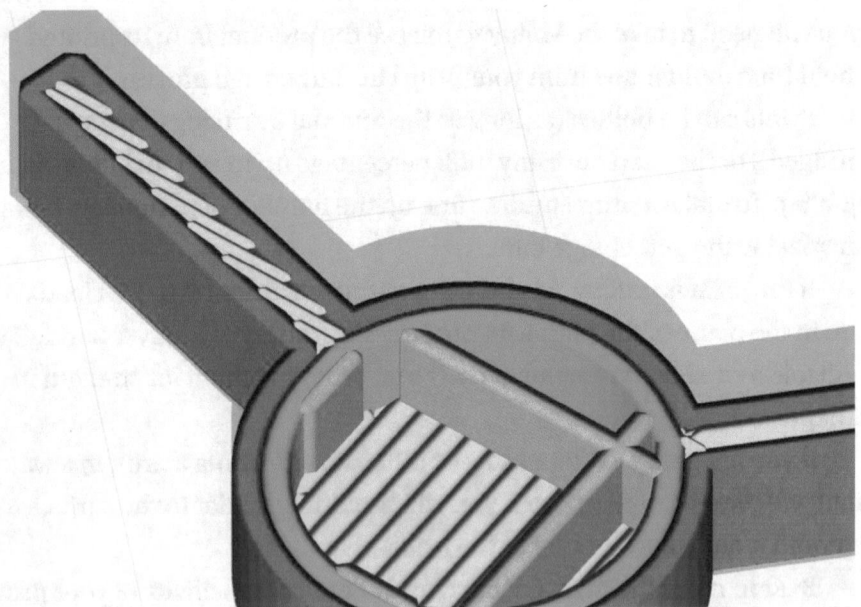

Figure 8-4. *Ultimaker Cura visualization of "wrong way"*

Figure 8-5. *Ultimaker Cura visualization of "right way"*

Caution   Designing models for printing with high-metal-content filament and subsequent debinding and sintering introduces a new set of design issues. Those are discussed in Chapter 11.

Resin Prints

Printing with liquid resin has some similarities with printing with filament, but not as much as you might think. For one thing, typically resin prints are created upside-down, and peel forces (Chapter 2) also will pull down or sideways on the print. Thus support is important for resin prints too. Typically, it is best to print a base (sort of a specialized raft) for a resin print and then print your object at an angle on top of support. A good base will help the print hang on, but have a good clean edge that you can get a removal tool underneath to get the print off at the end of the print.

Design and orient your model so that the contact area with the platform is minimal, because those layers may be compressed or distorted. To minimize support scarring and peel force, it is often best to print a flat object at 45 degrees in resin. Typically, support is thin and spindly and snipped off with a tool after the printing process is complete, so it is usually not as destructive to remove support from a resin print as it is from a filament one. You can see a typical print orientation back in Figure 3-10.

The primary purpose of infill for filament prints is to act as support for the internal overhangs of the top surfaces, but resin prints need support for different reasons. There also would not be a good way for resin to drain the uncured out of an infill pattern inside a resin print. For these reasons, resin printing software generally does not offer an infill option, and models are printed solid as they are designed. Printing a model hollow in resin requires modeling the interior hollow space, and your resin printing software may or may not have tools to help with this.

Resin prints should not have completely enclosed hollow spaces or bowl-shaped areas that could trap resin or air during the print. If they do, the geometry has to have a hole to allow the resin to flow out or air to escape. Software may refer to these areas that capture resin as "cups" and warn you about them. Reorienting might work, or you might need to go back to your design software and either add a drainage hole or rethink the print. Needless to say, solid prints use up a lot of (expensive!) resin, so you should consider whether your print geometry and intended use allows you to print hollow instead.

Because the prints are more isotropic and can handle smaller features, resolution and strength issues are less of a driver for most resin prints. Tall slender prints can break, and might be challenging to get off the support when they are printed at an angle.

Different thermal, chemical, and UV exposure issues affect resins. Because there are now many types of resin, you will need to understand the environmental requirements of your particular resin.

Powder Prints

Printing with powder is a more complex endeavor and often requires significant facilities preparation, as we have discussed earlier in the book. The big plus of powder printing with gypsum or plastics is that you can print without support. The powder in the bed will hold up the print so you will not need to use support at all. The forces on the print are relatively low, so it will not tend to pull off the bed the way that filament and resin prints will.

Powder prints also have far smaller minimum feature size than filament prints can, driven mostly by what will survive the subsequent handling of the print. (Resin can typically outperform powder in this regard, though.) Powder prints are at their best for very finely detailed latticework prints, or very elaborate, organic structures with gradual curves, like sculptures.

The prints are of necessity solid since there is no way to remove the powder inside a closed shell or a hollow print. They can be very fragile; often the plastic or powder-binder prints need to be infused with glue after the fact to make them stronger.

Since the entire print volume has to be filled with powder up to the print's maximum height each time a print is created, it is inefficient to create a print that is a tiny fraction of the print bed. Even though most of the powder can be recovered and reused from run to run, powder printing may make the most sense for applications where a larger number of prints can all be created at once. It is common for powder prints to include many objects, stacked on top of one another and carefully nested to leave as little unfused powder as possible.

Powdered materials are even more expensive than resins, and given that the prints have to be solid, prototyping this way can get expensive in a hurry.

Caution   Powder printing with metals has different requirements than printing with gypsum and a binder or sintering plastics. When metal prints are sintered layer by layer (DMLS), rapid heating and cooling introduce stresses that can make the print warp. To counteract these warping forces, powder metal methods require support that must be removed from the print and the platform with metal-cutting tools. For powder-binder methods, support is needed to survive the debinding and sintering stages, and other constraints are introduced as well. See Chapter 11 for more.

Summary and Questions for Review

In this chapter, we have looked at the design constraints on the geometry of a 3D printed part. We looked at the different issues that arise when printing with filament, liquid resin, or powder, like minimum feature size, the need for support, and keeping the print in place during the printing process. In later chapters, we will look at special cases (Chapter 9) and the functional design issues that arise for prints that need to withstand some force (Chapter 10).

Answer the following questions based on your understanding of the chapter:

1. If you wanted to create a very detailed model of a baroque building, what printing technology would likely give you the best replica of the building? What might be the most cost-effective way to get a reasonable replica?

2. What are reasonable infill percentages for resin and powder prints? Why are these infill percentages appropriate?

3. If you wanted to make a variety of different boxy, low-detail prints, what might be your best choice? (Define your criteria for "best.")

4. How do you think about support differently for a filament or resin 3D print?

CHAPTER 9

Special Geometries

Not every print is equally hard to create. There are a few special cases that require particular setups. These prints involve extremes in one physical property or another—hollow, or completely solid, or thin, or otherwise a shape that pushes the envelope of filament printing. On the other hand, sometimes a print that has an "obvious" straightforward way to print it can benefit from one of the processes in this chapter.

Vase Prints

3D prints take a long time to complete. One way to speed things up is to *vase print* it, if the geometry and application allow it. As the name implies, vase prints are shaped like a vase, with solid layers on the bottom, hollow inside, and no top layers. Typically, they are just one or two shells thick, and so they can both print fast and use minimal filament.

First, we will just make a cube into a vase. Slicing programs allow us to specify how many solid layers are on the top or bottom of a print, as opposed to the interior of the print that is partially filled with an infill pattern (Chapter 3). To make it simpler, most slicing programs have a "spiral vase mode" that prints a specified number of bottom layers and then spirals up an outer contour that is just one perimeter thick. In Ultimaker Cura this is a check box: Special Modes ➤ Spiralize Outer Contour. Figure 9-1 shows what a simple cube printed with this parameter checked would look like. The vases in Figure 9-2 were created this way, too.

© Joan Horvath, Rich Cameron 2020
J. Horvath and R. Cameron, *Mastering 3D Printing*,
https://doi.org/10.1007/978-1-4842-5842-2_9

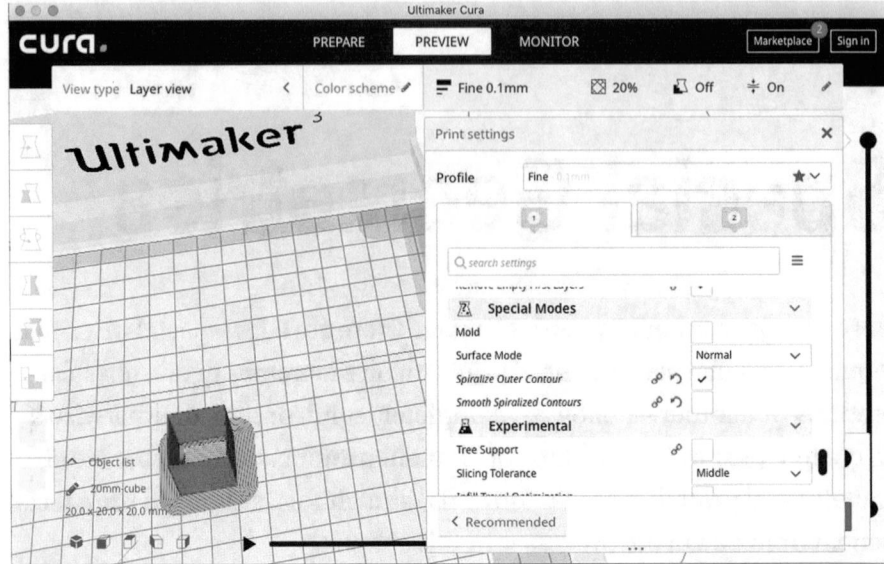

Figure 9-1. *Screenshot from Ultimaker Cura, Setting "Spiralize Outer Contour"*

Figure 9-2. *Two spiralized vases, the one on the right with "fuzzy skin"*

There is also a fun option to make a vase have an interesting surface in Ultimaker Cura: also select Special Modes ➤ Fuzzy Skin. The right-hand vase in Figure 9-2 used the two options together to produce a textured vase. However, this vase looks interesting but has many small holes where the fuzzy skin leaves gaps, so it can only be used for flowers that do not need water!

Vases have a seam. You can try to make it less noticeable by selecting the Special Modes ➤ Smooth Spiralized Contour setting (only visible when you have already selected Spiralize Outer Contour).

You can also create vases without this special mode, by explicitly specifying zero infill and no top layers, which is how vases were printed before slicers had special modes for that purpose. This is sometimes referred to as "old-school vase mode." The difference is that in old-school vase mode, you do not have the continuous spiral that theoretically removes all seams (though in some cases, spiral mode actually makes the seams more visible).

The old-school version also allows you to have layers with multiple islands (for example, more than one distinct part) or with holes. Either of those cases in spiral mode would result in unpredictable behavior or throw an error. You can also use multiple perimeters to create a thicker-walled vase, which also makes it easier to make it watertight. Working this way also allows you to use other features that might be overridden by the spiral vase option.

Other Uses of Vase Mode

Vase mode can come in handy if you are printing something very thin with surface detail on both sides. If you print such a thing vertically, you might find yourself with gaps and other issues. For example, the gravitational wave print from our book *3D Printed Science Projects Volume 2* (Apress, 2017) had areas where it was not quite the right thickness for either never or always having some infill, and some gaps resulted. We tried printing it with the spiralize outer contour feature and in essence created a "vase" with a 1 mm-wide opening at the top. Figure 9-3 shows this print, in silver silk PLA. As you can see, it is a very effective way of printing an object with very fine detail on two sides. We added a brim for stability during printing; you might want to use a raft.

Figure 9-3. *Gravitational wave, printed as a vase*

Printing Hollow

It is a short step from printing a vase to considering printing something hollow. Normally you would not want to do that, but if for some reason you do, just set infill to 0%. You may want to increase the number of perimeters for stability of the model. Figure 9-4 shows a hollow model with modest enough overhangs that it could be printed just as a shell.

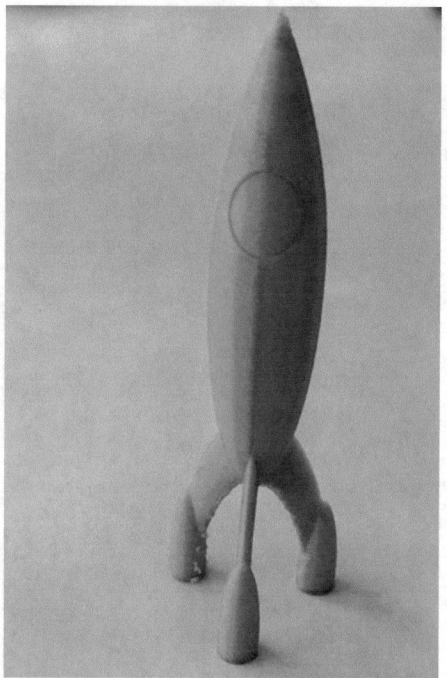

Figure 9-4. *A hollow print*

Printing Transparent (Solid) Pieces

There are now some filaments available that offer high degrees of transparency, but a typical print has too many air bubbles for you to see through it. If you print on a smooth surface, you may be able to see into the bottom of the print very clearly, but the top surface, where the print had to bridge over the infill, will be irregular enough that it will not be very clear. If you try to look through the side of the print, you will be able to see where the infill lines meet the wall, but the rounded edges of the layers will distort your view.

Even if you sand the sides smooth or use special transparent coatings to fill in the gaps and smooth the surface, the layer lines on the interior will still create this distortion. Only a print created completely solid can be as transparent as the ones shown in Figure 9-5.

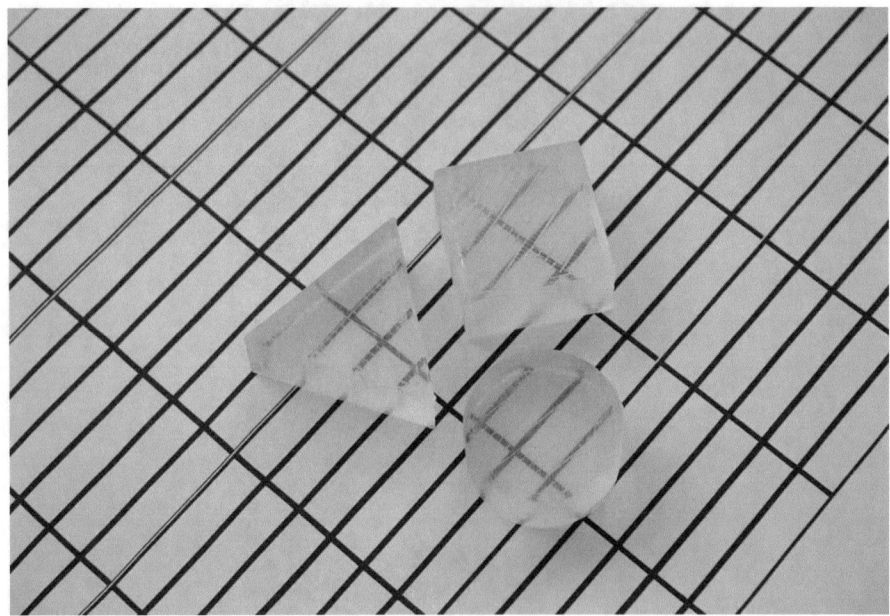

Figure 9-5.   *Transparent prints*

Therefore, the only way to print transparent objects is usually to print them solid. A 3D print generally consists of solid surfaces that are around 1 mm thick, with the interior filled with sparser infill structures. Your slicing software probably has a setting for how many solid top and bottom layers you want. To make a print solid, just increase this number until all layers are solid layers.

Printing solid can be finicky, though, because it makes the printer much more sensitive to small errors in the amount of plastic being extruded. If you are extruding slightly too much, melted plastic can build up around the nozzle. In a regular print, this buildup would even out once you got to the sparse infill, but that does not happen when you are printing solid.

It is also challenging to print a clear piece on blue tape or other textured surfaces, because the pattern from the surface will keep the print from being smooth. For best results, you may need a printer that has a heated platform and a surface that is not noticeably rough.

Printing solid is tricky. The relatively thin walls of a typical print give excess plastic somewhere to go, but just a little too much plastic in a solid print can create an error in the print that it will never recover from. You can lower the fudge factor called the *extrusion multiplier* in some slicers (it is called Material ➤ Flow in Ultimaker Cura) to a slightly lower number, like 95 to 98% from its default of 100%.

On the other hand, if your extrusion multiplier is a bit too low, you will end up with a print that has most of the strength of a solid print, but is full of tiny bubbles and air channels where there was not quite enough plastic to fill the space, and these will prevent the print from being transparent. Solid printing for transparency often requires a (carefully calibrated) flow multiplier 10–15% higher than what you use for most printing. It is also important to print slowly, to allow all the air to escape. If you want to do a lot of transparent prints, you may be better off using a resin printer with transparent resin.

Tall Pointy Prints

Prints that come to a narrow point (like the rocket in Figure 9-4) can be difficult to print because there is so little plastic being laid down that one layer does not cool before the next one starts. The Ultimaker Cura parameter Cooling ➤ Minimum Layer Time can help with this (make it a bigger number) but only so much, because the plastic will not cool very quickly when it is constantly in contact with the hot nozzle.

A way to solve this problem is to also print a disposable object called a *cooling tower* to slow down the process. This gives the printer something to do while your plastic is cooling, rather than either simply slowing down but continuing to conduct heat from the hot nozzle or moving the nozzle into open air and letting it ooze. Figure 9-6 shows a print that comes to a point along with a cooling tower. Another option is to print more than one of an object at a time to give the nozzle more to do per layer. This print is the orbit of Halley's Comet, from our *3D Printed Science Projects* book (Apress, 2016).

Figure 9-6. *A print with a cooling tower*

Printing on Fabric

It is possible to print on fabric to get some interesting effects. David Shorey has been experimenting with printing a few layers on a platform, laying fabric over the partial print, then continuing the print, fusing the layer of fabric in place. He has been getting progressively more elaborate in his designs. A set of his cosplay dragon scales is in Figure 9-7, and you can see more of his work at `www.shoreydesigns.com`. Some printers may be challenging to use this way, because you need to be able to pause the print at a specified height, and also clip down the fabric to the print bed in a way that does not interfere with the print.

Figure 9-7. *Cosplay dragon scales on fabric (courtesy of David Shorey/Shorey Designs)*

Printing Interlocking Pieces

One of the things that a 3D printer can do that is very challenging with subtractive technology is to create interlocking parts. For example, there are a lot of different chainmail designs out there on the various download sites if you want to experiment. Figure 9-8 shows an example designed by Rich in OpenSCAD. With care, these can be printed on a filament printer; fine-linked materials will need to be printed on a resin or powder (SLS) printer. There are service bureaus, like Shapeways, that will powder-print for you, but it is pricey.

If you create a design like this yourself on a filament printer, pay careful attention to maintaining clearances between pieces and avoid having features that fall below 1 mm or so, because they may not survive the printing process.

Figure 9-8. "Chainmail" printed in PETG

Note   Our book with Lyn Hoge, *Practical Fashion Tech* (Apress, 2016), discusses a variety of other techniques to create technical costumes that go beyond the 3D printing–centric suggestions here.

Mechanical devices that are printed all at once with interlocking parts intended to move freely after printing are called "print-in-place" mechanisms. Rich developed the 9-piece Arc Gimbal in Figure 9-9; each part of it can pivot freely. It is printed all in one piece, as shown in Figure 9-10. If you want to try it yourself, you can find it at www.youmagine.com/designs/arc-gimbal in .stl format.

Figure 9-9. *The 9-segment Arc Gimbal*

Figure 9-10. *The Arc Gimbal as printed*

Looking at the simulation of the print in Ultimaker Cura (Figure 9-11) makes it a little clearer what is going on. This cross section is about halfway up the print. Pointy cone-shaped pivots poke into depressions that are just a little bigger than they are, and the smaller arcs can turn freely inside the larger ones.

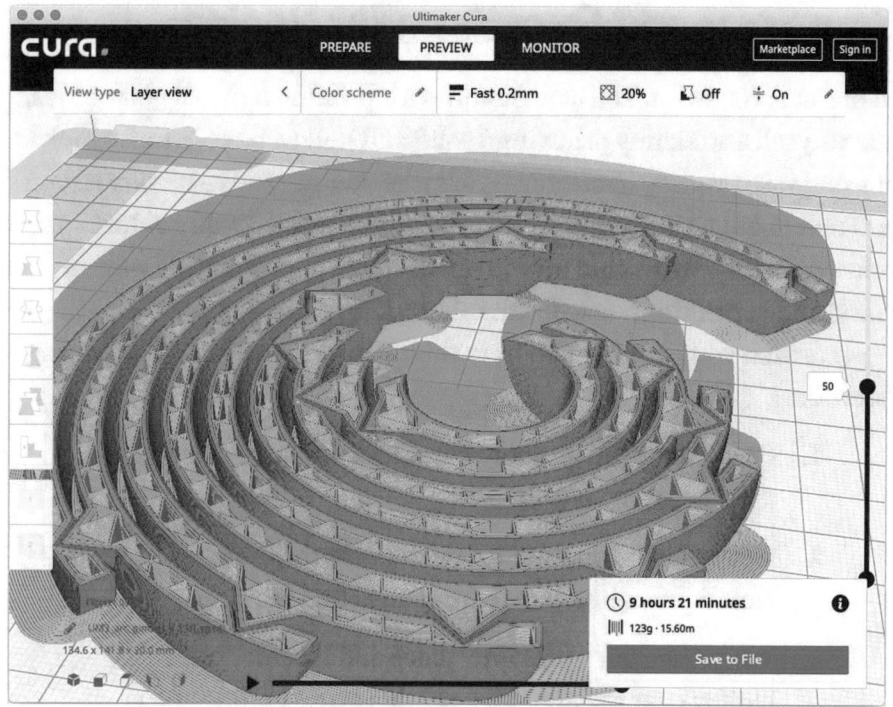

Figure 9-11. *The Arc Gimbal being sliced in Ultimaker Cura*

The clearances between layers should be so big enough that the parts turn freely, but do not just fall apart. In this case, the parts are held together by the springiness of the overall part and the symmetrical pivots. Too small a clearance and either stringing or inaccuracies might make your mechanism bind. Too big a clearance might result in the piece just falling apart. A bit of trial and error will be required. Be careful about scaling a print-in-place item, particularly scaling it smaller, since clearances might go out of the optimal range if you do.

Summary and Questions for Review

In this chapter, we looked at techniques for printing unusual geometries, like very tall and skinny prints, and solid and hollow ones. We also looked at using vase printing to create models that do not need to be very strong and that might be adequate for a purpose with just their outer shell printed. Finally, we wound up with an example of printing directly on fabric and of printing a piece with interlocking parts.

Use what you have learned from this chapter to answer the following questions:

1. How would you go about creating a print to make it as transparent as possible?

2. When might you want to use the vase-printing technique, other than to print an actual vase?

3. You print a tall and skinny piece and it comes out blobby near the top. What would you do to fix that the next time you tried?

PART III

Applications

This final section of the book looks at how to use 3D printing for practical applications. There are considerations for manufacturing plastic parts (Chapter 10) and a lot to think about with the many emerging options for printing in metal (Chapter 11). A traditional application, with some new twists available, is the use of 3D printing for visualization and prototyping (Chapter 12). Finally, we wind up with a discussion of 3D printing in the classroom (Chapter 13) and a survey of applications in their early stages now (Chapter 14) like specialty food printing and bioprinting.

CHAPTER 10

Manufacturing Plastic Parts

As 3D printers have become more ubiquitous and the lower-cost devices have become more reliable and capable, it has become more feasible to use these printers in a manufacturing environment. Here typically a *functional part* is required—that is, a part that is not just a decorative piece but one that is part of a bigger project or that is doing something that requires at least some mechanical strength. We address issues with metal 3D printed functional parts in the next chapter. In this chapter, we will talk about cases where plastic (perhaps with fiber enhancement) is enough for the job.

Sometimes a plastic part is not suitable for a workshop or factory use, and 3D prints can be used as molds or even as forms for fiberglass or other production molds. We will cover some common workflows in this chapter, ending with two case studies.

Functional Plastic Parts

One challenge with 3D printing functional parts is predicting how strong the part will be. Modern finite element analysis (FEA) programs that can assess stresses in a part are an engineering mainstay, and it is easy to rely on these programs and believe that if they say a part is strong enough, it is.

© Joan Horvath, Rich Cameron 2020
J. Horvath and R. Cameron, *Mastering 3D Printing*,
https://doi.org/10.1007/978-1-4842-5842-2_10

However, for 3D printing, that can be tricky. For printing with filament, the strength of parts varies a lot based on the manufacturer and variability in the qualities of the filament itself. Some manufacturers now quote strength parameters, but this tends to be based on expensive, specialty filament, typically tested after a tightly controlled printing process of a standard simple part. Chapter 2 has more discussion of material properties to help you think about a good choice given your printer's capabilities.

People are beginning to attempt to define standards, and there are papers being written on the strength of 3D prints. Appropedia and open access journal articles it references are a good free source of information to get started, at `www.appropedia.org/Tensile_Strength_of_Commercial_Polymer_Materials_for_Fused_Filament_Fabrication_3-D_Printing`.

But even if you do have nominal numbers for the strength of a filament and data from other people's tests, the temperatures used for printing, specifics of the printer, the settings you are using, and the geometry and orientation of the print itself all matter too. Even a printer putting out slightly more or less plastic than it thinks it is can have a huge effect on strength. As we saw in the "Shells" section of Chapter 3, your slicer will allow you to specify the thickness of the horizontal shell, either as a number of perimeters or in millimeters (which will be rounded to a multiple of your perimeter extrusion width). Two is typically a good number.

The width (in the *x-y* plane) of this perimeter is the extrusion width, which must be no smaller than your nozzle diameter, and might be larger. For a given extrusion width, if you are using thick layers, the interlayer adhesion might not be as good as it would be if you used thin layers, which will be more compressed and have more contact area. If the nozzle temperature is too low, that can lead to worse interlayer adhesion.

The bottom line is that filament prints will be stronger *within* a layer than *across* layers, in a way that is not entirely predictable. This is called *anisotropy*, meaning that the material has different properties in different directions. You can think of it as the grain in wood, which makes it break more easily in some directions than others.

A specific example may help show why this is true. Figure 10-1 shows a motor mount printed in three orientations. It would be used to hold a motor in the round hole with four screws, and then attach the motor to a wall or other surface with the part at right angles that has two holes in it. In what follows, we call the part with the two holes the "base."

Look carefully at Figure 10-1. Which one of these three parts would you expect to be the strongest and least likely to fail during its intended use? Where are the interlayer lines?

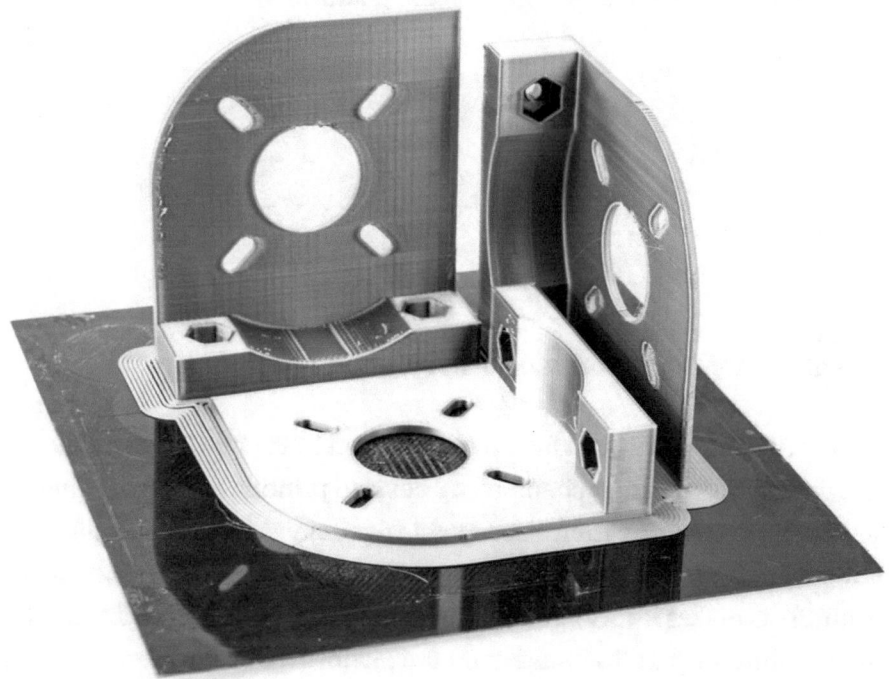

Figure 10-1. *Motor mount printed in three orientations*

Note   This part has been created to be too flimsy for its intended purpose so that we could make a point. It was printed in PLA, with the temperature deliberately a little too low to make this a more spectacular demo.

First consider the part on the upper left in Figure 10-1, printed upright with the base down. We might be concerned that this print might snap along the line between the base and the rest of the mount, since a layer line runs along the top of the base. It also has some unsupported overhangs, although all of them are small or climb at less than 45 degrees, so do not need support. When the print is flexed to destruction (by holding it in two hands and flexing it), it snaps easily at that point, as shown in Figure 10-2. Indeed, when we create a set of these for demonstrations, we have to be careful not to break it just getting it off the platform.

Figure 10-2. *Motor mount printed vertically, base down*

Next, consider the print flat on the platform in Figure 10-1, with the base poking up. In earlier chapters, we advised printing exactly like that—a nice, big base area, and minor acceptable overhangs. But Figure 10-3 shows that this, too, had one layer line between the base and the rest of the mount. This makes it very vulnerable to a critical failure, even if it is pretty strong within the part that was flat on the platform (which took much more force to break).

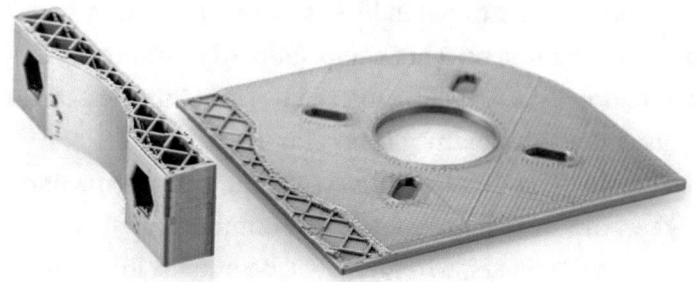

Figure 10-3. *Motor mount printed flat on the platform, base sticking up*

Finally, consider the print on the upper right of Figure 10-1, which was printed vertically with an L-shaped layer all the way up. This one is very strong—sometimes it is almost impossible to break it. It tends to also break in a way that might allow it to function for a while even after it broke (Figure 10-4).

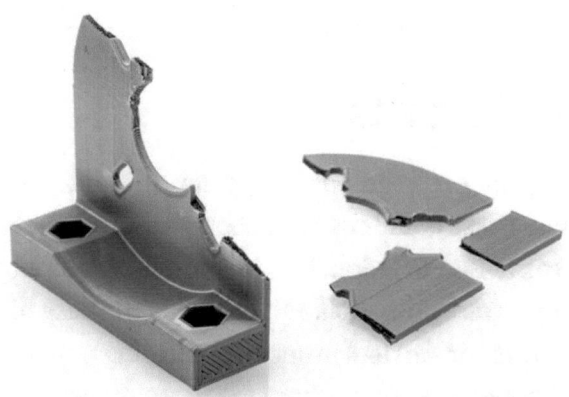

Figure 10-4. *Motor mount printed on its side, layer lines perpendicular to base*

These parts were all printed in PLA, so if the motor they were holding got hot (or if we left them on a hot car dashboard in summer), they would warp. UV radiation (like that encountered by something left out in the sun for a long time) degrades many plastics, too.

So, what to do? The simplest thing is to print a prototype part and thoroughly test the part before using it for something load-bearing. Consider how hot it will get, whether it will be outside for a long period of time, how it might be fatigued during operational use, and so on. As of this writing, most stress-modeling programs had limited or no ability to model material that is not isotropic, and so you are somewhat on your own. Hopefully this will change in the near future.

Note   Resin prints are more homogeneous than filament-based ones but have their own issues. Resin part strength is critically dependent on following the appropriate post-cure processes, and even then, standard resins can be very brittle.

Composite Filaments

If you want your print to be stiff but light, composite-filled filaments might be a good choice. These filaments have chopped carbon fiber embedded in a plastic matrix of PLA or nylon. Fundamentally, the strength of the material and its thermal properties will be that of the base plastic, but the fibers can make it stiffer and less prone to deforming under load. They can even distribute stresses throughout the part somewhat, which makes the part harder to break, though chopped fibers are much less effective than continuous ones for this purpose. Nylon with chopped carbon fiber is readily available. It can however abrade a nozzle, so you will need a hardened-steel or ruby-tipped nozzle to print with it.

Proprietary printers exist which have one nozzle laying down a plastic (like nylon) and a mechanism to lay down continuous fibers like carbon or fiberglass. This can be significantly stronger since the fibers are not chopped up and dependent on the plastic matrix for strength, but these are proprietary printers that will probably be pricier than one using composite filament.

Conductive Parts

If you have a printer that can lay down two materials at a time, you may be tempted to use conductive filaments to lay down conductive paths in your part. These filaments are made of PLA or another material with embedded graphite; this makes the filament somewhat abrasive for your nozzle. The graphite makes them mildly conductive, but the resistance can be pretty high. So, if you are trying to carry current—say, to light an LED—the material's ability to carry enough current might be a little marginal.

Filament manufacturer Proto-pasta, for instance, quotes a volume resistivity for its conductive PLA of 3D printed parts along layers of 30 ohm-cm and across layers of 115 ohm-cm (`www.proto-pasta.com/collections/exotic-composite-pla/products/conductive-pla`). Note that the ohm-cm units indicate that the resistance will be lower if the cross-sectional area of the conductive part of the print is bigger, but increases as the distance current has to travel through the print gets bigger.

The resistance is proportional to the cross-sectional area divided by that distance. However, if you have an application that does not require a lot of current, such as creating capacitive touch sensors, printing a conductive trace might allow you to create some interesting circuitry embedded in a housing. You could be better off, though, just leaving room to run wire or another conductive material through a gap in your print.

Tip   If you are developing Arduino electronics for a robot or similar project, you can make housings in Tinkercad. Tinkercad now has the ability to simulate a circuit and help you design enclosures around certain electronic components (`www.tinkercad.com/circuits`).

Printing Large Filament Parts

Printing large parts with a filament printer is not fundamentally different from printing smaller ones. However, the difference in scale means that issues that are minor annoyances in a print that is a few inches long can be expensive mistakes in a print that takes several kilograms of filament.

One method we have used to make a very large print easier to get off a platform is to configure it somewhat like a resin print. That is, as shown in Figure 10-5, to print it on top of supports and at an angle to the platform. Here we can see an aftermarket car part by Casale Design LLC printed on a MAKEiT, Inc. "2x4" printer. This technique makes it easier to get the print off the bed (cutting the sparse support with a hot wire if needed) and can more effectively manage the stresses on the print. A very big print bed is challenging to calibrate to perfect flatness, and this configuration makes the print less sensitive to that. If you want you can also add a raft, although as shown here just printing support straight on the platform is an option as well.

Figure 10-5. *Large print created on supports by MAKEiT, Inc. 2x4 printer (part by Casale Design LLC)*

Very big filament prints can also take several days. Thus, if you buy a large printer, be sure it has a filament-out detector and a means to restart a print. You will probably also be concerned about what happens if the power goes out. Since the peak heating for a big print bed is unlikely to be sustainable by an uninterruptable power source, one probably will not do you much good.

Additive Manufacturing at Scale

To this point we have talked about using 3D printing for one or a few prototype parts. However, as printer reliability improves and costs fall, it is becoming economic to consider 3D printing at scale. There are two basic approaches to scaling up. One can use a large number of smaller, low-cost printers (typically filament or resin) to print many parts in parallel, commonly called a "print farm." Or you can have one or a few high-throughput machines (often some variation of binder jetting) to print larger numbers of the same or similar parts at once. Depending on the material you need to use and the characteristics of your part, one or the other approach might make more economic sense.

Print-to-print consistency is important too, if you are going to scale up your printing. Differences in print temperature or other conditions can cause significant differences in the physical properties of a print, so you will want to make sure you understand the impact of any variability of your printer hardware and filament.

Print Farms and Service Bureaus

Small consumer 3D printers have fallen so low in price that it has become feasible to buy dozens or hundreds of them and print parts in parallel. This is usually called a "print farm." For example, Slant 3D (`www.slant3d.com`) states that they can do runs of 10,000 parts per week. They have an interesting twist on printing parts for others: they also sell the printer they designed for their farms, so that customers can get a print exactly how they want it and then submit a big run.

Some 3D printer manufacturers, like Prusa Research (`www.prusa3d.com`) in the Czech Republic, run print farms to print parts they use in their printers. They say they were using 500 printers to do this as of 2018, and had sold 130,000 printers as of mid-2019. In September of 2019, they set a Guinness World Record for having 1096 printers running at their facility at the same time. For a 3D printer manufacturer, running a print farm is also a way to thoroughly test and standardize their printers.

Service bureaus are businesses that do 3D printing (and sometimes design work) for others. They might have a print farm, but more often they have a variety of expensive printers that it does not make sense for other businesses to own. Metal 3D printing, for example, is often done by service bureaus.

Short-Run Manufacturing

Manufacturers often use "just in time" methods to keep parts in stock. This means that they do not keep a lot of inventory on hand, and sometimes a whole line will have to stop to wait for a part. To get through that and keep the line running, manufacturers turn to *bridge* parts, made in some other way than the regular process.

Since there are so many materials now, the bridge parts can often be 3D printed in the same material as the production part. This means, in turn, that the finished product can be shipped with the bridge part, and it might not need to be replaced (if quality control requirements allow use of a 3D printed part).

The next step up from bridge manufacturing is to plan to 3D print your manufacturing run of parts in the first place. Printing the same parts over and over can be pretty efficient, since it is worth it to really optimize the printer settings and then just launch the same job over and over. However, 3D printing can be slow for some applications, and the issues with being able to model a part's mechanical properties to a high enough fidelity might be problematic in some applications.

Tip   Because it is possible to 3D print shapes that would be difficult or impossible to manufacture by more conventional methods, you may be able to print what would otherwise be a complicated assembly in far fewer pieces, saving worker time.

Trying out 3D printed tooling or other in-house parts is a good way to test out 3D printing with something that is not going to a customer. Making conventional jigs and fixtures can be a significant expense and can have long turnaround times, and if they can be 3D printed in-house, they can be tweaked and adjusted relatively easily. If plastic can be strong or stiff enough for the task, and if the temperatures involved are not too high, this can be a low-risk way to get some experience with the technology. 3D printer maker Ultimaker has good case studies on its website (www.ultimaker.com) of its users' experiences.

Mass Customization

It is not a big step to go from manufacturing a small number of identical parts one at a time to asking whether one can make a standard part customizable instead. A CAD model might have just a few parameters that can be tweaked depending on what the user needs, or the individual product might be made from a scan.

Dentists have been early adopters of this approach, since almost all of what they do is custom to every patient. Most of the current dental applications use resin printers to create devices that do not go in the mouth themselves but are used as molds for casting, vacuum forming, or other technologies. We will go into that in depth in a later section of this chapter.

Moving to metal printing, orthopedists have been printing artificial hips and other implants. They are printed, typically in a titanium alloy, with surface texture that allows the bone to grow into and fuse with the implant, a process known as *osseointegration*. Moving beyond orthopedics, printing entire organs is an evolving field that has great promise for many medical conditions.

3D printed fashion (notably shoes and high fashion at this point) is in its early days, and is mostly used for prototyping or high-visibility pieces for celebrity clients or athletes. A 3D printed dress created by designer Michael Schmidt (www.michaelschmidtstudios.com) and technologist Francis Bitonti for Dita Von Teese was an early (rather revealing) printed lacework-like dress.

Designers Nervous System (https://n-e-r-v-o-u-s.com) created the "Kinematic Dress," which, like chain armor, folds up for printing (on an SLS machine) and then flows nicely for the wearer. Other novel, 3D printed high fashion has been created by Anouk Wipprecht (`www.anoukwipprecht.nl`)—famously, her "Spider Dress," which attacked anyone who got too close with animatronic legs. In the next section, we will look at creating jewelry by using 3D prints as a mold.

3D printing is also being used to create low-cost lab equipment. Scientists often are big consumers of duct tape, and 3D printing can create more opportunities to create one-off objects to hold things somehow. Of course, if there are chemicals involved, it becomes necessary to investigate whether or not the 3D printed materials involved are compatible with the chemicals in question. There are various open source science groups out there documenting their solutions, notably Joshua Pearce's group at Michigan Tech University. They maintain Appropedia (`www.appropedia.org/Open-source_Lab`), which has links to a variety of equipment, particularly for optics.

Note   We can think of these applications as "hardware as a service," in which a digital file can be tweaked and manufactured anyplace an appropriate fabrication machine exists.

Reverse Engineering and Spare Parts

People often think they can somehow just have a copy of a part pop out of a 3D printer. However, in essence, this means you need to somehow create a digital design of the part you are copying and replacing. 3D scans are imperfect, as we discussed in Chapter 3, and particularly so in areas where you might want precision like a part that interlocks with another one. Often people will scan a part and just use that as a guide to re-create a full CAD model.

The intellectual property issues here get complicated, too, and depend on jurisdiction. If your odd-shaped curtain ring breaks at home and you 3D print a replacement one, it is a somewhat different situation than doing that and then selling a copy of a distinctive product.

And of course, warranties might be an issue. If you are a manufacturer considering letting people create a replacement part on their own or a service bureau's 3D printer, what happens if they do a bad job and the part breaks?

GOING DIGITAL

3D printing has been used for prototyping for decades, and that remains a major application. Now that there are many materials that can be 3D printed (Chapter 2), it is a lot easier to create a model that mimics the form and fit of a product to see how it feels or works with other parts.

In industries where hand fabrication, particularly of prototypes, is common, CAD usage may not be a common skill. CAD drawings might be used to communicate with human fabricators who will fill out details based on common practice. In those cases, the biggest barriers to using a 3D printer (or other digital manufacturing tools) can be learning a CAD program. It requires getting used to the fact that a slicing program will not be able to interpret a drawing at all and will need every detail exactly as desired. As discussed in Chapter 7, some CAD programs are more 3D printer friendly than others. If you are going digital from scratch, you may need to do some optimization on the software that works best for what you produce vs. software that creates models that are easiest to 3D print.

Industrial Mold-Making

A somewhat more conventional application of 3D prints is as forms or molds. Either a 3D printed part can be used as the positive to create a negative mold or a negative mold can be created with 3D printing directly. PLA or specially formulated resins are commonly used to make jewelry from 3D prints via investment (or lost-wax) casting. In this process, a positive mold called a pattern is created, and then ceramic is laid up around it.

The ceramic is fired, and the wax, resin, or PLA melts out. Then metal is poured in to make the jewelry piece. Finally, the ceramic mold must be broken to remove the metal piece, so each one can only be used once. Figure 10-6 shows a resin-printed ring mold from Formlabs and the finished metal ring investment-cast from it.

Beginning the process again would traditionally involve carving a new wax pattern that will inevitably end up slightly different from the first. However, a 3D printed pattern can be reproduced precisely just by running the print again. You can change some numbers in the CAD file if it was not quite right and try again, or customize the design for another client.

Figure 10-6. *Ring mold and cast (courtesy of Formlabs)*

Formlabs (Figure 10-7) sells a high-temperature resin that can be used for injection molds. As this evolves, it might enable lower-volume injection molding runs, since this drastically lowers tooling costs and turnaround time.

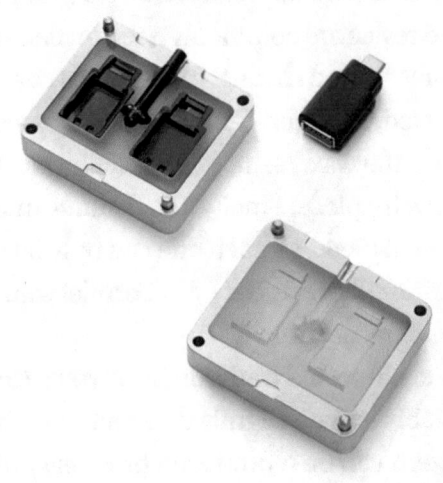

Figure 10-7. *3D printed injection molds (courtesy of Formlabs)*

Case Study: Aftermarket Automotive

Casale Design LLC (https://codycasale.com) makes custom aftermarket auto parts. These parts are challenging to create since they can be quite large by 3D printing standards (e.g., a car rear spoiler) and are typically organic shapes that are going to need to fit into other existing ones. Traditionally, a mold was created by hand, and fiberglass or other materials were laid up over it. Now, however, these large molds can be printed directly.

The red part in Figure 10-8 is being checked for fit in the larger white one. It was created with material laid up over a 3D printed mold. 3D printed parts can also be made in the same shape as the desired end part and used to lay up a negative mold. Then these negative molds can be filled with whatever material the final product requires.

In Figure 10-9, the white part was 3D printed, and the red mold laid up around it. The mold would then be used to make a production run of parts.

Figure 10-8. *A 3D printed prototype auto part by Casale Design LLC*

Figure 10-9. *Cody Casale shows a mold (red) and molded part (white)*

The full-sized spoiler in Figure 10-10 was printed in two pieces on a MAKEiT, Inc. "2x4" large format filament printer and then glued, filled, and sanded to a smooth finish.

Figure 10-10. *A 3D printed large part and smaller logo print*

The smaller part (shown in close-up in Figure 10-11) is used to create Casale's logo. The finished fiberglass part made from a mold using these pieces is shown installed on a car in Figure 10-12.

Figure 10-11. *Close-up of Casale logo print*

Figure 10-12. *A finished final custom part*

Case Study: Dentistry

Dentistry is a nearly ideal use of 3D printing. Every piece made is by definition custom for one patient, and there is an established workflow that starts with a mold of a patient's teeth and ends with a crown or other in-mouth part. Because of the precision required, dental applications are a good fit for printing with liquid resin (although some powder printing is used, too).

SprintRay, a manufacturer of resin 3D printers, has in fact decided to be a specialty manufacturer of an ecosystem just for the dental market (Figure 10-13). A curing system, printer, and specialized software system are all key parts of the workflow. Materials have to be approved by appropriate regulatory bodies (the FDA in the United States) to be used for certain applications.

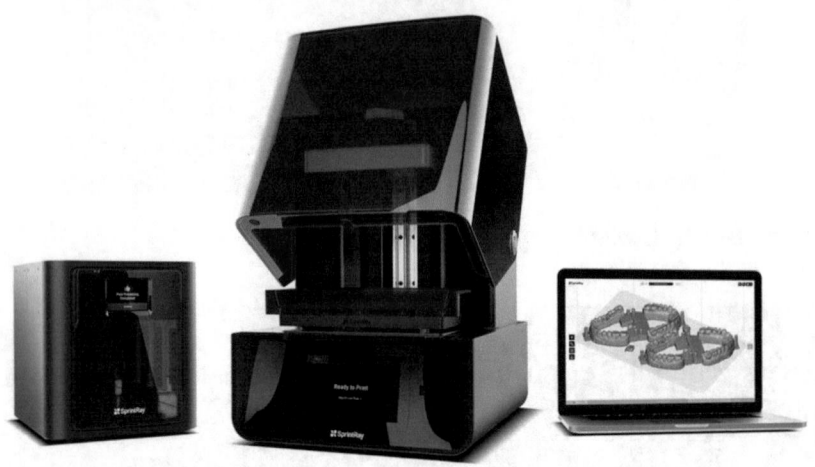

Figure 10-13. *SprintRay curing station, printer, and custom software (courtesy of SprintRay)*

The workflow can closely parallel the traditional one, which used to start with an impression of patient's teeth, which then was used to create a plaster mold. Then that mold was used as the basis for creating crowns or other appliances. Now, a 3D scan is taken of the teeth (a much easier process for the patient) and that scan is used to directly make a 3D printed "cast" (Figure 10-14) which can then be used to create the appliances, just as the plaster cast was. A large number of scans can be printed at once on a platform (Figure 10-15).

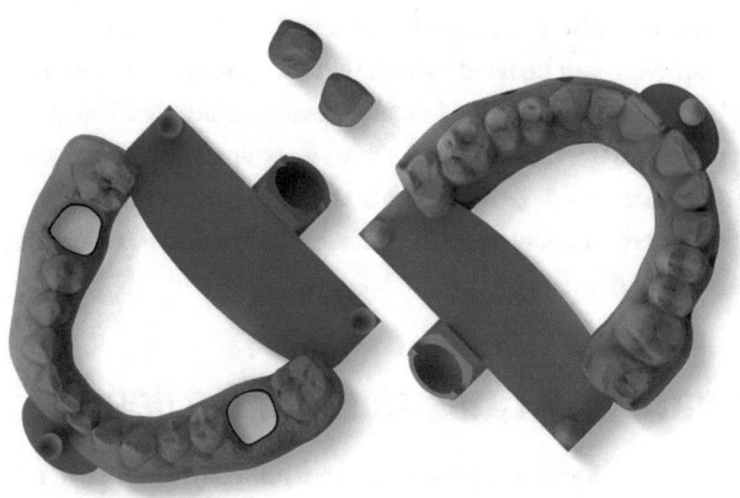

Figure 10-14. *A dental resin print (courtesy of SprintRay)*

Figure 10-15. *Material and prints on print bed (courtesy of SprintRay)*

This workflow also enables some innovative new products, too. For example, software can be used to start with the patient's current teeth and then move in small increments to a final desired configuration. Molds can be created for each of these intermediary steps and aligners vacuum-formed over each mold. This automates orthodontia significantly, but not without some controversy about how much interaction a patient needs at each step with a dentist.

Summary and Questions for Review

In this chapter, we looked at how to create strong parts for use in real-world situations. We also reviewed the creation of parts in quantity and for certain applications. The bottom line is that increasing reliability and consistency of lower-cost 3D printers may make small- to moderate-batch manufacturing far more efficient and cost-effective.

Consider your answers to the following questions based on your understanding of the material in the chapter:

1. What is a functional 3D print?

2. What considerations should you take into account when creating a functional part on a 3D printer?

3. You have a part that you have successfully printed once with a 3D printer. What further considerations should you keep in mind if you are now going to 3D print 1000 copies?

4. What other ways of using a 3D printer, other than direct 3D printing, might make sense for the 1000-copy case? What about 100,000 copies?

5. Why is dentistry a good fit for resin 3D printing?

CHAPTER 11

Metal 3D Printing and Casting

Metal 3D printing is the hot new frontier in 3D printing. 3D printing in metal is inherently harder than printing in plastic because of the far higher temperatures involved in melting (or, at least, sintering) metal at some point in the process. However, some clever crossovers with the technologies behind *metal injection molding* (MIM) are bringing a flurry of lower-cost metal 3D printing options to market. In this chapter, we will survey the current state of the art in metal printing.

We then talk about *casting* metal parts as an alternative—that is, printing a part in plastic and using the plastic part to create a mold for metal. This field is changing very rapidly, so there may be even more options by the time you read this.

Metal 3D Printing Technologies

Metal 3D printing can be broken into three categories: direct laser metal sintering (DMLS), binder-jetting methods, and what we will call "filament-like" printing, which some manufacturers refer to as "bound powder" printing. The latter two owe a lot to metal injection molding, so first we will have a little sidebar about that technology.

METAL INJECTION MOLDING

Metal injection molding, usually referred to by its acronym, MIM, is a technique very similar to plastic injection molding. Metal powder is mixed with one or more plastic binders, with the metal being a very high percentage of the mixture by weight but 60% or so by volume. Then this mix is injected at high pressure into a mold. This stage is called a *green part*. This part is then cooled and placed in a debinding agent to remove the binder. This can be a chemical bath, a catalyst, or just a controlled furnace to melt out the binder.

A large fraction, say 40%, of the part's volume is now empty space, and it is referred to as a *brown part*. Brown parts are very fragile, given they are almost half empty space. Some binder mixes keep a component of the binder—a *backbone* binder—in place until sintering starts to keep the print from disintegrating in the brown stage. The part is then *sintered*, or heated at high enough temperature that the outer part of each powder particle will melt into its neighbors. Sintering might take place in a vacuum, or in an inert or *reducing* gas. In the chemical sense used here, reduction means the opposite of *oxidation*—for example, avoiding rusting of iron.

The part will shrink significantly (but predictably) during this process. Figure 11-1 shows this shrinkage. The far left shows the original mix of 60% metal, 40% binder; the middle cube shows the resulting metal part (shrinking more in the vertical); and the far right shows the volume of binder that was melted out.

MIM is a mature technology that is used routinely. It can get away with powders that do not have to meet the very strict needs of metal powders for direct sintering, so its powders can be cheaper. The market for it is pretty big, so economies of scale also kick in. Generally speaking it is a very cost-effective means of making small, highly detailed parts.

It can be used for some metals that are very hard to work with otherwise, like high-carbon tool steels. These steels tend to oxidize or have other chemical problems if welded, but sintering can heat steadily and gently in a way that is more conducive to high-strength metal formation. The final parts can be more than 99% solid.

Figure 11-1. *Shrinkage of parts*

Traditional MIM requires making tooling (the high-pressure mold for the injected metal). Designs are limited to very small parts that are not very thick. 100 cubic millimeters per "shot" (part) is a common limitation on MIM service company sites. Because it does use a mold like plastic injection molding, MIM is good for making many of the same exact part, to amortize the cost of the molds.

Filament Metal Printing

A relatively recent technique for 3D printing metal uses MIM-like materials without the need for a mold. A mix of binder plastics is blended with metal powder. This mix is made into filament, pellets, rods, or some other feedstock that is fed into a 3D printer.

A number of metal-filled filaments are available, but most of these are only around 60% metal by weight and do not contain backbone binders. These are less than 20% metal by volume though, since the metals are usually about eight times as dense as the carrier plastic. Thus they do not contain enough metal to sinter into a fully metal part. Instead, these materials are intended to make parts that *look* like metal, in a process similar to *cold casting*.

In cold casting, a resin part is cast in a mold coated with metal powder. Once the resin cures, the surface can be burnished to expose and shine the thin layer of metal, and the exposed metal can even be allowed to oxidize for added authenticity. The same can be done with these lower-metal-content filaments. Unlike cold casting, these filaments include metal throughout the print, which still leaves them much lighter than a fully metal part, but does add a satisfying heft.

High-metal-content filament, on the other hand, is typically around 90% or more metal by weight, which makes it about 50-60% metal by volume. This technique goes by various names, including *bound powder*, and process names that are proprietary to one manufacturer or another. Other processes that use loose powder are inherently more expensive, since metal powder is hazardous to work with and needs to be managed and contained. Powder bound up in plastic, though, can be handled like plastic filament, with a few caveats.

Printing Process

When the metal powder and plastic mix is made into more or less conventional 3D printer filament, it can be used in a regular 3D printer like the ones we have talked about elsewhere in this book. However, these filaments are often very abrasive and will damage anything but an all-metal hot end, so you may need to swap out your nozzle to use these filaments. Other than that, typically the printing temperature is close to that of the plastic binder material, and so usually within the range of a low-cost printer. Obviously, check that before ordering any filament. Metal filament is very expensive as of this writing—typically five to ten times the cost of everyday filaments.

Parts are printed the same way as any plastic filament part, noting the nozzle temperature required and any suggestions about heated build platforms. You may have to adjust some other settings to allow for the increased viscosity of the melted plastic, due to the high ratio of filler material. The filler material may also make room-temperature filaments brittle. Some manufacturers suggest buying an add-on pre-warmer to soften the filament a little before it goes into your printer's extruder drive. Otherwise it might be prone to breaking in the printer, which would cause the print to fail (or at least pause, if your printer has a "filament out" sensor). Figure 11-2 shows a green part from The Virtual Foundry, a manufacturer of this type of filament.

Figure 11-2. *A green part made of high-carbon iron (part courtesy of The Virtual Foundry)*

Some systems designed for printing this way use an extruder designed to work with rods of bound metal powder instead of filament. These rods resemble the sticks used by hot glue guns and are pressed through the nozzle one after another. The larger diameter makes them less flexible, but also less likely to break, and this shape allows the printer to exert more force to push them through the heated nozzle.

As we noted in an earlier sidebar, freshly molded MIM parts are called green parts. This term is often used for bound-metal prints as well. The metal content in a green part is the same 50–60% by volume as the filament. However, printing with infill means that there may be significantly less of the metal/binder mixture than in a molded green part.

The printing process is hot enough to melt the plastic binder, but not nearly hot enough to fuse the metal particles inside. To create a metal part, you need to go through two more steps: *debinding* and *sintering*.

Note   If you want a print that *looks like* metal, but do not need the strength and thermal properties of metal, you can just use the part as it came off the printer and sand, coat, or otherwise cosmetically finish your print. The print will be approximately as strong as a print made of the plastic binder alone would have been.

If anything, the print might be weaker, since the metal particles are just taking up space that could be used by the plastic that actually hold the print together. For this reason (as well as cost), unless you really want the added weight, a higher metal content is probably not desirable for prints that you do not intend to sinter.

Debinding

To create a print with the structural qualities of metal, the next step after printing is to *debind* the part. As the name implies, debinding removes the binder while leaving behind the metal. Some binders are a mix of several compounds, and only one is removed during debinding. In those cases, part of the binder, a *backbone binder*, remains to hold the print together for subsequent steps. Depending on what the binder is made of and which metal powder is involved, debinding might be to use chemicals, a catalyst that interacts with the binder, or just heat to melt out the binder while not melting out the metal. After debinding you have a *brown* part. (These color names, incidentally, do not have anything to do with the actual color of the part at that point in the process and are used for historical purposes.)

Caution   A brown part is usually very delicate, since it will typically be about 40% small voids once the binder is removed. The part will need to be designed to survive its brown stage. Any supports that the print requires will be easier to remove before sintering, but this will make them even more delicate in the brown stage and vulnerable to sagging during sintering. Some systems are designed to have supports left on until after sintering and use a ceramic release layer to make them separable afterward. The ones that remove support early use a refractory material to support the print during debinding and sintering.

Debinding can take a while (overnight to multiple days) since fundamentally it is a diffusion process. Time to debind is an exponential function of the thickness of the part. MIM parts are usually small (volumes less than 100 mm^3) and have thin sections to minimize the internal travel of the debinder. Filament-type 3D prints usually quote less restrictive dimension limitations, particularly for technologies that allow infill.

The debinder only has to soak through the outer surface of a print before it can flow into the infill channels and reach the material at the core of the print. This is different from an MIM molded part, which is typically made solid, and therefore has strict limits on its thickness. To make sure this diffusion of chemicals is efficient, it is best to stick to infill patterns that do not create vertically isolated cells within the infill structure.

Caution   Some high-metal filament manufacturers suggest solid parts that will behave more like a MIM part after printing, and size requirements will thus be more restrictive.

Sintering

The final stage of the process is *sintering*. This process uses some combination of heat and pressure to force a powdered material into a homogenous solid. Sintering can take place in a vacuum, too. The particles and voids in a brown part are compressed down into a part that has voids of just a few percent (or even less than 1%). The temperatures in sintering may not be as high as they would be to melt the bulk metal.

However, sintering is a highly evolved process that requires a controlled temperature profile. Just a backyard kiln will not be sufficient; you need a furnace that can raise and hold temperatures in a well-defined profile. Sintering too will usually take a day or more, so the debind and sinter steps together can take from one to several days. This stage is sometimes referred to as *densification*. Figures 11-3 and 11-4 show finished 3D printed parts.

Figure 11-3. *3D printed metal part (part courtesy of The Virtual Foundry)*

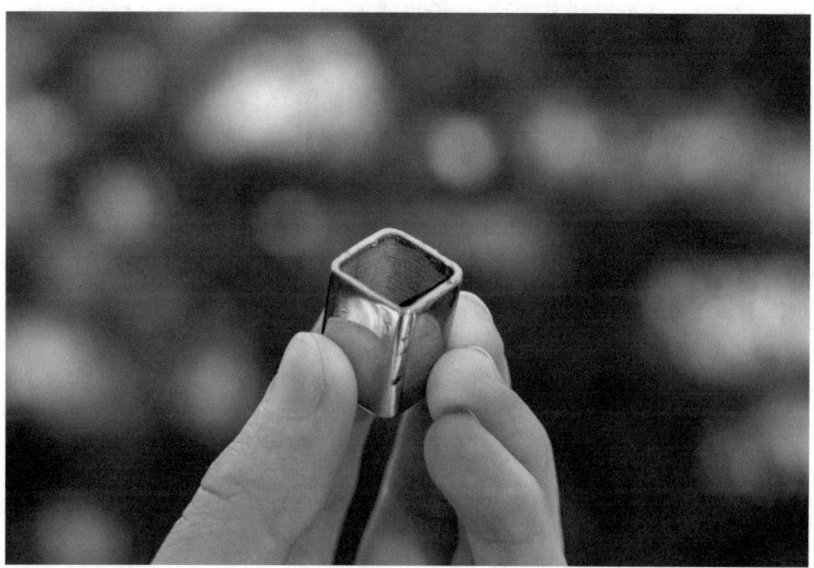

Figure 11-4. *3D printed steel tube (part courtesy of The Virtual Foundry)*

Debinding and Sintering Equipment

Debinding and sintering require equipment that is much pricier than the $200 printer you could, in principle, get away with for the beginning of this process. Like all things in manufacturing, how much pricier depends on the results you need. The capital investment you can make will drive how much work you chose to do in-house vs. vending it out.

At the moment, the cheapest end-to-end process for getting a metal part entirely in-house would be to use metal filaments which allow for heat-only debinding. The Virtual Foundry (www.thevirtualfoundry.com) was one of the first to market with this type of filament, and as of this writing, they have high-metal-content filaments with aluminum, bronze, copper, high-carbon iron, copper, tungsten, titanium 64-5, and stainless steels 316L and 17-4 filaments. Prices range from $66 for half a kilogram spool of copper filament to about $700 for half a kilogram of tungsten. The Virtual Foundry's binder is removed entirely with heat. Supports are removed after the green part stage; the part is packed in a refractory material (Figure 11-5). Then the part is taken through debinding with a process that heats the part enough to remove the binder, but not sinter the metal. Finally, the temperature is increased enough to sinter the metal and complete the part. They also sell furnaces capable of debinding and sintering their filament for around $30,000.

Figure 11-5. *Parts packed in refractory material (courtesy of The Virtual Foundry)*

Another alternative is to outsource the debinding and sintering parts of the process, and to just print the green part. BASF is currently selling Ultrafuse 316L stainless steel filament, which requires a chemical debinding. Retailer MatterHackers sells the filament with a coupon for outsourced debinding and sintering of parts at a collaborating MIM facility. The part has very stringent geometric requirements and has to be free of contaminants, like other filament material, to be processed at this MIM facility.

Finally, end-to-end integrated processing systems are coming on the market which include a printer, chemical debinder, and sintering furnace. These also have proprietary software to manage the process. Desktop Metal (www.desktopmetal.com) and Markforged (https://markforged.com/) have similar integrated systems. Desktop Metal uses rods of powder/metal material, while Markforged uses a conventional filament. Both have two nozzles in their printer, one of which lays down an interface layer between the part and any support. The support stays on through the debind and sinter process, but it crumbles to dust during sintering. The manufacturers do not post prices directly, but reseller prices and reviews indicate that these systems will run in the low six figures. Markforged has a variety of filaments including A2 and H13 tool steels, Inconel 625, and 17-4 stainless steel. Desktop Metal's offerings include 17-4 and 316L stainless steels, H13 tool steel, Alloy 625 and 4140 steels, and copper.

Shrinkage and Part Accuracy

If a part is 40% voids at the end of the debinding process, and the final product is over 99% metal, the part has to shrink between those two points. Naively, if we just ask ourselves how much a cube has to shrink to have 60% of the original volume, we would just take the cube root of 0.6, which is 0.84, and say each dimension would be 84% of the original, or a shrinkage of 16% in each axis. Gravity comes into play though and shrinks the dimension that is vertical during sintering a little more than the horizontal ones. Thus, the part will shrink maybe 20% in the vertical and 14% or so in the horizontal directions. Manufacturers of filament will give you an estimate for their material and recommended process, as well as an estimate of the density of the finished part.

The good news is that this usually happens in a repeatable way for a given metal/binder combination, if the debinding and sintering are done consistently. Thus, you can allow for it at the CAD stage, or by scaling the axes in your slicing software.

Other than that, part accuracy is a little complicated, as is always the case for filament-using printers. The smallest feature you can print will be around 2 nozzle diameters. The surface smoothness will be a function of the metal particle sizes. Some filaments are made from powder close to that used for direct metal laser sintering, and others use powder more like that for MIM. MIM powder does not have to be as regular in its shape as does DMLS powder, for reasons we will discuss when we get to DMLS later in this chapter. The surface roughness will thus be a source of inaccuracy, although a minor one.

Note   For many 3D printed parts, you will still need to polish or machine fine details after the fact, and avoid punching through the walls of the part.

Binder Jetting

The binder-jetting technique is a hybrid technique that lays up powder across a print bed (like SLS does, as described in Chapter 2), but instead of sintering it with a laser, a layer of binder is sprayed onto the area that will become the printed part. A big block of powder is generated, with its base being the area of the print bed and its height being the top of the tallest print on the bed. Prints are excavated out of this block of powder. The binder is removed in a debinding process appropriate for the binder and metal involved and the part sintered more or less the same way as for the filament-like prints.

These prints are supported by the unbound powder while printing, but may still need support structures to help them maintain their shape during sintering. These prints also cannot have infill the way filament prints can, because the empty spaces would be filled with powder instead of air.

This technique is most efficient if the print bed is entirely full of prints. The whole bed has to be covered with powder no matter what. After being filtered and mixed with fresh powder, most of the unbound powder can be reused. Manufacturers usually quote a percentage of used and new powder that is acceptable. If the bed is pretty full of prints, this method can be very fast. The metal is not being melted, and the binder can be sprayed from an array of nozzles like those of an inkjet printer. Manufacturer Desktop Metal is pitching using its filament-like printer for prototypes or small runs, and then using essentially the same materials in powder-binder forms for mass production.

Prints will need to be fully supported so that they will survive sintering, when the bed of powder will no longer be there. In the case of Desktop Metal's systems, what they call an "anti-sintering layer" is put down on the interface between the part and support structure so that the supports are easily removed after sintering. There is not very much binder, relatively speaking, and it is removed in the sintering process.

The big minus, though, is that you are dealing with unbound metal powder. This has to be handled with great care and personal protective equipment. Unless the system is very carefully designed to keep all the metal powder in modular components, changing from one type of metal to another can be a big deal. The printing process has to happen in an inert atmosphere, to avoid igniting the metal particle accidentally. As of this writing, metal binder jet systems were just starting to ship, and systems were reported to be in the approximate $1M range. These parts still need to go through the sintering process, so each part will likely still take several days from start to finish. Higher throughput is achieved by printing many parts in parallel.

Note   Other manufacturers use a similar process that infuses stainless steel prints with hot bronze instead of sintered.

Part Accuracy

Since the proportion of binder is small, so too the shrinkage will be small. Resolution will be limited by the binder droplet size, so it can be very fine. Features still need to be thick enough to survive the delicate brown stage, and these parts will need to be handled carefully in the depowdering step. The surface however will be a little rough, because you are sintering from a powder.

Direct Metal Laser Sintering

Direct metal laser sintering (DMLS) has been around for a while, relatively speaking. It has the simplicity of one-step processing. Like binder jetting, a layer of powder is spread over the entire surface of a platform. Then a laser sinters the metal powder to create a part in one step. However, the cost of that is applying high laser energy to powders that are very flammable. DMLS has to happen in an inert atmosphere, and powder management is a real challenge. For that reason, DMLS (and the facility support that a machine needs) is very expensive, in the multiple millions of dollars.

DMLS is a slow technique, since you are sintering metal with one laser spot as you go. (Some new machines from 3D Systems have multiple lasers running in parallel to speed this up.) The other techniques we have described in this chapter sinter the whole part at once, which speeds up this step considerably. A side effect of this spot heating during fabrication is that stresses can build up in the material. Depending on the intended application, the part may require heat-treating to reduce stresses that build up during the printing process and to give the print the desired microstructure.

The print needs support, even though the powder will surround a part for the whole print, to avoid warping due to these stresses. The support needs to be cut off after printing. Because the entire print, including its supports, is made of solid metal, this requires metal-cutting tools.

Like binder jetting, DMLS is most efficient when the whole block of powder at the end of the print is packed with parts. Some powder can be reused, but new powder has to be added each print.

Powders suitable for DMLS are challenging to produce as well. To sinter reliably, the powders for DMLS have to be more uniform in shape and in size distribution than MIM powders. This makes the raw material more expensive to produce.

DMLS is the way to go if the part has some very thick sections that would be challenging to bulk sinter, or even a wide range of thicknesses within a part. Since everything is sintered as you go, there are no issues with thick sections. High complexity parts are well served by DMLS too, if support can be removed.

Finally, DMLS is more or less welding. Materials that are hard to weld because of oxidation (like high-carbon tool steels) are not good candidates for DMLS, and will be better served with one of the filament-like processes or binder jetting, to avoid high-speed melting. Steels available from various manufacturers include stainless steels 1704PH and 316L; aluminum AlSi10Mg; nickel alloys 718 and 625; Titanium Ti64, Gr5, Gr23, and Gr1; cobalt chrome molybdenum alloys; Monel K500; and Copper C18150.

DMLS parts do not have to be sintered after the printing stage, but they may need to be annealed or otherwise heat-treated to relieve mechanical stresses that built up in the course of printing.

Accuracy

DMLS parts have very high accuracy. Since there are no binders, there is no shrinkage. The resolution and smallest feature size will be of the order of the laser spot size, and surface finish will be determined by the powder diameter. Extremely intricate parts can be created with DMLS.

Pros and Cons, Printing Techniques

Given all these options for printing with metal, what is the best way to choose among the options? The main criteria will be

- Budget

- Which metal you need to use

- How many copies you plan to make

- Geometry of the part

None of these trade-offs are entirely independent of the others. Cost per part may be lowest with an expensive machine if the part is being produced in large numbers that make it worth it to buy a binder jet machine. Printing with filament and outsourcing the debinding and sintering will be the lowest capital cost, but it loses some of the advantages of doing printing in-house. You might just want to vend out the whole thing.

Binder jetting can be much faster than DMLS in the printing stage, but DMLS does not have the additional processing that the other techniques require to get to a sintered part. Some metals that are not easy to weld will not be suitable for DMLS. If you want to print in a tool steel, most likely you will be looking at one of the powder and binder options. If you are working with a very reactive material (like aluminum), bulk sintering may be easier to deal with.

Machining is always a competitor, too. The more complex the part is, the less advantageous machining becomes. However, if the part is very complex, it may be challenging to cut off the DMLS support.

Parts with some thick sections are not a candidate for the filament-like or powder and binder metal 3D printing systems, because the debinding might take too long. However, if you can redesign your part to avoid these thick sections (or to use an infill pattern that allows good drainage), you may be able to use the filament or powder/binder techniques.

If the parts are high value, complex, and unique, but there are a lot of them, you might want a DMLS or powder/binder system, depending on part thickness since filament printing might be too slow for production. Many medical devices are 3D printed with DMLS, for example.

Many early adopters are using metal 3D printing to make jigs and fixtures for their own internal use. The ability of common software tools to model the strength of parts made with 3D printing is still a bit limited, and so applications where it is annoying—but not a customer-relations disaster—might be a good first choice.

Note   If you want to create an STL file and have someone else print the file in metal, there are service bureaus that will do that for you. Search online for "3d printing metal services." Service bureaus that can print metal usually publish *design rules* that explain what they can and cannot do (including material properties, feature size, maximum part size, and so on). Some service bureaus, like Shapeways (www.shapeways.com), also let you publish your design so others can print it and pay you a royalty.

Specialty Applications

The increasing availability of metal 3D printing opens up some novel applications, beyond the tooling, fixtures, and medical devices that one might expect. It can also create opportunities to use materials in ways that one would not conventionally think about.

Generative design is a computerized part generation process. Based on the loads expected in a design, the software will generate the part to have members where it needs to support those loads, and nothing anywhere else. (Using these tools to make a part lighter is sometimes called *lightweighting*.) Finite element stress modeling of a 3D printed part is still a maturing capability, so one will still need to leave some margin for error. However, this capability is a natural partner to 3D printing in metal, and the market is likely to push those capabilities in the coming years.

Another area that metal 3D printing enables is the use of old materials in new ways. Traditionally radiation shielding, for medical applications, for example, was created out of lead. However, lead requires special handling now that its toxicity is appreciated more than was the case in the past. This means that an alternative to lead with similar properties is an attractive concept. Tungsten, it turns out, is very good at blocking radiation and can be made into a high-metal filament. The Virtual Foundry, for instance, advertises the use of their tungsten filament for this application.

Casting

Another option for "printing" metal is to print a plastic part and then use it as a mold, form, or pattern for a traditional metal casting technique. The *casting* process is very old, its origins lost in antiquity. It is still used today in many applications, from one-off casts through mass manufacturing. In brief, one creates a *pattern*, traditionally in materials like wood, clay, or wax, but 3D printable materials work just as well. The pattern is a positive mold of what you want to cast in metal. Various techniques are used to pack sand or ceramic around the pattern. The pattern is then removed (*sand casting*) or melted away (*investment casting*), and metal fills the void where the pattern was.

Caution   The material in this chapter is intended to give you an idea about how an experienced artisan can create a metal piece based on your 3D print. It should give you enough information to create a part that will cast well. It is not a do-it-yourself guide to casting, though. You need to know more about safety procedures and equipment, which you should learn directly from an experienced artisan. We appreciate the insights of foundry artisan Peter Dippell.

Designing Models for Casting

This section gives some design rules for castable patterns, 3D printed or otherwise, in case you want to have someone cast a metal part from a print (pattern) that you make.

Sand Casting

The sand casting process is used in many applications, from one-off casts through mass manufacturing. A pattern is created (e.g., by 3D printing) and then sand infused with a binder is packed around the pattern. Channels for pouring molten metal are carved into the mold, and the pattern is extracted. Molten metal is then poured into the empty space where the pattern was, and the final metal piece is extracted from the sand when it is cool enough.

Sand cast patterns traditionally have been carved out of wood or another material that would survive the required number of uses. Because traditional patterns are used multiple times, being able to reprint them is not as much of an advantage as it is in investment casting. There, the pattern is lost each time (more on that in the next section). However, the channels needed to spread around the molten metal (called *sprues* and *runners*) need to be re-created each time in sand casting.

With careful thought (to avoid lots of support and other additional work), it may be possible to print these sprues and runners as well. Depending on your comfort with your chosen CAD program and its capabilities, it may or may not be easier for you to figure out how to make an STL file with the appropriate plumbing in addition to your main model. Bear in mind, too, that whoever casts your model will need to extract what you build from the sand, which could get tricky if you also want to avoid support.

For 3D prints that will be used for sand casting, you will want to use a bit of *draft*. That means that instead of having vertical surfaces intersect horizontal ones at right angles, surfaces that would have been vertical instead are tapered a bit to facilitate removal from the sand. In the case of the heart pendants in Figure 11-6, it would have helped to have a little bit of draft (just a few degrees) rather than the crisp verticals everywhere.

Right angles can be printed by well-made 3D printers, but in sand casting the sand tends to get stuck in corners and edges and results in some imperfections. As you can see, the place where the vertical half-heart pokes upward is a little rough at its base because of the sharp edge there in the 3D printed version.

Tip   Engineering-style CAD programs (like SolidWorks, Onshape, or Autodesk Fusion 360) have the ability to add draft to an object. It is difficult to do with beginner programs, however. If you are doing serious work that you want to be able to cast, you may need to step up to one of these more industrial-strength programs.

Figure 11-6. Heart patterns and finished aluminum cast pieces

An *undercut* in the mold-making world is the equivalent of an *overhang* in 3D printing. It is a part of the model that (in this case) would pull out sand when the pattern is pulled out. Just as it is difficult for the printer to create an object that does not build up smoothly from the platform, it is hard to sand-cast an object that cannot be pulled out of the mold smoothly. If a mold is made up of two pieces, those pieces also have to fit perfectly, with appropriate tolerances. As mentioned in the previous section, higher-end, engineering-oriented CAD programs have tools to separate parts for 3D printing and subsequent casting with the types of considerations noted here.

Because metal contracts when it cools, your finished cast part will be smaller than your 3D printed part was. Be sure to account for this. You can look up the shrinkage (usually stated as a percentage) for your material and plan your 3D printed part to be a little bigger if your cast part needs to fit into something else precisely.

Think through *how* precisely parts need to fit together; do not make holes exactly the same size as the objects that need to fit into them. A little experimentation may be required to engineer your process end to end.

Tip   A manufacturing engineering textbook may be helpful to get a structured overview if metal casting and working with metal is new to you. One of the classics of the genre is *DeGarmo's Materials and Processes in Manufacturing, 12th Edition* (Wiley, 2017) by Black and Khoser, with new editions appearing regularly.

Investment Casting

Sand casting is very versatile, but it is not good for capturing fine detail or for pieces that have complex geometries, such as a sculpture of a person. For that type of work, investment casting, sometimes called *lost-wax casting*, can be a good fit. With those advantages comes additional complexity.

Investment casting has more steps and for high precision can take a lot longer than sand casting. Professional sculptors producing bronze statues typically use investment casting. The process is pretty laborious, particularly if many copies are being made, because nothing survives the melt-out.

First, a piece is carved in wax. Typically, sprues are also carved in advance and attached to the piece so that there are strategic paths to flow in metal and to allow air (and wax or, in our case, 3D printed plastic) to escape. This wax piece is then coated with several layers of ceramic or plaster, or alternatively a plaster cast is made around it. The plaster or ceramic is allowed to harden. The wax is "burned out" (melted away, hence the name *lost-wax*, since the pattern is lost each time), leaving the plaster cast. The hollow empty mold then is filled with metal. After it hardens and cools somewhat, the ceramic mold is broken open, and the piece is removed and cleaned up. 3D printing gives the option of printing the investment over and over, which might be a huge time-saver. Wax has been used for the investment casting process for centuries because it burns out at a relatively low temperature and leaves a clean mold.

Investment Casting with Resin

If you want to do investment casting professionally, you are probably going to wind up using a resin printer that has a resin designed for the purpose. Special wax-like castable resins have been developed for resin 3D printers that are particularly good for investment casting. They melt at a low temperature and melt or burn away with very little residue.

Dental applications (discussed in more detail in Chapter 10) are a natural application for investment casting with resin. By definition, every dental appliance is different, so 3D printing is a natural fit. Teeth are 3D scanned, and special software is used to make CAD models of dental appliances, which are 3D printed with resin and then cast in metal. Figure 11-7 shows one dental appliance printed in resin that is intended to be cast in metal.

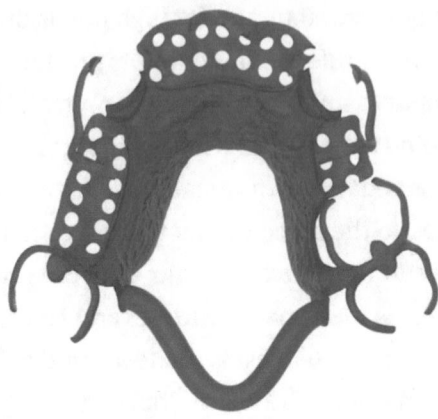

Figure 11-7. *A resin print intended for investment casting to metal (courtesy of SprintRay)*

Figure 11-8 shows the material and how several of these would appear on the print platform just after printing. Dentistry is not the only industry enthusiastically embracing resin printing. Jewelry-making has been an early adopter of resin printing investment casting, too.

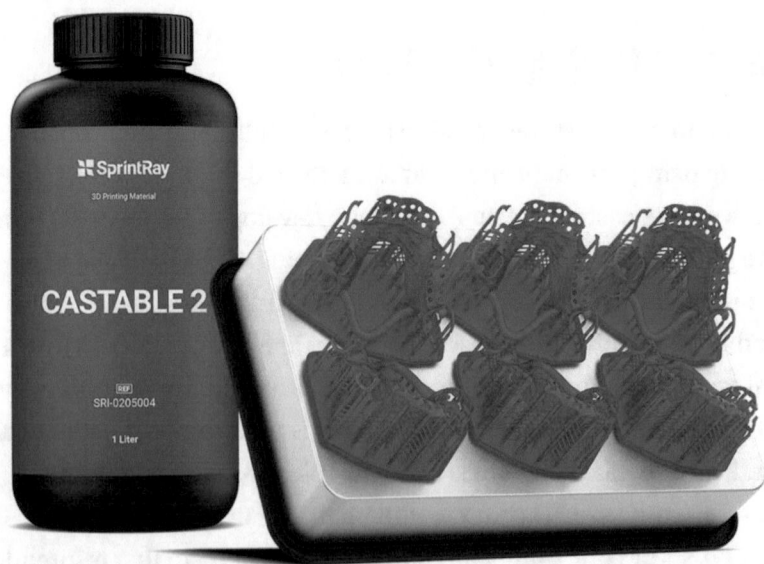

Figure 11-8. *Resin bottle and resin prints as they are on the platform after printing (courtesy of SprintRay)*

Investment Casting with PLA

As it happens, PLA also works for investment casting, although with the lower resolution inherent in filament printing vs. resin printing. Some people in the 3D printing community have referred to using PLA in place of wax in lost-wax as a "lost-PLA" process. You cannot carve PLA easily, but you can definitely print multiple patterns to melt out.

The sculpture in Figure 11-9 was created by Peter Dippell using a "lost-PLA" process starting with a 3D print. The subject was scanned with a 3D scanner (Chapter 3), which created an STL file (Chapters 3 and 7). The STL file was then converted into G-code (Chapter 3) and printed in PLA on a consumer-level printer. After that, it was pretty much the standard lost-wax process described earlier.

Figure 11-9. *An aluminum, investment-cast statue of Rich*

In Figure 11-9 you can still see the 3D printed layer lines. Whether this is a big problem or a charming reminder of where the piece was "born" is in the eye of the beholder. One can look at it as the "brush strokes" of a new medium. Alternatively, the piece could be sanded lightly before casting, or the piece could be polished at this point. However, sanding or polishing risks losing some of the very detail that investment casting seeks to preserve.

Low-Temperature Metals

Some metals and alloys have particularly low melting temperatures, allowing them to be cast in other types of molds. Some room temperature–vulcanizing silicones can handle temperatures high enough to be used as a mold for casting pewter. Silicone is a popular material for mold-making because its flexibility allows it to handle some geometries that would be a problem for sand casting, making it possible to create reusable molds for some shapes that would otherwise require investment casting.

Finding Casting Services

If you want to cast a part in metal, search for "metal casting" or "investment casting" and your city name in your favorite search engine. You can also see whether your local community college or high school has a jewelry design program; if it does, the program likely knows of a small-batch casting service or may offer the service for a fee itself. You can also talk to a shop teacher at your local high school or the people at a makerspace to find an artisan.

Professional foundries may or may not be comfortable using PLA or resin in their investment casting workflow because it is not a medium they have used before. They may have evolved proprietary wax formulations they do not want to change or risk contaminating. They may want to do the intermediary step of taking a mold from the 3D print, making a wax part, and then burning out their wax as usual.

Casting vs. Printing Metal

Casting a part is a well-understood process. Being able to 3D print a part that can then be cast may avoid hand-carving of patterns or repetitive hand operations for investment casting. Casting metal is likely to be cheaper than 3D printing it for some time.

However, not all geometries can be cast easily. For geometries that would traditionally be machined or more recently made by MIM, 3D printing may avoid tooling costs and lead time to give a similar or better result. Relative cost, though, will depend on size of the part, how many of a given part will be produced, part geometry, and materials. There is not one simple formula about when it is more cost-effective to 3D print metal, but there are more and more options to consider.

Summary and Questions for Review

This chapter discussed 3D printing metal, as well as the alternative of 3D printing a mold or pattern to use in variations on traditional metal casting. Metal printing can use something similar to filament-based 3D printing, but then a debinding and sintering step like MIM will be required. Or a binder jetting or direct laser sintered system can be used at more expense, but requiring less work down the road.

Answer the following questions based on your understanding of the chapter:

1. Imagine you want to make five copies of a metal part that would require five-axis machining. How would you decide whether or not to 3D print it, and which metal 3D printing technologies would you consider?

2. The same situation as in question 1, but now with a run of 5000 parts or 50,000.

3. Which 3D printing technologies can be used to 3D print metals that do not weld easily? What metals fit this category?

4. When does DMLS win out over filament-like printing, and vice versa? What criteria would you use to declare a winner for a particular situation?

CHAPTER 12

Prototyping and 3D Visualization

3D printing has long been used for prototyping. Although CAD models are very good, often it is not very clear how well a prototype device works until you have a physical model. Whether a 3D printed model is really needed or just a cool thing to have depends on the circumstances. In Chapter 1, we talked about when to use a 3D printer vs. other technologies (or just cardboard and duct tape). How accurate and how functional your model needs to be should drive your choice of technology.

People often ask why a prototype on a screen is not good enough. For many things, it might be, but it is challenging to imagine how a consumer product will feel in your hand or to explain how different parts of a landscape will fit together. Architects usually build models of their projects so that people can see how the parts fit into each other and into the scenery around it, but now they can use 3D prints instead of foam board. Unless the 3D print requires a lot of post-processing or is large and time-consuming to reprint, it is likely to be easier to change a 3D print than a hand-sculpted model.

© Joan Horvath, Rich Cameron 2020
J. Horvath and R. Cameron, *Mastering 3D Printing*,
https://doi.org/10.1007/978-1-4842-5842-2_12

Prototyping

One thing to consider when creating a prototype is the level of detail required and the budget. If both the fidelity can be low and money is tight, you should probably just use some cardboard and duct tape. If the accuracy needs to be higher than that, a filament-based print is a good next step. Finally, a resin or powder print and some post-processing might to be in order if the model needs to have fine detail and look like the real thing.

Another reason to create a prototype that can be 3D printed is that it makes it easy for remote collaborators to have their own copies. Instead of shipping around fragile and expensive models, everyone can print one locally. A model can be iterated internally on a $200 filament printer using cheap PLA. Once form and fit are settled, a final version can be printed in another material, painted, and so on. Or for that matter, the CAD file can go on to be fabricated using a different technology altogether.

As we discussed in Chapter 10 about short-run manufacturing, many common injection-molding plastics now are available as filaments. It may be possible to 3D print a functional prototype or a small production run using an in-house 3D printer. The one thing to be cautious of though is that the mechanical properties of an injection-molded and 3D printed part will be different. Even though they are of the same plastic, the 3D print will be stronger within than across layers, but the injection-molded one should have the same properties in all directions. Some printing technologies, like resin printing, produce more isotropic parts than filament printing. The increasing variety of 3D printable materials makes it more likely that the feel of a prototype can also be close to the final product.

Science and Math Modeling

3D printing can create a model of something that is inherently 3D, but perhaps not readily available at human scale—a single molecule, for instance. Figure 12-1 shows a 3D model of an ice molecule from our 2016 Apress book, *3D Printed Science Projects*. The model creates one water molecule which you then have to assemble into ice crystals.

Two of us started working on part of an ice crystal model thinking we would combine them into one big one. However, we each made a different structure. We discovered that there were indeed multiple ways of assembling this model that were accurate models of ice. It was much more visceral to discover this by creating a molecule than just reading that ice has several crystalline structures.

Figure 12-1. *Ice crystal model (model from 3D Printed Science Projects)*

A first question to ask is whether the model you are considering creating really is inherently three-dimensional. We have seen people make flat 3D printed versions of diagrams. You can do that, but why? Even for the visually impaired community where that might make sense, there are faster and cheaper solutions for that sort of thing, like swell paper. For example, 3D printing an essentially 2D periodic table without adding any insights does not make a lot of sense, but for some reason it is one of the first things people think of creating. On the other hand, adding another feature to the table for the third dimension might be interesting, like ones on www.thingiverse.com that use the third axis to show how properties of the elements like reactivity and density vary.

If a concept is abstract and naturally three-dimensional, as long as the relationships among the axes are correct and line up with the math, or physics, or what-have-you being described, a model can bring a lot of insight. Figuring out how to create the model is a learning experience, too, as you (or your students) wrestle with how to have the model's geometry show the concept you have in mind.

Tip   As we discussed in Chapter 13, a free program exists to 3D print terrain (although the software noted there is limited to a resolution of a few city blocks). This makes it possible to create very accurate models of watersheds or wetlands for urban planning or public information purposes.

Mathematicians have always created models for their own use and to teach students. However, the ability to have a 3D printer on your desk or in your department can be a game changer. Many mathematical modeling programs will directly export a 3D printable file. The challenge can be the complexity of the print and possibly extracting support from very intricate models.

Medical Visualization

3D prints are increasingly being used for planning surgeries. Full-color models of a patient's anatomy can be created based on CAT scans or other imaging data. At the high end, multicolor resin prints (including clear or translucent parts to show relative position of the skull) can be created for complex surgeries like brain tumor removals.

These models can also be used to train medical school students about what various pathologies look like, based on real patient data. Some practitioners also like to use 3D models to discuss upcoming procedures with patients. Unlike dental 3D prints which are actually part of the procedure and devices like 3D printed metal artificial hips, these models are used purely for information and training purposes. Figures 12-2 and 12-3 are examples of anatomical models.

Figure 12-2. *SLA anatomical model (image courtesy of 3D Systems)*

The model in Figure 12-2 was made with a 3D Systems SLA resin printing process and the one in Figure 12-3 with a 3D Systems full-color powder and binder-jetting process (which they call *CJP*, for ColorJet Printing).

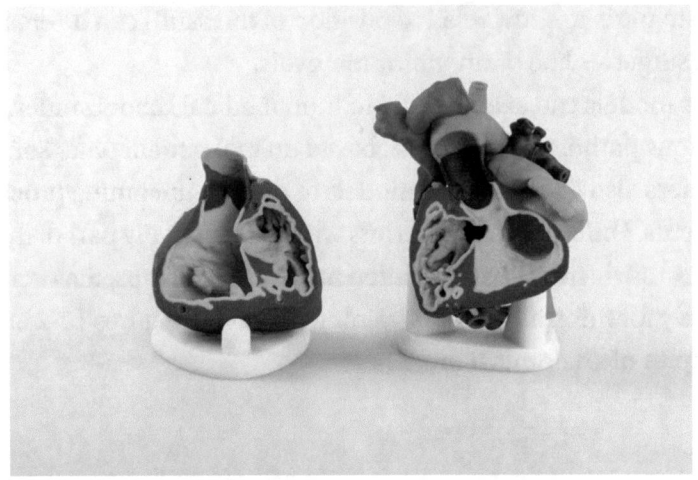

Figure 12-3. *CJP anatomical model (image courtesy of 3D Systems)*

Visualization Best Practices

Making a 3D model is harder than it looks. Most textbooks have more or less the same 2D projection of 3D objects, and you may have to do a surprising amount of research to get the 3D form factor. If you want your model to come apart in a way that reflects the real system, you will find you need to research the physics or chemistry or anatomy in question thoroughly.

There are no hard and fast rules for this. Blind users of our models from our Apress *3D Printed Science Projects* books have taught us that tactile models need to tell a story, and there needs to be an obvious and unambiguous beginning point for exploration of a model. A good test of this quality is to imagine how you might explain the model to someone blind. If they pick up the model and have a written explanation of what the model is, will they know where to start their tactile exploration and what the important features are?

Tip   We have found that thinking about making the models accessible to tactile-only users leads to designs that are good for all users, visually impaired or not. The broader name for this way of thinking is *Universal Design*, if you want to search on the term for more inspiration.

Similarly, there is often a temptation to add a lot of detail to a model to show off your 3D printing skills. However, this can make a model overly complicated and fragile and even can hide some of the simple elegance of many science and math concepts. This is a tactile equivalent of using ten fonts and sound effects on a PowerPoint slide; you can do it, but your message will be lost in the racket such techniques create.

Consider how to make your model as simple as possible rather than trying to have as much information shown as possible. Our blind friends, for example, did not like Braille labels on their models since they are hard to distinguish from physical features. Make sure your model has a point that it is making, and design the minimal form that gets that point across.

When we develop models for publication that we intend others to be able to print, we try to make them easy to print. For example, we avoid support and small features if at all possible. We also assume that many users will have poorly tuned printers and so do not publish models that are a 3D printed tour de force.

Summary and Questions for Review

In this chapter, we discussed the use of 3D prints for visualization, either as a form and fit prototype, or to help students or professionals think about a system in 3D. We also discussed that less can be more when designing a physical model of a concept and that there is a lot to be gained by thinking about what story the model will be telling its users.

Answer the following questions based on your understanding of the material in this chapter:

1. You are creating a model of a museum building's exterior that will be about four inches on a side to use in a fundraising display. Describe what details you would feel are necessary to include and why.

2. Imagine a 3D printed model of a human blood cell. What are a few key features you would include? How would you describe what the model is showing to a blind person? Where would you start and then how would you guide an exploration from there?

3. What are two or three principles to keep in mind when you design a 3D printed prototype that will make the transition to production as seamless as possible?

CHAPTER 13

3D Printers in the Classroom

Most teachers have not dealt with digital fabrication tools (3D printers, CNC machines, laser cutters, etc.) before encountering them in a school makerspace. Marketing videos usually show a time lapse of an object magically appearing on a build platform. The reality, though, is different. A modest print can take hours or even days, depending on the printer, the material, and the geometry of the print.

Resin and powder printers have messiness issues, as discussed in several chapters earlier in this book, and are at any rate out of the price range of many schools. For that reason, we will focus on lower-cost filament printers in this chapter, other than to note that specialized classes (like jewelry-making or advanced biology) might be able to do sophisticated project with a resin printer.

Logistics Issues

For filament-based printers, there are limits to how much faster the technology will get, based on physics. One layer has to cool enough for the next one to be laid down, and fans can only do so much. So these will always be slow. There are (currently exotic) techniques to do resin prints faster, but they are extremely expensive.

© Joan Horvath, Rich Cameron 2020
J. Horvath and R. Cameron, *Mastering 3D Printing*,
https://doi.org/10.1007/978-1-4842-5842-2_13

Time to Print

Most methods of one-at-a-time 3D fabrication are pretty slow, even for a professional practitioner. We talked about laser cutters and CNC machines vs. 3D printers in Chapter 1 and will not repeat those trade-offs here. Consider the time it might take for a person to carve the same shape with hand tools, and perhaps it might not seem slow at all. All this does not help, though, when you have a fifty-minute class period with 30 students and you want to involve all of them in making a 3D print. Here are a few options:

- Have each student make something small, and print them in batches. Because of the cooling-time issue, often several small objects may take the same time to print as one small object.

- Only 3D print what really needs to be 3D printed. If a student is making a sculpture that will stand on a big cube of a base, use something else for the base and only print the sculpture.

- Have 3D printing as part of a group project, and have one 3D printed part per group.

- Ideally, have class projects spread over several weeks or stagger group project stages somehow to spread out demand.

- Teach good design practices that minimize support (Chapter 8).

- Have a review process that bounces prints that will fail or use inordinate resources, with feedback and an opportunity for the student to fix the design problem. This also spreads out the load on the printers if a lot of prints bounce on first submittal, but overall class timelines will need to allow for this.

There are philosophical questions to consider, too. For example, will you allow a student to print something they have downloaded from a database and not changed in any way? Can they include such a file in their projects, or do you want to require that anything they print on a school printer has at least some original work? Or, perhaps, will you only allow them to print things they have designed from scratch? Are there things you will forbid your students to print? If you are new to this, you might check with a peer school who is ahead of you to see what has worked for them.

These issues are compounded somewhat for resin printers, where significant (and messy) post-processing is also required. However, if you are looking at making undergraduate-level experimental devices that require fine detail or that might get hot, you might have to consider resin printers. Most likely you will need to have a staff member run a resin printer.

Print Queue Management

If you have a lot of students creating files to print, managing the optimal use of the printers you have can be challenging. You will need to create a priority system. Even if it just "first come, first served," write it down and post it. Do classroom projects have priority over after-school activities, like the robotics team? Here are some options for managing priorities based on the type of print job:

- Short jobs cut the queue ahead of long ones.

- Small jobs wait until they can be plated together and printed at once.

- Risky experiments might wait until no class projects are due for a few days.

You will also need a way to track which prints are waiting to be printed, have been printed, have been attempted but have had the print fail, or have been rejected without printing for technical reasons. It is best to keep the sliced file until you are sure the print worked; otherwise you might need to waste time slicing it again if something went wrong (like a power outage) that does not require changing anything before printing again.

Finally, you will need to decide what to do about prints that take more than one school day. Will you allow overnight (or over-weekend) printing? If, say, the robotics team meets after school and only has a few hours, can they start a print and have it finish unattended? At any rate, you should get a fair amount of experience before leaving a printer unattended for any length of time.

Many people put a webcam on their printer so they know if something has gone very wrong, so they can sprint over and deal with it. If you have a remote interface like OctoPrint (Chapter 3), you can even stop the print remotely if you see that something has gone wrong. You will still have to remove the print and clean up before you can try again, though.

Curriculum Issues

We are often asked where to find "maker curriculum" materials. We always find the request a little odd, since it seems to us that the right thing to do is to use tools like 3D printing to enhance learning in the typical subjects, rather than treat it like something to be learned per se.

Constructivist learning advocate Seymour Papert famously suggested that student projects needed to have a low floor and a high ceiling, by which he meant that students should be able to at least get a toehold in a concept if they are struggling, but that there should be flexibility for stronger students to explore to the limits of their ability.

Right now, 3D printing's "low floor" is seen as finding and downloading an existing model. This is unfortunately a common model of "using 3D printing in the curriculum." We feel that designing a model—or perhaps altering ones that get you started—is where a lot of the learning takes place.

Except in some specialized cases (like teaching the visually impaired), just downloading a model and printing it probably does not add much value and is more or less a new version of ordering a model from a supply house. (Potentially cheaper, of course.) Free database models can be misleading or represent a concept incorrectly, too.

So the question becomes: can students use Tinkercad, say, to have just a bit higher floor to visualize something they have just learned about, or to express themselves creatively? But, more importantly, how does doing this serve having them learn what they are trying to learn?

What "Design Thinking" Means

Joan is trained as an aeronautical engineer, and she worked for 16 years as a rocket scientist. In that role, she participated in many design meetings. Rich designed one of the earliest ancestors of today's consumer 3D printers, as well as a modern consumer device. If you are teaching "design thinking" in a middle-school context, you may be confronted with many charts of the process that are wonders of color and complexity. Some we have seen would have given people planning missions to Venus pause, or made them roll their eyes.

Design is something we all do every day, and it does not have to be, well, rocket science. A generic design process goes something like this.

First, figure out what you want to do, or what problem you are trying to solve (without stating, yet, how you want to do it). Engineers call this "Specifying requirements and not implementation," which means "Tell me what you need my design to do, and stop telling me how to do it." Once these requirements are defined, think about what makes a design "the best" for this purpose and what "success" is and how to measure it. (Who decides what is "best"?)

Next, come up with some ways to do what needs to be done. Pick the one that seems "best" and try it. If it worked, by your definition of success, you are good. If not, roll back as far as you have to and try again.

Making the process itself something to learn, with terminology and vocabulary and many steps and arrows, seems to us to defeat the purpose of encouraging students to explore and prototype, not to mention intimidating teachers. Keep it simple and commonsense; we like to use cooking as an analogous process. Clear metrics of success can help with figuring out how to grade a project, too.

One reason that 3D printing and its sister digital fabrication technologies are challenging is that they require fluency in both digital design and the realities of what will happen when that design is created (or not) with an imperfect machine using real-world materials. The latter takes some amount of experience and willingness to live with failures along the way. Being able to live comfortably in both these worlds—to be able to design something that will actually work—will always be an in-demand skill, and a key preparation for many STEM careers. But it requires an orderly approach and some discipline to get things to work.

The maker movement has resulted in the democratization of CAD tools, discussed in depth in Chapter 7. Tinkercad (`www.tinkercad.com`) and Morphi (`www.morphiapp.com`) are common choices for the younger set. Tinkercad has the virtue and problem that it is entirely web based, but it is free and always adding new features. Morphi is a downloadable app, available at a modest price per student.

Younger students, though, tend to make unprintable designs in Tinkercad. Often, they will have pieces of "one part" hovering over one another or poking below the level of the platform. A discussion of basic design constraints, at an age-appropriate level, can help. (Have a large, flat base, avoid overhangs, be sure features are not too small, and so on;

see Chapter 8.) We have found that pictures of "the right way" to design something for 3D printing (or any fabrication technology), along with what happens when things are created "the wrong way," are valuable to learners of all ages.

Tinkercad used to operate purely by dragging, dropping, and adding and subtracting prefabricated shapes, but it has now added a "Scribble" function. This allows you to do a limited amount of freehand drawing, such as Joan's name on the side of the roof in Figure 13-1, and add these freehand parts to other shapes. We describe Tinkercad in more detail in Chapter 7.

Even if young students do not have access to a 3D printer, learning CAD programs early will give them a head start later on if they do have access to digital fabrication tools when they are older.

Figure 13-1. *Tinkercad Scribble function*

Tip   For examples of successful projects, consider reading blogs with real stories of life in educational making. You might enjoy Lucie deLaBruere's "Create, Make, Learn" blog at `http://createmakelearn.blogspot.com`. Lucie often collaborates with Rodney Batschelet, whose work you can read about and see in Chapter 6 (we appreciate their suggestions). John Umekubo's eponymous website, `https://johnumekubo.com`, is another elementary-focused source of maker-educator news and practical ideas.

Art and Theater

We have found that art and technical theater departments are often early adopters of 3D printing. Frequently they have learned CAD in other contexts, so it is not such a big learning curve as it might be for other faculty. 3D printing is used broadly in *cosplay* (a combination of costuming and role-playing). Art pieces can be 3D printed and then either painted or otherwise post-processed, as described in Chapter 6.

For theater, props and parts of costumes are commonly 3D printed. Printing on fabric (Chapter 9) is an option, too. Figure 13-2 shows a 3D printed Samurai and Knight designed and created by the team at CoKreeate (`www.cokreeate.com`) as demonstration pieces.

Figure 13-2. *The CoKreeate 3D printed Samurai and Knight*

Math and Science

Science, technology, engineering, and math (STEM) classes are usually what people think of first as applications for 3D printing. Interestingly though once students get past middle school, there is often reluctance to use 3D printing in the classroom because it is perceived as a distraction that takes away from time needed to cover material. We think this is misguided, though, because changing and creating a model is a very natural way to learn many science concepts intuitively.

We have developed many models in the OpenSCAD programming language (Chapter 7), which allows creation of *parametric* models. These models can be altered by changing parameters (like the dimension or type of a wing.) A well-designed model will have parameters that allow a user to change the model based on the math or science involved, rather than just scaling it up or down.

Tip   We have written two books of 3D-printable science projects: *3D Printed Science Projects* (Apress, 2016) and *3D Printed Science Projects Volume 2* (Apress, 2017). Both would be suitable for high school students; the first volume has more options that could be used with students younger than that.

We have been using a parametric wing model from our 2016 book to teach about aerodynamics. The model creates wings that are based on NACA airfoils. NACA (the National Advisory Committee for Aeronautics, a predecessor to NASA) standardized airfoils in about 1935. Airfoils are the cross section of a wing, which is a major determinant of how much lift a wing can generate. Students can create a wing using different airfoils and other features of an airplane wing like how much it is swept back and how much it tapers.

This model is printed on a support (called a sting). We put the wing on a postal scale and zero out the scale. Then when we blow a fan on the model, it will register a change in weight, which is equal to the lift of the airplane. Figure 13-3 shows one of the models and Figure 13-4 the setup. Students can change how much the wing is tilted (known as "angle of attack") and see how the lift changes when this parameter is changed, and when the wing might stall out and lose lift.

Figure 13-3. *NACA wings*

Figure 13-4. *The wing's lift being determined*

3D prints can be used to create lab equipment, or used in conjunction with open source electronics to make field equipment. Student projects can be build using an Arduino or other low-cost processor to collect data and return it via a Wi-Fi or other module. 3D printed cases and mounts can make these experiments more robust, particularly outdoors.

Finally, as discussed in Chapter 12, 3D prints are also effective to visualize abstract concepts, whether in math or science. Creating a 3D model is often invaluable in user interface design and engineering visualization in general.

Robotics

The international organization FIRST Robotics (For Inspiration and Recognition of Science and Technology, www.firstinspires.org) is making robotics a school sport, like basketball, with several leagues aimed at different age brackets. At the high school level, teams build robots that might weigh as much as 150 pounds. Many of them use 3D printing for a few components. Common applications are camera mounts and protective (and/or decorative) mounts or cases for small electronics.

Learning Differently

What about using 3D prints for other students who need to learn differently? For students who learn best by assembling or making things, a 3D printed model can be a game changer. The two of us, for example, learn and think very differently, and we have found that the process of creating models and talking about how to use them makes us both learn a lot more than we might otherwise. Joan learns reasonably well by reading books or going to traditional lectures, but Rich does much better if he can create a 3D model and manipulate it, even if only on a screen.

We have also been working with teachers of the visually impaired to understand how to create models that are effective teaching tools for their students. We report on this effort in more depth in our 2018 Apress book, *Mastering 3D Printing in the Classroom, Library, and Lab.* Briefly, our key lessons learned are that one should make a model's orientation clear and have some natural "narrative start" point that allows you to describe how to use the model. Generally speaking, you will want to avoid 3D printing Braille labels, since it can be hard to distinguish between Braille and features of the model. Tactile maps are a common use of 3D printing.

With some creativity, blind users can do their own 3D printing, particularly from the few CAD programs that describe models as code rather than only through 3D renderings. At least a teacher or parent might be able to create a tactile model of a key concept for the visually impaired student. There are several efforts ongoing to create indexes of models useful to visually impaired students. You can check out a Google group `https://groups.google.com/forum/#!forum/3dp_edu_models` which we manage to share ideas.

Creating Terrain: Geography and History

Creating 3D terrain is a powerful application of 3D printing for geography, history, and other applications. At some level, you can accomplish the same insight from a topographical map, but we have found that having an actual 3D model of a mountain range or varied terrain like the Los Angeles basin makes it much easier to see large-scale geology and also to imagine the sweep of historical events taking place on the landscape.

A wonderful free program that lets you print anyplace on Earth is Thatcher Chamberlain's Terrain2STL, at `http://jthatch.com/Terrain2STL/`. An equivalent program for the moon can be found at `http://jthatch.com/Moon2STL/`. The program creates an STL file of an arbitrary-sized area and allows you to exaggerate the vertical.

Vertical exaggeration is useful not only to accentuate terrain features, but also because the print's layering is less obvious on the steeper surfaces that it creates, and subtler features may be lost entirely if they are less than one layer high.

With little or no vertical exaggeration, you will likely find that the print quality is better if you rotate the models to print on its edge. Oriented this way, only the most extreme terrain features will produce unprintable overhangs, and the printer will be able to reproduce much finer variations in elevation.

Figure 13-5 is a print of the area around Pasadena, California, with a vertical exaggeration of around ten times, making the San Gabriel Mountains and their floodplain clearly visible. If you want more vertical exaggeration than the program offers, you can always do more in your printer's slicing software, which usually will let you scale in just one axis.

Figure 13-5. *Pasadena terrain model created by Terrain2STL, high vertical exaggeration, printed flat (as shown)*

Figure 13-6 shows the area around Mt. Whitney in California with no vertical exaggeration (the valley floor is at about 4000 feet, and the mountain peak is 14,000). The Mt. Whitney print was printed vertically (i.e., with one side of the print on the platform).

Figure 13-6. *Mt. Whitney area, no vertical exaggeration, printed vertically*

Terrain model files can get too large for slicing programs to handle easily, and it may be necessary to clean them up a little. Doing so might lose some fine detail, but it makes them easier to use in other programs later.

Tip   To fix problems with STL files (called *meshes* in other software), we often use the open source, free program MeshLab. MeshLab is not the friendliest program on earth, but it does work well. You can download it from `www.meshlab.net`. If a model just looks funny in your slicing software, open it in MeshLab, accept any suggestions the program makes, and export it to try again in your slicing software. We describe how to use MeshLab in Chapter 3, "Mesh Repair Programs."

If you want to model a large area, you can carefully make adjacent sections in Terrain2STL and print them out in pieces. There are also software tools that will let you cut an STL into parts, including Autodesk Meshmixer (`www.meshmixer.com`).

Teaching Coding

Teaching CAD can be part of teaching coding. Tinkercad has recently added CodeBlocks, which are based on Scratch blocks. This feature, in beta as of this writing, is a way to tie in coding and design.

At a more sophisticated level, OpenSCAD (also discussed in Chapter 7) enables you to develop models based on code rather than drag-and-drop objects. It may not be appropriate for the average elementary student, however; it is a C-like language (a family of languages that also includes Java and Python) and requires being able to handle coding at that level.

Examples of Student Projects

Many have fond memories (or not) of making a shoebox diorama at some point. It is not big step to imagine making 3D printed pieces to include in a traditional diorama that is otherwise made with craft materials. If part of the point of an assignment is to have students learn some digital manufacturing techniques across the curriculum, one option is always to require that some part of a traditional diorama-type assignment be constructed that way.

A discussion of Tinkercad or a similar program and design rules for 3D printing (Chapters 7 and 8) is probably enough to get students started for something like this. In our experience, most schools and libraries have a staff person slice and print the file, although some high schools have programs that train self-selecting students to own that process.

3D Vermont

3D Vermont competition (http://3dvermont.org) asks students to create a model of a building of historical interest with supporting information and then gather together to present their model and discuss its importance. They to place it in the appropriate spot on a giant model of the state of Vermont. Rules are written up on the site, and prizes are involved.

If you want to see some examples of the competition, look on Twitter (twitter.com) for posts with the hashtag #3dVermont. Clearly this works best in a region (like Vermont) where it is plausible for students to travel to get together and compete, but one could imagine more local variations.

As an aside, if you are thinking about starting a modest competition of your own, we would suggest standardizing on Tinkercad rather than SketchUp (which 3D Vermont uses). SketchUp is intended as an architectural tool and so makes sense from that perspective, but it is notorious for making models that have printing issues because it was not primarily designed for the purpose.

Relitigating Historic Battles

The Battle of Agincourt in 1415 was a key turning point in the Hundred Years' War between France and England. England won this battle on French soil against a vastly numerically superior French force. There were several reasons for this. The English army was much reduced by disease and fighting its way across France, but it still had many archers armed with the longbow, which was a fast-loading weapon that could send out a volley of arrows. The French, on the other hand, saw archery as a lesser fighting technique compared to armored knights.

It had rained the night before, and the armies met on a muddy field where the French knights bogged down. The longbowmen were able to pick off the trapped knights. There were some complex rules of engagement at the time that also favored the English. The battle has been remembered in songs, poems, and Shakespeare's play Henry V. The play in turn was the basis for a classic movie starring Sir Laurence Olivier, meant as wartime propaganda to cheer on the British during World War II. (There is a good Wikipedia article on the subject if you search on "Battle of Agincourt.")

We decided we would try a pilot with three students attending classes at the Academy program at Pasadena's Institute for Educational Advancement (`www.educationaladvancement.org`) to relitigate the battle. First, they studied medieval defensive technology and fortifications. They then used this knowledge as the basis of castle designs in Tinkercad (Figure 13-7). The real battle had no castles, but we used them as markers for army home encampments and to focus learning on defensive strategies.

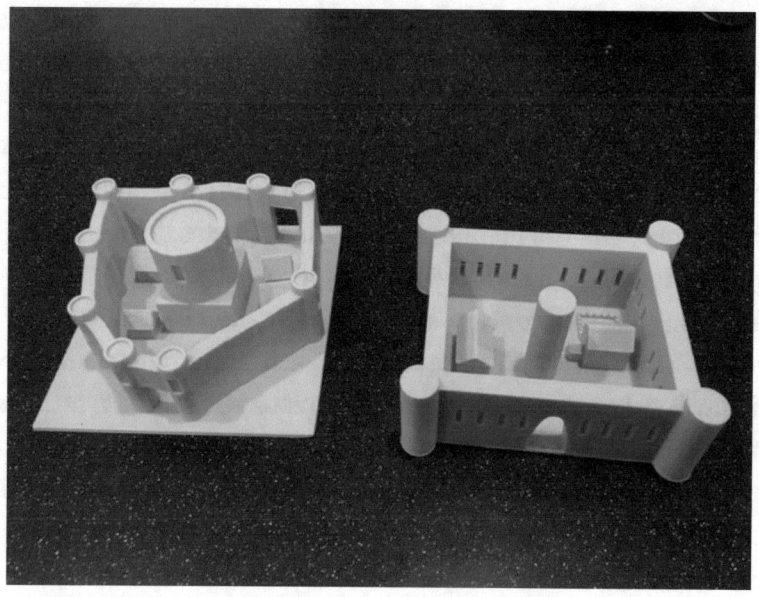

Figure 13-7. *Castles by students Baxter and Ellis at IEA*

Next, we gave them the task of studying the technology at the time and coming up with a "secret weapon" on both sides. The requirement was that it had to be plausibly inventable with the technology of the time. (We had them look at Leonardo da Vinci's work, 100 years later, for inspiration.) They fabricated a model of it using 3D printing and craft supplies. This caused the students to enthusiastically research what was available at the time, and the military history of the rest of the fifteenth century to look for ideas.

Then, we laid out a "battlefield" and created a role-playing simulation where we estimated how much damage each weapon would cause to the other side, rolling dice to see how much damage was done. We used slips of paper for troops (keeping track of how many were left after each round) and a mix of dominoes and LEGOs to designate battleground features other than the "secret weapons." One student was Henry V, and another the French Constable Charles d'Albret, acting for King Charles the Mad of France. A third student was the Duke of York, in charge of the English longbowmen.

We ran the simulation twice (ninety minutes each time). The first time through students just had the historical weapons (not their "secret weapons"), and not surprisingly the result was the same as the historical one, except that the French surrendered when class was over and it was clear they were going to go down. The second time the simulated battle ended in a draw, and the French allowed the English safe passage go home to England. Figures 13-8 and 13-9 show aspects of the battle.

We ran this simulation with just three students, but it could scale up pretty easily. The trick was to make sure that each "turn" did not take too long to work through, because it became a little tedious otherwise. If you have a student who likes to run tabletop role-playing or strategy games like Dungeons and Dragons or Warhammer 40K, they will be a natural ally in setting this up.

Role-playing more generally lends itself to creating 3D printed miniatures and symbolic game pieces, not to mention various-sided dice. Side lessons in probability, strategy, and many other topics are possible.

Figure 13-8. *King Henry V plans his attack*

Figure 13-9. *Rich with the students in the thick of "battle"*

Tip   Creating a castle is one of our standard exercises to teach Tinkercad or OpenSCAD. It is a very good "high ceiling, low floor" since a plausible castle can be just a few cylinders and blocks or can be an elaborate work of art. Rich likes to use crenellations as an exercise in OpenSCAD to teach about loops.

Elementary Students

Most 3D printers are designed primarily for the adult market, or at least are recommended for age 13 and over. Generally speaking, this feels about right to us. Most schools designate a staff person, a teacher, or (if they have one) a makerspace manager to deal with the equipment. In some cases, this falls to the school librarian. If the school is K-12, though, older students may be able to undergo some extra training and earn a defined role in a makerspace—perhaps managing the queue of jobs to 3D printers, doing quality control on CAD files, or slicing the files.

Another thing to consider is whether 3D prints can be part of a larger fabrication project. Maybe a project is mostly cardboard, but a decorative or functional part is made with a 3D printer. Having students think about what tool to use for what job is a key part of the real-life design process, but too often we see teachers trying to find a reason to use a 3D printer and constructing an artificial project. It is better, if possible, to let an organic design need create a use case for a 3D printer (or any tool).

The right project prompt is important, too. It should be neither too specific nor so broad that students do not know where to start. This is a natural way to fit design into other subjects (e.g., illustrating part of a story, or solving a problem a character encounters in a story).

Note   We go into the topics in this chapter in far more depth in our 2018 book *Mastering 3D Printing in the Classroom Library and Lab*, also from Apress.

Summary and Questions for Review

In this chapter, we discussed issues that arise in working with 3D printing in a school setting, starting with printing policies and workflows. Printer time needs to be managed, and makerspace managers need to decide whether or not students need to develop their own designs vs. just printing something that already exists. We then gave some ideas for applying 3D printing in service of various academic disciplines, ending with specific projects.

Answer the following questions based on your understanding of the material in the chapter:

1. What type of printer (filament, resin, or powder) makes the most sense for a middle school? Why?

2. How might you handle the print queue for a class of 30 students?

3. Give an example of how 3D printing might be used to support teaching history.

4. Give an example of how 3D printing might support students creating instruments to study their local environment.

5. Describe a simple design process using a concrete example.

CHAPTER 14

The Future

In the first edition of this book, published in 2014, we also had a chapter about future trends. Six years later, a lot of the predictions have come true, some remain in "the future," and new frontiers have developed. In this final chapter, we will give you some insights into how the field has evolved in recent years and our best guesses about what near-term priorities will be.

User Experience

In 2014, low-cost 3D printers were still very much a hobbyist product. For the most part, people built their own printers out of kits. These early adopters were tolerant of printers that were finicky and that required fiddling to get to work. At the same time, there was a lot of hype about how every home would have a 3D printer, drawing analogies with the personal computer revolution.

This expansiveness created an expectation in many buyers' minds that one would be able to buy a printer, turn it on, and have 3D objects come out. This has not really come to pass, although it is closer to the truth for industrial-level printers with five figure price tags than it is for low-cost printers. In 2015 or so, the entrance of extremely low-cost producers from Asia into the market also led to many people who really did not have an immediate use for a printer buying one. Many of these users also expected something that would "just print" and were disillusioned, particularly since many of these ultra-low-cost printers had sketchy, if any, tech

© Joan Horvath, Rich Cameron 2020
J. Horvath and R. Cameron, *Mastering 3D Printing*,
https://doi.org/10.1007/978-1-4842-5842-2_14

support. The fallout of all these factors, as far as the market is concerned, was that many 3D printer companies went out of business or were acquired by bigger players.

With all that said, printer interface design and robustness should continue to improve. Many printers have features like LCD screens or Wi-Fi onboard to allow use without a computer connected. Software improvements have continued to make the printing process more reliable. Some machines—particularly the larger ones capable of very long-running prints—have begun to be equipped with features like filament-out detectors and the ability to save their state in the case of a power failure, so that prints can be resumed later.

Materials

As we have noted many places in this book, advances in 3D printing are tightly tied to advances in 3D printable materials. One of the most striking trends in the last five years has been the vast increase in the number and type of 3D printable materials. As we noted in Chapters 2 and 4, the choice of a printer now is largely driven by what materials you want to print. We expect that more industrial plastics will become available in 3D printable form to make the transition from prototype to finished part more seamless.

Printing Food

One area that has been a little slower to catch on is 3D printing food. The long print times, and the fact that extruding food at high volume is pretty evolved already, makes it attractive mostly for niche applications. Dessert printing (e.g., printing in chocolate) is one application that remains, with several competitors in the space. One challenge is that all parts of the machine that touch the food have to be food-safe.

Since most of these materials cannot be made into a food-safe filament, these printers typically use materials delivered in the form of a paste or gel. Chocolate printers have to carefully manage the precise temperature profile of the raw material too, so that it hardens in a way that is strong and looks good. Commercially available printers exist for chocolate and marzipan, butter, and similar extrudable foods. For example, Procusini (Figure 14-1) has been around for a while with a printer that uses packaged extrudable materials, aimed at food professionals (`www.procusini.com`). The Procusini printer can be used to create chocolate prints that are complex 3D structures (Figure 14-1) or to enhance other more fanciful desserts (Figure 14-2).

Figure 14-1. *Chocolate shapes made by Procusini (courtesy of Procusini)*

A consumer-oriented version designed just to print in chocolate, the Mycusini (`www.mycusini.com`), has an associated template library and tools to generate text or line drawings (Figure 14-3). This is intended to allow a user who wants to avoid learning to use 3D CAD to still be able to make interesting things in chocolate.

Figure 14-2. *Fanciful desserts with chocolate part printed by Procusini (courtesy of Procusini)*

Figure 14-3. *The Mycusini printer line (courtesy of Mycusini)*

Extruding food is not new, of course, even at home; pasta machines have been around for a long time. What is new is the ability to make complex shapes for decorative purposes. We expect that that commercial food-printing machines, particularly for the home market, will experiment with the user experience. As with all 3D printing, there are challenging trade-offs between letting the user do anything they want to do and making the learning curve as shallow as possible.

Printing Medications

There is interest in the medical community in 3D printing pills to have precise, customized medications. The intent is not to print these at home, but rather for the manufacturer to be able to create exactly the dose a patient needs. Epilepsy treatment Spritam (`www.spritam.com`) from Aprecia Pharmaceuticals is the first 3D printed drug approved by the US Food and Drug Administration (FDA). They 3D print pills of the dose needed by a patient in a way that will dissolve very quickly when the patient takes it. Several other startups exist to try to create personalized medications, and this area is likely to see growth in the coming years.

Since these are likely to be industrial processes at scale, there may also be innovations in how to get medications into 3D printable forms and then to produce and distribute them accurately. Or, of course, this might be a modern reemergence of the neighborhood compounding pharmacy, but with a printer instead of a mortar and pestle. The regulatory environment around all this will need to emerge as well.

Bioprinting: Printing Living Tissue

Another medical application of 3D printing is printing living tissue. For this purpose, a printer typically has two nozzles. One lays down a biocompatible matrix, like a hydrogel alginate. The other nozzle is used to lay down a mix of living cells and other materials (sometimes called *bioink*) in such a way that the cells stay alive and vital through the printing process and beyond.

Some companies are aiming at creating tissues that will be used to test tissue responses to drugs or other stresses. Others are hoping to replace human tissues altogether. In that case, the tissue is implanted in the patient and then the matrix will dissolve. One of the big challenges with this is vascularization–finding ways to help blood vessels to grow to nourish the new tissue.

Speed of printing is an issue too; if it takes too long and the temperatures or chemical environment get out of the range where the cells are happy, there are problems. There are many research groups and companies exploring different avenues in this space. Like all medical research, the path to real clinical trials is always long and arduous.

Architecture and Printing Concrete

Architects use 3D printers in several ways. First, they can use them to visualize buildings and environments, using whatever 3D printing technology is most appropriate. However, there are now several groups exploring using 3D printing to create structures directly by 3D printing concrete. Like a food printer, concrete printers use a thick slurry that is either printed in place (to create a house) or printed elsewhere and shipped in completed form. The result looks like a scaled-up filament 3D print, with visible layer lines.

Here too, materials are critical. The concrete needs to be stiff enough to hold its shape after extrusion without a form, and needs to harden quickly enough to support the weight of subsequent layers. The key advantage of the technique is that one can create complex concrete shapes without needing to build forms. Most concrete printers are some sort of large gantry that is assembled on-site. Other fixtures, like rebar or plumbing, need to be inserted somehow during creation or added after the fact. ICON (`www.iconbuild.com`) has developed a printer it calls the Vulcan II, and as of this writing, it says on its site that it has built a small community in Mexico. The company feels that it can build shelter at lower cost than competing techniques.

There are other innovative options, too. A multi-university European project called 3DPARE is creating artificial reefs to deploy in the Atlantic. Reefs are particularly vulnerable to climate change. The project is exploring material choices to make the artificial reef components as low-impact and bio-receptive as possible. The project is piloting printing parts of the reef in concrete and then shipping them out to test in the ocean. You can read more at `www.giteco.unican.es/proyectos/3dpare`. We expect to see many more applications of 3D printing in construction as more and more materials become available and the industry gets more experience with it.

Test and Validation

Because many 3D printing techniques generally cannot create a model that has the same material properties in all directions (an *isotropic* part), it can be very challenging to create a trustworthy computer model of the strength of 3D printed parts. Normally 3D prints created from filament will be stronger within a layer than across layers, because the bond between layers is not as strong as the material strength within a layer. The extruder temperature and inconsistencies in filament properties from batch to batch, among different colors of the notionally same filament make it challenging to predict the properties of the final part.

Resin prints are dependent on post-curing for some of their material properties. If a print is somewhat under- or overcured, it may not have the desired properties. A large solid print might not be fully cured in the middle or have some uncured pockets. Similarly, prints made with a binder that is removed somehow afterward need careful design to be sure that the material distribution is adequately consistent for the part's ultimate purpose.

Modeling and Simulation

If you are making a part conventionally out of a common metal, you can create a simulated model of the expected forces on the part and see if you are going to have problems. As of this writing, that is not the case for 3D prints, since these programs assume an isotropic part. The programs also will want to know bulk properties of the material, which requires more assumptions.

Joshua Pearce's group at Michigan Tech University has been doing testing of 3D printed parts to establish a baseline of mechanical properties of various 3D printed materials. If you search on their group, you will find publications reporting on tests they have performed on how mechanical properties of 3D prints vary. Their site at www.appropedia.org/Pearce_ publications_in_materials_science_and_engineering is a good place to start. A part is only as strong as its weakest point though, and small variations in the filament or printing process can produce variations that are difficult to predict or detect.

Some 3D printer manufacturers and vendors are also starting to characterize their materials more thoroughly. Of course, there will always be a trade-off between low cost and reliable, predictable materials. It is likely that the market will split into cheap filament and high-cost validated properties filament over time.

Generative Design

A new type of design software is emerging that "grows" a design based on the loading and environment the part being designed will encounter in its service life. These programs lay down (computer-generated) material only where it is needed to support a load. This could potentially be very interesting for 3D printed parts, since a part could be aligned with differential strength in mind. There are some early-stage programs out there, but this is likely to be a growth area if users can become comfortable that the models are creating designs that really will stand up to the predicted environment.

Autodesk is, as of early 2020, including generative design capability in the high-end version of its Fusion 360 software. They discuss using it to create complex structures such as lightweight, latticework parts, and structures with tiny holes to mimic bone. For more, see `www.autodesk.com/solutions/generative-design`.

Standards

One of the challenges in using 3D printed parts is that filament's mechanical properties can vary widely, even with the colors of a manufacturer's PLA, for instance. For filament-printed parts especially, the part geometry and the relative direction of forces to layer lines matter a lot. Resin print properties can depend both on the resin's formulation and on how well the curing process followed specifications. Parts may shrink or warp during post-processing too.

Various groups have been wrestling with testing common 3D printing materials for qualities like strength and chemical interactions, but it is challenging. Some groups working in this space include the American National Standards Institute (ANSI) and various collaborators (`www.ansi.org/standards_activities/standards_boards_panels/amsc/`) and ASTM (`www.astm.org/Standards/additive-manufacturing-technology-standards.html`). There is a lot of work to do here, and thorough characterizations of materials and geometries will be a research effort for some time to come.

Manufacturing Without Molds and Forms

Creating up to about 100 units of an object, or over 100,000, has established manufacturing paths. Making between a few hundred and many tens of thousands of units used to be awkward. Higher-run production techniques, like injection molding or other techniques that required molds, tooling, or other forms, were not cost-effective below many tens of thousands of parts, unless the parts themselves are pricey. This is because these techniques have a large initial cost to develop molds and other tooling, and a very low per-part cost after that. However, 3D printing is changing that calculation on several fronts.

It is often seen as a disadvantage that the cost of 3D printing one part stays more or less the same regardless of the print run size. However, this cuts both ways, and since there is no part-specific investment ahead of time other than a CAD file, runs of 1000 or so parts are perfectly economically feasible, if the printing infrastructure is reasonably cost-effective. CAD files can also be created and updated much faster than molds, and the increased agility of this manufacturing technique may offset the difference in cost.

A side effect of plummeting prices of consumer and prosumer grade 3D printers is that it now is pretty cheap to create a *print farm*, a gang of printers that might all be printing the same part in parallel or different ones. Some 3D printer manufacturers, like Prusa Research, use their own printers this way to manufacture their own parts. The capital outlay can be surprisingly low, and if business picks up, it is pretty easy to scale up proportionately by adding more racks of printers. Many *service bureaus* (companies that 3D print for other people) traditionally positioned themselves as makers of very small numbers of parts, but this may start to change.

Manufacturer Slant 3D (www.slant3d.com) has positioned itself in higher-volume printing of parts that might otherwise have been injection-molded. Figures 14-4 and 14-5 show sample print runs from their factory.

Figure 14-4. *3D printed brackets (courtesy of Slant 3D)*

Figure 14-5. *3D printed parts (courtesy of Slant 3D)*

One of the problems that arises doing printing for others is that customers inexperienced with 3D printing can pretty easily create parts that will not print or otherwise will not work out well. To mitigate that, Slant 3D also sells printers that they use as modules in their factory, the Mason (Figure 14-6) so that a customer can get a part exactly how they want it and then send off their big order to be printed remotely with more peace of mind.

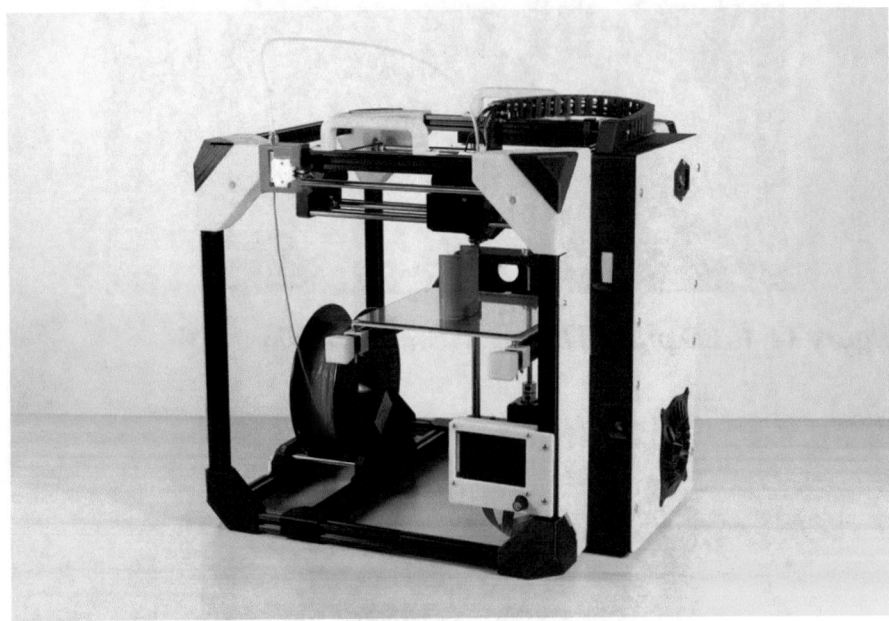

Figure 14-6. *The Mason printer (courtesy of Slant 3D)*

As we mentioned in Chapter 11, metal 3D printing based on metal injection molding (MIM) is in a similar way allowing creation of some metal parts that might have been created with MIM to be made on lower-cost printers instead. Similarly, concrete structures without the need for forms may change the price point in that industry as well. We expect that more and more fabrication will move to some sort of additive manufacturing as the materials to make it possible come on line. Creating gangs of low-cost, reliable printers is no longer challenging, but many advances in materials are still to come.

Printing is still pretty slow. Some filament printers are designed for very high linear motion speeds, but that only goes so far. Printing with larger nozzles, and specially designed extruders that can heat more material faster, makes it possible to print large objects in a reasonable amount of time (at the cost of some loss of detail).

Resin printing provides more opportunities for speed improvements. Some resin printers have managed to speed up the printing process significantly by skipping the peel step between layers, allowing continuous build rates on the order of one minute per centimeter of model height. Some experimental resin printers are even taking cues from CT scanning technology to illuminate and cure the entire volume of a resin print at once, leading to print times of a few seconds. Here too, materials innovation will probably define what capability is possible.

3D Printing in Remote Environments

3D printing is a natural fit for remote environments, where it might not be practical to have all the spare parts one might want and it can be very valuable to be able to print anything on demand. Storing CAD files is a lot easier than storing a warehouse full of parts that might never be needed.

Issues to consider are transporting and storing materials (filament may have natural advantages here), stability and availability of electrical power (for remote or high-poverty areas on Earth), and of course the knowledge required to design and print parts reliably. It is not a stretch to imagine an astronaut can handle a 3D printer, but a technician at a remote research or medical station might need some support.

The idea of 3D printing habitats on the moon and Mars has been the subject of explorations and contests of late, and we expect that this will continue and grow as interest in living and working off-Earth moves closer to reality. We hope that there are spin-offs, too, to help house those on Earth more affordably, particularly after natural disasters and other displacements.

Summary and Questions for Review

In this chapter, we surveyed the current boundaries of 3D printer technology and applications and speculated about the future. In particular, we reviewed how user interfaces have evolved and are likely to continue to do so, and the increasing trend for improvements to be enabled by materials innovation. Finally, we looked at how racks of 3D printers can be harnessed to create product in moderate quantities.

Answer the following questions based on your interpretation of the chapter:

1. If you needed to manufacture 2000 plastic pieces, how would you go about it? What factors would you consider in selecting a technology?

2. How would the answer to the first question change if the items were similar, but not quite identical?

3. Why is generative design a good fit for developing 3D printable parts?

4. Why is it a good idea to 3D print structures on the moon or Mars rather than build them conventionally?

5. Give some examples of the challenges in definitively testing the strength of a 3D printed part.

APPENDIX

Links

About the Authors

Nonscriptum LLC: www.nonscriptum.com

Chapter 1

RepRap project on Wikipedia: http://en.wikipedia.org/wiki/RepRap_Project
Prusa Research: www.prusa3d.com
Kickstarter: www.kickstarter.com

Chapter 2

BuildTak: www.buildtak.com
Markforged: www.markforged.com
Formlabs: www.formlabs.com
PancakeBot: www.pancakebot.com
Organovo: www.organovo.com

Chapter 3

3MF file format: https://3mf.io/what-is-3mf/
MeshLab: www.meshlab.net
Thingiverse: www.thingiverse.com

© Joan Horvath, Rich Cameron 2020
J. Horvath and R. Cameron, *Mastering 3D Printing*,
https://doi.org/10.1007/978-1-4842-5842-2

YouMagine: www.youmagine.com
Instructables: www.instructables.com
Pinshape: www.pinshape.com
GitHub: www.github.org
Yeggi: www.yeggi.com
Creative Commons: www.creativecommons.org
The RepRap project: www.reprap.org
Slic3r: www.slic3r.org
MatterControl: www.mattercontrol.com
Ultimaker Cura: https://software.ultimaker.com
Linkedin Learning: https://linkedin.com/learning/
RepRap G-code reference: http://reprap.org/wiki/G-code
OctoPrint: www.octoprint.org

Chapter 4

3D Hubs: www.3dhubs.com
MakeXYZ: www.makexyz.com

Chapter 5

Tinkercad: www.tinkercad.com
Blick Art Materials: www.dickblick.com

Chapter 6

No links

Chapter 7

Protein Data Bank (PDB): www.rcsb.org/pdb/
Chimera: www.cgl.ucsf.edu/chimera/

Visual Molecular Dynamics (VMD): www.ks.uiuc.edu/Research/vmd/

National Institutes of Health (NIH) repository of medicine-related models: https://3dprint.nih.gov

Smithsonian downloadable collection: https://3d.si.edu

OpenSCAD: www.openscad.org

Tinkercad circuits: www.tinkercad.com/circuits

Morphi: www.morphiapp.com

Inkscape: https://inkscape.org

Onshape: www.onshape.com

Fusion 360: www.autodesk.com/products/fusion-360

SolidWorks: www.solidworks.com

SketchUp: www.sketchup.com

Mathematica: www.wolfram.com/mathematica/

ZBrush: www.zbrush.com

Blender: www.blender.org

Maya: www.autodesk.com/products/maya

Chapter 8

No links

Chapter 9

David Shorey: www.shoreydesigns.com

Arc Gimbal: www.youmagine.com/designs/arc-gimbal

Chapter 10

Open access article on strength of 3D prints: www.appropedia.org/ Tensile_Strength_of_Commercial_Polymer_Materials_for_Fused_ Filament_Fabrication_3-D_Printing

Proto-pasta Conductive PLA: www.proto-pasta.com/collections/
exotic-composite-pla/products/conductive-pla
Slant 3D: www.slant3d.com
Prusa Research: www.prusa3d.com
Ultimaker: www.ultimaker.com
Michael Schmidt: www.michaelschmidtstudios.com
Nervous System: https://n-e-r-v-o-u-s.com
Anouk Wipprecht: www.anoukwipprecht.nl
Appropedia open source lab: www.appropedia.org/Open-source_Lab
Casale Design LLC: https://codycasale.com

Chapter 11

The Virtual Foundry: www.thevirtualfoundry.com
Desktop Metal: www.desktopmetal.com
Shapeways: www.shapeways.com

Chapter 12

No new links

Chapter 13

Lucie deLaBruere's "Create, Make, Learn" blog: http://createmakelearn.
blogspot.com
John Umekubo: https://johnumekubo.com
CoKreeate: www.cokreeate.com
FIRST Robotics: www.firstinspires.org

3D Printed Education Models Google Group: https://groups.google.com/
forum/#!forum/3dp_edu_models
Terrain2STL: http://jthatch.com/Terrain2STL/
Moon2STL: http://jthatch.com/Moon2STL/
Autodesk Meshmixer: www.meshmixer.com
3D Vermont: http://3dvermont.org
Twitter: twitter.com
Institute for Educational Advancement: www.educationaladvancement.org

Chapter 14

Procusini food printer: www.procusini.com
Mycusini home chocolate printer: www.mycusini.com
Epilepsy treatment Spritam: www.spritam.com
ICON concrete printing: www.iconbuild.com
3DPARE artificial reefs project: www.giteco.unican.es/proyectos/3dpare
3D print properties mechanical testing: www.appropedia.org/Pearce_
publications_in_materials_science_and_engineering
Autodesk generative design: www.autodesk.com/solutions/generative-
design
ANSI 3D printing material testing: www.ansi.org/standards_activities/
standards_boards_panels/amsc/
ATSM 3D printing material testing: www.astm.org/Standards/additive-
manufacturing-technology-standards.html
Slant 3D: www.slant3d.com

Index

A

Additive manufacturing, 4–5, 54
Appropedia, 240, 251

B

Batschelet, Rodney, 173–175
Battle of Agincourt, 313
Binder jetting, 271, 272
Bioprinters, 323, 324
Bitonti, Francis, 250
Bowyer, Adrian, 6
Brown part, 262, 267
Butterfrog, 173, 174

C

CAD software
    Blender, 196, 197
    Fusion 360, 195
    Morphi, 191
    Onshape, 195
    OpenSCAD, 188–191
    Tinkercad, 188–191
    Zbrush, 196
Cameron, Rich, xv
Casale, Cody, 254–257
Casale Design LLC, 246, 247, 254, 255

Casting
    3D printing patterns for, 279
Chimera (software), 185
Computer-aided design (CAD),
    3, 4, 52, 177, 179
Computer numerically controlled
    machine (CNC), 10
Creating a first 3D print, 130–131
Creative commons licenses, 56–57
Cricut Maker, 12
Crump, S.Scott and Lisa, 5

D, E

Dental additive manufacturing, 54
Desktop Metal, 271–274
Dual-extruder machines
    settings in Ultimaker Cura, 203
Digital manufacturing, 10, 15, 17
Direct metal laser
    sintering (DMLS), 275–276

F

Fabric, 3D printing on, 230–231
Filament
    changing, 131–134
    composite, 244–245
    composite-filled filaments, 244

Printed in the United States
By Bookmasters